KU-053-021

ENVIRONMENT AND ECONOMICS

**RESULTS OF
THE INTERNATIONAL CONFERENCE
ON ENVIRONMENT AND ECONOMICS**

18th-21st June 1984

© OECD, 1985

Application for permission to reproduce or translate
all or part of this publication should be made to:
[...]

ORGANISATION FOR ECONOMIC CO-OPERATION AND DEVELOPMENT

Pursuant to article 1 of the Convention signed in Paris on 14th December, 1960, and which came into force on 30th September, 1961, the Organisation for Economic Co-operation and Development (OECD) shall promote policies designed:

- to achieve the highest sustainable economic growth and employment and a rising standard of living in Member countries, while maintaining financial stability, and thus to contribute to the development of the world economy;
- to contribute to sound economic expansion in Member as well as non-member countries in the process of economic development; and
- to contribute to the expansion of world trade on a multilateral, non-discriminatory basis in accordance with international obligations.

The Signatories of the Convention on the OECD are Austria, Belgium, Canada, Denmark, France, the Federal Republic of Germany, Greece, Iceland, Ireland, Italy, Luxembourg, the Netherlands, Norway, Portugal, Spain, Sweden, Switzerland, Turkey, the United Kingdom and the United States. The following countries acceded subsequently to this Convention (the dates are those on which the instruments of accession were deposited): Japan (28th April, 1964), Finland (28th January, 1969), Australia (7th June, 1971) and New Zealand (29th May, 1973).

The Socialist Federal Republic of Yugoslavia takes part in certain work of the OECD (agreement of 28th October, 1961).

Publié en français sous le titre:

ENVIRONNEMENT ET ÉCONOMIE

© OCDE, 1985
Application for permission to reproduce or translate all or part of this publication should be made to:
Director of Information, OECD
2, rue André-Pascal, 75775 PARIS CEDEX 16, France.

An International Conference on Environment and Economics was held at the OECD Headquarters in Paris, France, on 18-21 June, 1984.

The Conference addressed a range of issues in eight main Sessions, namely: Environmental Trends, Costs and Policy Issues Through 1990; The Impact of Environmental Measures on Growth, Productivity, Inflation and Trade; Environmental Policies: A Source of Jobs?; The Impact of Environmental Policies on Industrial Innovation; The Benefits of Environmental Policies; More Effective and Efficient Environmental Policies; Economic Instruments: Alternatives or Supplements to Regulations?; and Future Directions for Environmental Policies.

The Conference was attended by Delegations nominated by Member Governments of the OECD and was made up of ministers, parliamentarians and high-level officials responsible for policy-making at the national level. Delegations also included representatives of industry, trade unions, environmental groups and acknowledged authorities in environmental economics and related fields. The Business and Industry Advisory Committee and Trade Union Advisory Committee to the OECD also participated in the Conference, as have those international organisations which have traditional links with the Environment Committee of the OECD.

This report on the Conference is published under the responsibility of the Secretary-General of the OECD.

Also available

ECONOMIC ASPECTS OF INTERNATIONAL CHEMICAL CONTROL (October 1983)
(59 83 02 1) ISBN 92-64-12508-6   96 pages   £5.50   US$11.00   F55.00

COAL AND ENVIRONMENTAL PROTECTION. Costs and Costing Methods (October 1983)
(97 83 09 1) ISBN 92-64-12513-2   132 pages   £6.00   US$12.00   F60.00

ENVIRONMENTAL POLICIES IN GREECE (October 1983)
(97 83 07 1) ISBN 92-64-12503-5   142 pages   £7.00   US$14.00   F70.00

ENVIRONMENTAL EFFECTS OF ENERGY SYSTEMS. The OECD Compass Project (August 1983)
(97 83 03 1) ISBN 92-64-12470-5   138 pages   £6.00   US$12.00   F60.00

EMISSION CONTROL COSTS IN THE METAL-PLATING INDUSTRY (February 1983)
(97 82 07 1) ISBN 92-64-12342-3   98 pages   £4.30   US$8.50   F43.00

THE COST OF OIL SPILLS. Expert Studies presented to an OECD Seminar (November 1982)
(97 82 05 1) ISBN 92-64-12339-3   252 pages   £7.40   US$15.00   F74.00

COMBATTING OIL SPILLS. Some Economic Aspects (November 1982)
(97 82 06 1) ISBN 92-64-12341-5   140 pages   £4.70   US$9.50   F47.00

ECONOMIC AND ECOLOGICAL INTERDEPENDANCE. A Report on Selected Environment and Resource Issues (May 1982)
(97 82 04 1) ISBN 92-64-12311-3   96 pages   £2.90   US$6.50   F29.00

Prices charged at the OECD Publications Office.

*THE OECD CATALOGUE OF PUBLICATIONS and supplements will be sent free of charge on request addressed either to OECD Publications Office,
2, rue André-Pascal, 75775 PARIS CEDEX 16, or to the OECD Sales Agent in your country.*

TABLE OF CONTENTS

INTERNATIONAL CONFERENCE ON ENVIRONMENT AND ECONOMICS

CONCLUSIONS

Leaders of Government, Industry, Trade Unions and non-governmental organisations joined by internationally recognised experts in economics, environment, science and other fields concluded a four-day Conference at OECD in Paris on environment and economics. The Conference Chairman was the Hon. Pieter WINSEMIUS, Minister of Housing, Physical Planning and the Environment of the Netherlands, and the Session Chairmen included:

-- Hon. Mrs. Huguette BOUCHARDEAU, Secretary of State for the Environment and the Quality of Life, FRANCE;

-- Hon. Charles CACCIA, Minister of Environment, CANADA;

-- Hon. Koji KAKIZAWA, Vice-Minister, Environment Agency, JAPAN;

-- Sir Rupert MYERS, Chairman, NSW State Pollution Control Commission, and Chairman, National Conservation Strategy Committee, AUSTRALIA;

-- Hon. Karl-Heinz NARJES, Member of the Commission, COMMISSION OF THE EUROPEAN COMMUNITIES;

-- Hon. William RUCKELSHAUS, Administrator, UNITED STATES Environmental Protection Agency;

-- Mr. Janez STANOVNIK, Former Executive Secretary, Economic Commission for Europe, and Professor at the University of Ljubljana, Yugoslavia;

-- Hon. Antonis TRITSIS, Minister of Physical Planning, Housing and Environment, GREECE.

Mr. Emile van Lennep, Secretary-General of the OECD, drew attention to the prominence that was recently given to the international dimension of environmental problems and the role of environmental factors in economic development at the London meeting of the Heads of State or Government of seven Member countries. It was for him a welcome indication that governments, learning the lessons of the past, were determined that environmental issues should be "in at the ground floor" in the process of economic recovery now under way.

The Conference met at a time when, although unemployment remains unacceptably high, overall economic conditions are improving -- with growth, on average, foreseen at a rate above 4 per cent in the OECD area this year with wide variations around this average. This growth, if sustained and extended, will inevitably have both positive and negative implications for the environment. The Conference was thus particularly timely and provided an opportunity to review the work of the OECD on environment and economics over the past 10 years and to identify issues and appropriate policy responses through the 1990s.

Emerging Trends

The Conference recognised that renewed economic growth, whilst bringing benefits, leads to higher levels of conventional pollutants, thus imposing greater pressures on environmental resources, with higher damage costs, unless environmentally favourable measures are taken. Renewed growth will also accelerate the emergence of new and complex pollution problems, linked to new technological developments. A number of delegations stressed the need to reduce emissions below current levels.

The Conference further recognised that the traditional scope of environmental policy is expanding to embrace quality of life issues (especially urban amenities) and critical issues in natural resource management which are increasingly important for sustained economic development, but where the lack of adequate scientific and other data and the long time scales involved pose special difficulties. In certain cases, present policies, sometimes reflecting inadequate valuation of resources, are leading to actions (for example, in relation to water, soil and forests) that are not only environmentally unacceptable, but may also undermine the basis for sustained economic development.

Industrial innovation and the development of new technologies carry significant implications, both positive and negative, for environment and resource issues by inducing changes in the structure of economic activity, and in patterns of consumption, investment, employment and trade. Appropriate structural adjustments, which respond to environmental requirements as well as to market forces and technological developments, should be promoted especially at the beginning of the business cycle.

The growing regional and global dimension of many of these issues and their potential economic and financial consequences, whether action is deferred or taken, calls for their urgent and continuing examination on an international basis, as well as increased action at national and local levels.

Environmental Management and Economic Growth

Continued environmental improvement and sustained economic growth are essential, compatible and interrelated policy objectives for OECD Member countries. This, the major conclusion of the Conference, means that the environment and the economy, if properly managed, are mutually reinforcing; and are supportive of and supported by technological innovation.

The Conference noted that, in most OECD countries, public demand for better environmental quality remained high during the recession. Renewed economic growth is likely to increase this demand and to broaden it; and, at the same time, to make it politically and financially more possible for governments to respond to it.

The resources of the environment, which are the basis of economic and social development, are scarce. Inadequate environmental policies may have adverse consequences in all fields. Improved management of environmental resources is therefore necessary. Strengthened international cooperation, both within and beyond OECD, is essential to develop the appropriate tools and to put them into use.

The Conference recognised that environmental policies must be justified on their own merits for environmental reasons. However, on the basis of the substantial evidence available to it, the Conference concluded that the benefits generated by environmental measures (including the damage costs avoided) have generally been greater than their costs.

The macro-economic effects of environmental policies on growth, inflation, productivity and trade have been minor, whilst some positive effects on employment and technological innovation have been demonstrated. At the level of individual firms, industrial sectors or communities, cost impacts can be substantial and can lead to environmentally desirable structural, process or product changes. The impacts of these changes can fall unequally on different groups and regions and environmental policies should consider equity aspects.

Towards More Effective and Efficient Environmental Policies

The Conference concluded that OECD Member countries are at a watershed in the evolution of environmental policies. New directions are needed in order to achieve a continuous improvement in environmental conditions and to avoid irreversible damage to the environment.

Three such directions were identified as fundamental at both national and international levels:

-- Integration of Environment and Economic Policies;

-- "Anticipate and Prevent" Strategies;

-- More Cost-effective and Efficient Environmental Policies.

Integration of Environment and Economic Policies -- Development trends in all OECD Member countries offer significant opportunities for long-term economic gains through sound management of the environment, as well as risks of major losses. If these gains are to be realised and the losses minimised, including those of a social character, the Conference concluded that environmental considerations should, as a matter of priority, be brought effectively into the centre of national decision-making on overall economic policy. They also need to be fully integrated with other policies such as agriculture, industry, energy, transportation and land use management.

The means to achieve this integration are available and include:

-- Improving institutional arrangements: with planning, programme review and budget procedures that ensure continuing interaction between the environmental authorities and other government departments, especially at early stages of policy development;

-- Improving aids to decision-making: amongst them, environmental impact assessment, cost-benefit analysis (in both physical and monetary terms) and risk assessment;

-- Extending effective forms of environmental impact assessment to proposed policies, as well as programmes and projects, that have potentially significant implications for environmental and resource management;

-- Including environmental considerations in planning: especially land use planning, zoning and development control schemes;

-- Increasing public information and involvement: by making available to the public relevant facts about risks, benefits and costs, thereby ensuring that it is in a position to express its preferences.

-- Adopting a multi-media approach to management, in order to treat pollution problems that occur in different environmental media, air, water or land, in an integrated manner.

A Stronger Basis for "Anticipate-and-Prevent" Strategies -- Although "react-and-cure" strategies remain necessary to deal with existing problems, "anticipate-and-prevent" strategies which are attractive from the point of view of economic efficiency and cost-effectiveness, will increasingly be needed. By their nature they are difficult to apply because they often call for action in advance of demonstrated damage, scientific certainty and public support and require a strong data and knowledge base.

The Conference concluded that strengthening this knowledge base was necessary, urgent and cost-effective and that the means were available to do it, including:

-- Economic evaluation of the potential advantages of anticipatory action;

-- Improving inter-disciplinary scientific research on priority environmental issues;

-- Improving the collection of data on environmental quality, resources, benefits and expenditures at national, regional and local levels;

-- Improving public understanding of environmental objectives and policies through environmental education and training.

More Cost-Effective and Efficient Environmental Policies -- The Conference noted the substantial evidence demonstrating that the effectiveness and efficiency of environmental measures can be improved by various means, and concluded that the following were of special importance:

-- The consistent application and extension of the Polluter-Pays
   Principle, which aims at ensuring that polluters bear the costs of
   pollution control and consequently that they are not subsidised nor
   given unfair trade advantages over their competitors;

-- More effective use of economic instruments, with their reliance on
   market type mechanisms, as complements to regulatory instruments;

-- Streamlining and improving institutional and regulatory systems with
   a view to improving coherence in policy, consistency in regulation
   and decision-making processes, to ensure adequate enforcement and to
   avoid negative side effects.

-- Encouraging consultation between regulatory authorities and industry
   in order to increase the understanding of environmental policy
   requirements and of problems in their application; and to provide
   appropriate time schedules for compliance;

-- Encouraging employee participation in environmental protection
   measures undertaken by firms (including those affecting working
   conditions), through the provision of adequate information.

Strengthening International Co-operation

The growing interdependence of the world's economic system has become a
central question for governments as they examine the critical issues likely to
dominate the world scene to and beyond the turn of the century. This
interdependence is seen to cover not only population, energy, food and
technology, but also the environment, which constitutes the resource and
ecological base for sustainable future development. The Conference recognised
the need for increased international co-operation in relation to key problems
of a global or regional character or where direct impacts on neighbouring
countries arise. Furthermore, at a national level, environmental policies
should reflect the reality of global environmental interdependence. The
Conference noted that in many cases these problems stem from the activities
and policies of the advanced industrial societies; but that rapid industrial
and population growth in developing countries will also be increasingly
important. The special responsibility of OECD Member countries to co-operate
in seeking solutions, especially with developing countries and relevant
international organisations, must be acknowledged.

The Conference concluded that several forms of co-operation on
environmental and resource issues have proved effective and could be extended
and deepened through the use of the OECD in providing a forum for the early
recognition, analysis and resolution of these issues. These include:

-- Encouraging the development of an improved capacity on the part of
   Member governments to undertake co-ordinated and integrated policy
   analysis, including the development of appropriate methodologies and
   of long-term scenarios at global, regional and national levels;

-- Preparing periodic State of the Environment Reports as a basis for
   evaluating progress in the implementation of environmental policies;

-- Identifying and assessing those economic, investment, trade and other policies of the OECD area that have the greatest potential environmental impact, both within and beyond the OECD;

-- Promoting the greater integration of environmental assessment in the development process;

-- Encouraging harmonized approaches to environmental policy with a view, _inter alia_, to minimising trade distortions;

-- Developing better information on economic, social and trade dimensions of environmental policies; and sharing that information widely.

INTRODUCTION

Hon. Pieter WINSEMIUS

Minister of Housing, Physical Planning and
the Environment, the Netherlands

This Conference, our first International Conference on Environment and Economics, comes at a highly opportune time. For the last 10 years, environmental measures in OECD Member countries have had to find funding against a background of economic recession and tight public and private finance. With economic recovery, the outlook for environmental policies is changing, and this time, unlike 1974, for the better. Economic growth, rising output and higher consumption will put new pressures on natural resources and the environment, however. This will confront us with demands for improved environmental policies, demands that represent a special challenge to the advanced industrial societies of the OECD. The future demands and opportunities call for changes in existing approaches and strategies, guided by new and creative directions which this conference can help to provide.

In facing the changing economic, social and technological perspectives, we should not counterpose environment and economics. All of us, and especially the advanced industrial societies, carry the responsibility of pursuing both environmental quality and economic development; not one at the expense of the other, but both in mutual support. This is no easy task, as we all realise. At the same time, we all recognise that we must deal with this challenge. This important responsibility is the basis of our joint motivation to contribute to the success of these four days. The agenda provides us with further stimulation, presenting us with important issues for discussion between old friends and friends to be -- who are here as individuals, rather than as representatives of their governments, industries, trade unions, environmental organisations or whatever.

Personally, I am deeply honoured by your confidence in allowing me to preside over your Conference. With your help we can guide this Conference to a successful conclusion. Therefore, I am grateful to the Secretary-General for his inspiring remarks. My recognition also goes to the support that I will have from the very distinguished Members of the Bureau that has been appointed, from ministerial colleagues seen throughout the Salle, from the excellent keynotes speakers, discussants and rapporteurs, from the Rapporteur-General, from the members of the media and from all those whose efforts the Chairman would acknowledge in advance. A special word of thanks is owed to the Secretariat and to all of those who have been working and will be working to make the Conference a success.

15

Challenges

Our Conference is focussed on the future. It examines what new directions should be given to policies to deal with environmental issues in a more effective and economically efficient manner. In doing so, we can look back upon the experience of more than a decade of environmental action in OECD countries. We can undoubtedly learn from past trends in environmental issues and policies. We can also draw some valuable guidance from our shared experiences and our shared research, based on more than 10 years of work at OECD. But the essential question remains: how can we influence future environmental trends by applying new strategies at the national and the international level?

We deal with this question against the background of some important developments that have changed societal positions on environment. Allow me briefly to discuss four of these developments.

Changing attitudes

First, more than ever, the people, the industries and the governments of advanced industrial societies are deeply committed in their concern for our environment. During the late 1970s public support for environmental issues remained high, and in some countries it even grew, in spite of an economic recession. Today, environmental issues have become an enduring social concern, much like health care, education and other basic issues. The challenge for environmental policy makers is to benefit from this change in attitudes and to build on it in designing new strategies.

Changing management behaviour

Second, management itself, not only in public institutions, but also in private corporations, has grown to become more and more environmentally responsible. Environmental concerns are increasingly taken into account in overall economic policy-making processes -- although still not frequently enough.

Belatedly, many private companies in advanced industrial countries are embedding environmental management in their overall strategic philosophy, planning and research -- but, again, still not enough.

The challenge for environmental management is to reinforce these behavioural changes and to take them into account when re-examining existing regulations and designing and enforcing new regulations.

Changing relations between environment and economics

Third, we have come a long way in our understanding of the relationships between environmental protection and economic development. Fifteen years ago there was great concern that environmental action could impose a heavy, if not intolerable burden on economies, slowing growth, aggravating unemployment, adding to inflation, inhibiting innovation and distorting trade. That concern now appears misplaced. Our work together in this house has demonstrated that it was also misconceived. The Conference will prove that many traditional issues in actual fact are non-issues. We have, for example, found that the benefits have generally exceeded the costs, even in strictly economic terms -- which many, myself included, would argue are not the most important from a long-term perspective. We have also found, as the Secretary-General said, that environmental protection and sustainable economic development are not only compatible but also interdependent and mutually reinforcing. The remaining challenge is how we can achieve sound environmental management in the most effective and efficient manner possible. That is the crucial question we will be exploring in depth during this Conference.

Changing environmental issues

Fourth, there have been major shifts in the portfolio of environmental issues. For example, consider the changes that have taken place in scope and scale of the environmental issues that confront our societies. Environmental issues are no longer limited to environmental pollution alone.

Today, the scope of environmental concerns has widened to embrace the utilisation and management of natural resources and urban issues, especially amenities and questions concerning the quality of life. While most of these issues remain local in occurrence, that is, they have localised sources, their effects are increasingly regional and global in scale. In addition, the economic and social implications of many of the new issues are greater than ever before -- just think of the threat of contamination and depletion of underground water, of erosion, desertification, acid rain, the loss of soil fertility or climatic change induced by rising levels of carbon dioxide in the atmosphere. A great number of new tasks lie ahead of us, while at the same time the battle against more conventional pollutants that were already on our agenda is far from won. Let me illustrate this by a few examples:

-- Regarding traditional water pollutants, great progress has been made. Yet, the papers for this Conference indicate that the load of biochemical oxygen demand (BOD and COD) could rise in almost all regions of the OECD in line with industrial and population growth. And, at present, even in a country with a long tradition of water quality management like the Netherlands, 40 per cent of the total BOD production is still discharged into surface waters without treatment.

-- In the field of hazardous waste, we are faced with a massive clean-up operation. In the Netherlands alone, we have identified 4 000 soil sites polluted with hazardous waste. The clean-up at one site, Lekkerkerk, has already cost 50 million US dollars, and one company faces claims valued at 35 million dollars. Clean-up costs ould run as high as 700 million dollars per year for 13 years in OECD Europe and about the same in the United States. We could be talking about 0.25 per cent of GNP to deal with this one problem alone. And still, the OECD economies are generating 180 million tonnes of new waste each year -- which requires policies to prevent the escape of this waste to areas beyond control.

-- Chemical control is another area full of uncompleted tasks. Many

17

harmful chemicals like PCBs are still present in the environment. On top of that, between 1 000 and 2 000 new chemicals are introduced each year by OECD's chemical industry for which pre-market testing should be a prerequisite.

-- Wind and water erosion affect more than 60 per cent of the agricultural land of countries such as Canada, the USA and Spain. Losses in nutrients in some cases reach rates higher than the rate of natural soil regeneration and can reach 2.5 times the annual consumption of nutrients in fertilizers. Desertification, or the sustained decline of the biological productivity of arid and semi-arid land caused by man-made stresses, primarily affects Australia, Canada and the USA, as well as some of the Mediterranean countries of the OECD. The sources of these issues and the solutions to them lie in management practices encouraged by policies in other sectors, like agriculture and forestry.

In selecting just a few examples of problems to be solved, I have limited myself to those of OECD countries. However, most of the key developments that I just mentioned are issues of concern not only within and between OECD countries but also between OECD and non-OECD countries. The Third World comprises three-quarters of the planet's population, and in many parts thereof population growth and poverty conspire to place destructive pressures on the environment. Ecological destruction in the Third World will not leave OECD Members unaffected. Furthermore, many environmental issues in developing countries stem largely from the activities of advanced industrial societies. Hence, many environmental issues in the Third World cannot be addressed effectively in the absence of concerted actions on our part.

The Policy Life Cycle

The question that we will be dealing with at this Conference is how can we take these developments and challenges into account in formulating future directions.

I have given this a lot of thought and I have developed a concept that I call the Policy Life Cycle and which I would like to share with you briefly. I think it offers some insights into the politics of the problems we will be discussing and how governments may have to deal with them.

What do I mean by the Policy Life Cycle? I mean simply that public policy on environmental issues, as on other issues, inevitably proceeds through various stages of development. I have identified four distinct stages.

-- The first is recognising the problem. At the start of the Policy Life Cycle, there is usually great dissension. Debate centres on the nature of the problem, its sources and effects and its scale. This may go on for years, depending on the complexity of the problem, on the extent of the damage costs and who is suffering them, and on the nature of the control costs and who would have to pay for them. Concern grows, and an issue is fully recognised as a policy problem, only when more evidence - which may consist of information on risks, damage costs and control costs - becomes available and widely accessible or when a scare, an incident or an accident serves to dramatise the problem.

18

-- The second stage is <u>gaining control over the problem</u>. We now agree there is a problem; the question is how to handle it. During the course of this stage, debate and dissension over the magnitude of the problem decrease, although there may be considerable disagreement over the appropriate policy measures to take. This stage ends when the authorities succeed in introducing policies and programmes to deal with the issue. In doing so effectiveness, not efficiency, is the name of the game.

-- The third stage involves the actual <u>solving of the problem</u>. Policies and programmes now are in place and it becomes obvious that the problem can be mastered. The public's attention therefore begins to wane and, with it, political attention. As programmes are implemented and heavy investments are carried out, the problem appears more and more manageable. Enforcement rather than legislation is the key. Debates about the macro- and micro-economic impacts of environmental policies are typical of this stage. Attention also begins to turn to questions of efficiency.

-- Finally, when the problem is reduced to environmentally acceptable limits, society faces the continuing need <u>to maintain control over the problem</u>. This is the fourth and final stage of the Policy Life Cycle.

The challenge, of course, is to choose the most adequate mix of approaches for different issues at different stages in the Policy Life Cycle. This will, of course, vary from country to country, since the same issue may be at quite different stages in different countries, and thus it will require quite different policies for monitoring, research, planning, financing, implementation and maintenance. This underlines the need for some appreciation of just where in the Policy Life Cycle an issue stands at any point in time.

Some illustrations may serve to clarify the concept and at the same time provide an indication of the enormous complexity of international cooperation in the field of environmental policy.

-- Currently, a number of issues are struggling to gain recognition as issues requiring action. Acid rain, for example, or groundwater pollution from nitrates in fertilizers, or the need for prior environmental assessment of development projects, or carbon dioxide and climatic change. These examples illustrate the fact that when a problem requires action at the international level, recognition in one country may have to wait a long time for recognition in the other countries concerned before joint action can be taken. Some of you may remember the attempts by Sweden to put Acid Rain on the agenda of the 1972 Conference on the Human Environment. Another way of saying this is that at different times different countries act as sort of "lead countries" in gaining recognition of an issue as a policy problem requiring action.

-- As a second set of examples, issues that have reached Stage 4, that of "maintaining control", in certain advanced industrial societies are often moving towards the stage of "solving the problem" in countries which are still in the middle of the industrialisation process. The differences with non-industrial Third World countries can be even more pronounced. The problem of providing water and sewerage systems is in Stage 4 in much of northern Europe and in Stage 3 in southern Europe, but in many Third World countries it has only reached Stage 2, that of gaining control.

The fact that our countries are normally somewhat out-of-phase in the Policy Life Cycle underlines, among other things, the potential cost-effectiveness of international co-operation. Lead countries must be willing to "pull", by sharing information, by providing expertise, by helping others in any way possible. This is not only because of the evident needs of the other country, but also because it is in their immediate self-interest: international solutions to international problems must be based on international co-operation. In this area, we have hardly begun to scratch the surface.

Challenges, Strategies and the Policy Life Cycle

A few moments ago, I discussed some of the environmental challenges confronting the advanced industrial societies. When one considers the trend of each of these challenges, and the stage of the Policy Cycle in which we find them in each of our countries, one is struck by the need for greater imagination in developing future strategies and policies. During the past decade, governments have staggered from stage to stage, reacting to issues long after they should have been recognised, and often after it was too late to require or induce those responsible for specific economic activities to build-in measures to prevent the problem. Think, for example of the failure of chemical waste management in the past -- which has confronted us today with a massive and expensive clean-up operation. As a result, in sector after sector, policies have focussed largely on curative measures which are, as the documentation before this Conference demonstrates, generally less effective and less economically efficient than preventive measures.

For achieving improvements in effectiveness and efficiency, it is, as I said earlier, of vital importance to choose the most adequate mix of policies. Which policy instruments we should choose is one of the subjects that we shall be considering over the next four days. Let me, taking advantage of my privilege as Chairman, offer you my views on certain directions we should take. I will limit myself to three but hope and expect you to add and refine wherever possible.

First, in all our countries and internationally, we must develop a stronger basis for anticipate-and-prevent strategies. When you consider the scope and scale of the environmental challenges before us, and the economic consequences both of reacting and of failing to react, one realises that society cannot afford not to shift from a reactive track to a preventive track.

In order to get on a preventive track, we must shorten as much as possible the time it takes to get through the first stage of the Policy Cycle and to gain recognition of an issue as one requiring action. One way to do this is to strengthen our common knowledge base on long-term environmental trends, costs and benefits. Failure to gain early recognition of an issue stems from many factors, of course, some of them political. Those who bear the damage costs of environmental pollution are usually dispersed -- sometimes across several states or countries -- and they are often unorganised. Those countries and industries that would have to bear the control costs are not, and one cannot really expect them to be as quick to recognise an issue as those who are now paying the damage costs.

In the light of this, it seems to me that three actions could serve to accelerate recognition of an issue.

First, we must ensure that environmental considerations are integrated at an early stage in the policies of the sectors most concerned; for example, industry, agriculture, energy, transportation and urban development.

Second, we must minimise the area of dissension. During the early stages of the Policy Cycle, policy is handicapped by scattered and imperfect information and, with increasingly complex environmental problems, it usually is most difficult to decide upon a proper course of action. Rather, the call is for further study, a call that is hard for politicians to resist, especially when it stems from evident uncertainty and comes from scientists. Dissension might be managed much better than it is by a proper use of a range of techniques, including risk assessment. Most importantly, however, I feel we must learn to work more closely and openly -- usually also at an early stage of policy development -- with all other parties involved in finding the best solution to an environmental problem.

As a third step, we must share experience and knowledge. The more effective use of international co-operation can play an important role, by establishing the "state-of-the-art" on the science of an issue, and by marshalling the evidence on risks and on damage costs and control costs. This is especially vital where the issues are common to several countries.

A second direction we must take -- and will be discussing throughout the Conference -- is to <u>promote greater efficiency in environmental policies</u>. Let me emphasize that -- as always -- effectiveness of a policy comes first: the world is filled with policies that are executed in a highly efficient manner but do not serve any purpose. Still, economic efficiency is needed at all stages but particularly in the "solving-the-problem" stage, when investments made by the public and private sectors are at their peak.

There are several ways in which this might be done.

Apart from those mentioned in the documentation, I would again stress integration at an early stage in overall economic and sectoral planning as well as in investment planning in the private sector. As one aspect, this requires forward looking environmental policy plans, in which clearly defined and measurable targets are formulated.

During the planning process, much more could be done to establish clear priorities for action. Governments cannot require that everything be done at once, although it is sometimes politicially very difficult not to pretend that one is trying to do so. Formalising priorities makes obvious what we might call the posteriorities: those issues that did not make the list or were ranked in lower positions. The political unpopularity of this does not need any explanation. As a consequence the word "posteriority" is hardly known.

The periodic streamlining of regulatory systems and institutional arrangements is critical to efficiency, and, may I add, in my view also to effectiveness. When a new issue is tackled, the approach agreed upon usually reflects negotiating and compromise and almost inevitably crystallises in some rather strange constructions. Partially, I think, this is explained by the fact that environmental policies are usually of a relatively recent date and had to find a place in legislative frameworks created by other policy fields over a much longer period. When polarisation is reduced later in the Policy Cycle, especially during the "solving-the-problem" stage, this can permit these constructions to be unfrozen and re-crystallised according to the latest insights. Properly speaking this is not deregulation but re-regulation.

Similarly, at this later stage in the Policy Cycle, it may be possible to supplement blunt regulatory systems with more sophisticated and efficient economic instruments and with more effective measures of enforcement.

I now come to the third and last of the directions that I, as your Chairman, would like to present to you: managing the organisational culture. I think it is essential. I also think it is forgotten too often. We tend to focus on studies, on plans, on techniques, on laws and licences. However, the one essential element that distinguishes "good" policy making from "average" policy making is people: the organisation and its culture. Culture -- the system of values, styles, symbols and ideology -- is an essential aspect of every organisation. The environmental organisation is no exception to this rule. Thus, the effectiveness of an environmental organisation heavily depends on maintaining the appropriate culture within the organisation.

In doing so we must realise that each phase of the Policy Life Cycle sets its own demands with respect to culture. In the first phases of the Life Cycle the name of the game is "results under uncertainty". Our people must be good at ad hoc improvisation, at crisis management; they must possess a fighting spirit. From the point of view of personnel, we will need an emphasis on managing technology and legislation. In the later phases of the Life Cycle on the other hand, other cultural elements will be more effective, such as planning orientation, ability to make compromises, skill at decentralised control, emphasis on cost-consciousness and efficiency. The overall theme becomes "no-nonsense execution".

There is a lesson to be learned from this. At transitions of the Policy Life Cycle we must make choices regarding the type of culture and organisation that we need in the future. For example, do we still need the "tigers" that have been effective in the policy start-up stage, or do we need excellent executors, "people to man the store"? Should we decentralise certain responsibilities and task areas, with respect to issues that have reached the solving stage? Of course, there are no simple and clear-cut answers to these types of questions. It is my conviction, however, that environmental policy today needs a culture that is characterised by a quest for excellence, both at the lowest and at the highest level of the environmental organisation. Policy makers should stimulate a "we-will-control-the-problem spirit", by identifying and rewarding good examples, by selecting promising people, and, above all, by stimulating everyone to work very hard.

Successful policy making is 98 per cent a question of perspiration and 2 per cent inspiration. The organisation should concentrate on the perfect execution of key tasks. This requires mostly a strong team spirit, room for entrepreneurial initiatives and experiments (the "do it, fix it, try it" approach) and a clear and simple organisational structure. It is crucial that we realise the importance of these aspects. Without the necessary cultural and organisational changes, other improvements in effectiveness and efficiency might not be achieved. The price of such a failure would be far too high.

Concluding Remarks

Environmental management today requires a thorough examination and a good understanding of the interrelationships between environment and economics. During the coming days we will discuss the many complex aspects of this interrelationship. We will be frustrated, no doubt, as we will not find all the answers, or a complete consensus on all the issues. I expect us, however, to leave Paris with a gleam in our eyes, as we realise that we have taken significant steps forward.

The advanced industrial societies must start to do what they have all too often failed to do in the past; that is, to anticipate the environmental consequences of their economic activities and to take measures to prevent them, not only within their own boundaries but also with regard to their neighbours and with regard to the global commons.

And we must succeed. As a group of advanced industrial nations we share a collective responsibility to the people of our own generation and to the people of the generations to come. When -- in 15 or 20 years time -- we pass the baton of responsibility to the next generation, we must be able to say: "We are proud of our environmental inheritance, it is clean, intact, beautiful and productive. Go out and make it even better yet". It is this unique feature, this concern for our planet's future, that distinguishes environmental policy from other fields of policy. If at this Conference you and I can take even a small step forward in this direction, our gathering will have been successful. The challenge is with us.

ECONOMIC PROSPECTS AND THE ENVIRONMENT

Mr. Michael POSNER

Economic Director, National Economic Development Office, London

Ministers, and the public they serve, are more aware than professional economists of the misleading nature of official statistics. Figures for "gross domestic product", even "personal consumption per head of population", do not stir the imagination of ordinary families. The quality of life, the security within which we work, the prospects for our children, our opportunities for leisure and relaxation, are all more important than crude measures of income or wealth.

The scepticism which greets economic arithmetic should also be applied, therefore, to conventional indicators of environmental comfort or health. Measures of the emission of pollutants, or of waste to be disposed of, of areas of land to be used for industrial building, of new motorways to be constructed, are no more conclusive in the evidence they offer than the economic series which they seek to modify. The quality of life is not easy to capture with numbers.

There is a well-known sense in which economic progress is competitive with environmental goods. More chemical works mean more effluents to dispose of. More electric power means either more hydrocarbons to burn or more nuclear waste to dispose of. And more travel by richer industrial workers means more road congestion and more road building. Economic growth is, for these reasons alone, a less attractive prospect to sell to our brightest young people in universities than it was two or three decades ago.

On the other hand, we must not forget that most environmental changes which our fellow citizens seek cost money to achieve and require the absorption of resources which are competitive with other final uses. In my country a certain amount can be done by using unemployed young people to clear mountain paths, or to improve the amenity of wasteland of one sort or another. But in general, to clean rivers, to transform industrial desolation into parkland, to rejuvenate ancient but decrepit city centres, requires modern machinery, skilled manpower, all the apparatus of a modern industrial economy. I would myself guess that if present distress about the state of European forest systems is sustained by further research findings, it will turn out that very heavy expenditure is required to reverse or offset the damage. Although some of the interesting papers prepared by officials under OECD guidance show the considerable sums of money that would be required to control industrial pollution which results from the process of economic growth itself, the absence of economic growth would make it more difficult, not less difficult, to improve the environment.

In elementary economist's language, therefore, I suggest that economic growth and environmental protection are complementary goods, not competitive goods. In one sense that is a source of comfort -- participants in this Conference need not feel that they are getting their left hand to struggle against their right hand. But it is also bad news, because we are unable to console ourselves or our fellow citizens with the thought that failure on economic growth can be compensated by successes on environmental matters.

Three Types of Environmental Issues

In the boom of the late 1960s, fear was often expressed that "Spaceship Earth" might run out of this, that or the other source of raw material. The most potent fear was of a shortage of energy, although as soon as we remembered to stick to individual types of fuel rather than the physicist's concept of "energy" in the abstract, the fear was somewhat diminished. But it was seriously suggested, first by the Club of Rome and then by many other commentators, that a serious brake on economic progress would be applied by raw material shortage.

This fear was not a new one: it has long been discussed under the heading of "changing terms of trade between manufactured goods and primary products". There is undoubtedly an important matter for analysis here, and the need to ensure balanced developments of industrial and primary production remains an important concern. As an energy economist myself, I would not wish to deny the importance of looking far ahead in energy matters, and envisaging the way in which balance between supply and demand might be achieved at dates in the future.

But this type of concern has given way in popular thinking to a second group of topics, on which the OECD experts have themselves assembled important facts and arguments: the issue of pollution and its control. Undoubtedly, the treatment of the external diseconomies of profitable industrial activity had been too little noticed in the whole period since the first industrial revolution, and the sudden upsurge of interest in this topic in the OECD world in the last two decades is to be welcomed. A lot can be achieved through the changing of the rules of the economic game, at least in advanced market economies, so as to achieve the internalisation of the costs of environmental damage caused by particular industrial activities. "The polluter must pay" is from that point of view an excellent slogan which diminishes the public expenditure consequences of environmental protection.

But that principle does not take us far enough. Specifically, it fails to ensure that remedial action, which might be in the public interest, is in fact taken -- the tax penalities, paid to the government, or the private damages exacted through the legal system, by damaged private persons, need not be applied to the repair of the environmental harm. Moreover, in many cases the damage caused to the community as a whole may be greater than the total of the individual identifiable losses caused to particular persons. And, most important of all, the definition of pollution, the fixing of the target at which we aim, is itself subject to change and argument.

This leads to the third type of environmental issue, which I believe is insufficiently stressed in most of our papers, largely because it is difficult to measure and even more difficult to control or reverse. If I may be autobiographical, when I was a boy in suburban south London, there were red-backed shrikes in my back garden, and there were nightingales on Shotover Hill overlooking Oxford. Both are now gone, and losses even more severe than that are to be found all over the OECD world; even in the United States, where for so long the wilderness was a "free good", both the Adirondacks and the Rockies are at risk. Of all the OECD countries, it is perhaps only Australia which is so far exempt from the creeping loss of our natural environment as our grandfathers knew it.

We cannot expect Ministers from very poor countries to take this sort of fear to heart, and even in the OECD world many of our fellow citizens have greater concerns than the disappearance of green fields and butterflies. But looking ahead into the next century, as is the theme of this Conference, our grandchildren will hold it against us if we fail to seize hold of this problem and begin to envisage the appropriate action.

The Good Environment: A Moving Target

One way to look at environmental damage is that of absolute purism, of conservation at any cost. No more land to be built on; no more hedges to be uprooted; no more power stations to be constructed; no emission of sulphur oxides or particulate smoke. In parish pump terms, "the field at the bottom of my garden must never be built on".

Any economist and I hope most Ministers would rebel at such an absolute approach on any topic, although I am somewhat more inclined to favour a rigid line on environmental issues than on any other: "No further high-rise building within sight of Notre Dame" would be a rigid principle worth fighting for. But for the most part, we must be prepared to trade off environmental benefits against other goods, provided that we strike a very tough bargain.

"The polluter must pay" is, however, an absolutist doctrine. It requires that an absolute unshakable definition is given to the notion of pollution. In practice pollution, or rather the state of absolute purity which we might call "non-pollution", is a moving target. Legislation, popoular understanding of the issues and popular sentiment in favour of a better environment are effectively tightening our grip on polluters all the time. The British approach, which requires of industry that they use the "best practicable measures" to avoid pollution gives just the flavour of systematic ambiguity that we need: the best available measures are always improving; the best that we think we can afford increases all the time, not least in response to increasing economic prosperity; and the latest equipment always embodies more anti-pollutant devices than do its predecessors.

An economist should insist that a trade-off between environmental benefit and economic cost is always necessary: the adoption of the test of "best practicable measures" is not a method of avoiding the necessity for choice. The speed at which we approach better practice, the cost per year of improvement, is a variable, open to political choice. It is not an absolute, and not every technical advance in pollutant control is worthy of purchase.

There is a real role for technical experts here. They can illuminate, by their studies, the financial cost of different possible actions: they can put a price-tag on particular goods. They can evaluate the nature and extent of the environmental benefit to be expected from particular measures. And they can, therefore, arrange a comparison between the cost-benefit ratios for particular actions. Such cost-benefit analysis cannot ever be conclusive: techniques can never give ultimate answers to this type of question. But they can arrange the argument in a way that can enable sensible decisions by others.

International Collaboration

There are at least two ways in which these issues can be better handled in an international, collaborative way rather than country by country. First, within any one geographical region, costs and benefits may be external to individual nation states, but internal to the region as a whole; for example, tall smoke-stack emissions, effects of pollutants on river basins, wind-blown micro-organisms, and so on. These issues transcend national boundaries but require regional rather than international frameworks for their settlement.

Secondly, however, the cost of environmental protection may be, for individual industries in individual countries, large enough to influence their competitive position. The reluctance of any one government to enforce new, higher environmental standards will be greater if it feels it is acting on its own; the willingness of governments collectively to make environmental progress will be greater if they work together.

I must try, in this talk, to be neutral on the matter of the amount of resources that should be put into environmental protection. But it is reasonable to ask for the choice to be posed in an unbiased way. The resource cost of environmental improvement cannot be avoided; it must be recognised, and faced squarely. That cost may be too high, in the minds of decision makers, to justify a particular slice of the expenditure. But it is only the resource cost which has to be borne by the international community as a whole, not the additional costs caused by the loss of competitive position by the home industry in the country that first makes the stop. In old-fashioned language, we must consider the costs (and benefits) for the international society as a whole without adding in the private costs for particular industries in the particular countries. And, indeed, those additional private costs will not be suffered at all if the move is made simultaneously by a group of countries which are highly competitive with each other.

OECD is such a grouping. It is, therefore, highly appropriate that OECD should give great weight to environmental issues.

How Rapid Should Environmental Progress Be?

The argument above does not, I must emphasize, constitute a bias towards environmental spending. All that emerges from the argument is a need to organise the analysis so as to exclude issues extraneous to the case that is being examined. Not all the set of possible environmental improvements can be bought by the international community simultaneously. It might be best not to buy some of them at any time, now or in the future; that is for discussion, case by case.

In asserting earlier in this contribution that environmental improvement and economic progress are complementary goods, I implicitly made

27

an underlying technical assumption, namely:

    i) That an additional marginal dollar of GDP can be generated with an amount of damage to the environment which would require less than a dollar of expenditure to correct.

Perhaps a rather stronger form of this assumption is appropriate, namely:

    ii) That an additional dollar of GDP can be generated with an amount of damage to the environment which would require so little expenditure to correct that it would be possible to pay all the normal marginal rewards to the factors of production involved in the activity and meet the cost of correcting the environmental damage.

If the first condition cannot be satisifed, economic progress may have to be stopped in its tracks. If the second condition cannot be satisfied, then we can expect trouble with the "Greens" (indeed I might become a Green myself), but a political settlement will in general be possible. This will have the effect of reducing the perceived economic benefit to the individual member of society from economic growth but still registering some benefit.

To test for either of these assumptions, we must impose a criterion of "environmental damage" which, as I argued earlier, cannot be absolute, is a matter of judgement and opinion and involves hunting after a moving target. I shall, if I may, offer a comment which I hope you will regard as wordly-wise rather than cynical: the criterion of environmental damage which I would expect to emerge from the political process is that which would just permit us to satisfy assumption (ii). I expect society, by and large, taking one OECD country with another, taking the swings of political fashion into account, to decide to seize with moderate enthusiasm such economic growth as is available; to spend, out of the incremental output, as much on environmental improvement as we could afford; and to accommodate the necessary environmental change with a shrug of the shoulders.

That would be my general expectation. But this would not apply equally for all economic "improvements", across the board. Some changes -- in agricultural land use, in strip-mining of coal, in the use of water resources, in the emission of pollutants to the atmosphere -- will frankly be ruled out. Well-informed economic agents should already be budgeting for that eventuality.

That is one "threat" to economic progress. Another more important danger is that the pressure to improve the environment will increase faster than the availability of resources to satisfy it. While it would be wrong to exaggerate this risk, and wrong also to suggest that any significant part of the environmentalist lobby would press their case to extremes, I am concerned that poor economic performance and fierce environmental pressures could work together in a vicious spiral. The lower the rate of economic growth, the less can be afforded for environmental improvement; the less we spend on environmental improvement, the greater will be the resistance to industrial developments that seem to require environmental damage; and the slower in consequence will be economic growth. The circle of causation is complete.

This danger is significant chiefly where economic growth is concentrated on the older "smoke-stack" industries, concentrated in old-fashioned urban developments. That type of growth is most unlikely in most OECD countries in the next two decades; our fears on this front need not, therefore, be great.

But it does not follow that fears of incompatibility between economic performance and environmental pressures can be put entirely aside. While the extreme incompatibilities of the past -- urban sprawl, industrial wastelands, inner-city decay, polluted atmospheres -- will not be recreated, it would be naive to suppose that the next 20 years will give rise to no environmental problems. Our Victorian great-grandfathers were as confident as we are that all change was progress, and it is sobering for us now to remember that many of today's environmental problems arose from errors made in our lifetimes by men and women of enlightened outlook, filled with good will for environmental issues.

Conclusions

I offer the following tentative conclusions which might stimulate useful discussions during the proceedings of this Conference:

i) Pressure for environmental improvement will increase through time, whatever happens to the availability of economic resources, whatever the growth rate of GDP as conventionally measured.

ii) It will in general be possible to generate at least sufficient "surplus" from economic growth, after financing the increased commercial expenditure that normally accompanies growth in income, to cure whatever damage growth inflicts on the environment.

iii) Provided that we do not allow the political process to move the ever-shifting target of environmental purity too rapidly away from where it stands at the moment, it should be possible for us to do even better than (ii) suggests: environmental conditions should actually improve faster the more rapidly the economy grows.

iv) There is much to be gained by international collaboration in environmental matters, both within regions (because environmental causes and effects cross national boundaries freely) and more widely (because the costs of imposing environmental standards can adversely effect the competitive position of any one country acting on its own).

v) In encouraging discussion of these issues by an informed public, we should emphasize that environmental benefits often need to be traded off against other desirable outcomes. There are, or should be, very few "absolute" goods.

vi) But some absolutes should be recognised. We should require resistance to irreversible changes in the environment, the destruction of natural or human ecologies that are irreplaceable. These assets, which a celestial Guide Michelin might designate as 4-star "Gloires de la création humaine", can be only few in number, and must be chosen with great caution. Where their preservation requires significant expenditure, this should perhaps be a charge on the international community.

SESSION ONE

ENVIRONMENTAL TRENDS, COSTS AND POLICY ISSUES THROUGH 1990

CHAIRMAN'S OPENING SPEECH

Hon. Dr. Karl-Heinz NARJES

Member of the Commission, Commission of the European Communities

Mr. Chairman, Mr. Secretary-General, ministerial colleagues, ladies and gentlemen, we have all listened attentively to the wise and far-sighted statements made earlier this morning which have launched our Conference. They have clearly set our agenda for the next few days.

As I see it the basic task of our Conference is to address the question of whether economic growth and development is compatible with necessary environmental protection. My answer to that is clear and simple: Yes, it is. It has to be made to be. Because the world needs both.

In developed and in developing countries we are faced with a deep-rooted structural adjustment process. Of course, in industrial countries the structural problems have been accompanied by a severe cyclical crisis. Nevertheless, the task is to respond to a series of new challenges. These are -- and I am just limiting myself to some of these ideas -- adjustment to shortages in raw materials, for example the high price of oil, the increasing scarcity of water, in particular in developing countries, and perhaps the scarcity and rising costs of cereals in eastern countries and worldwide.

One of the factors which has become scarce and which will become much more expensive is a clean environment. There are several pressing problems which illustrate this trend, such as deforestation and desertification in developing countries, air pollution, in particular acid deposition, throughout the whole of the northern hemisphere and an increasing problem of waste.

It is in that sense that we all know well -- if we are being honest -- that we have no real choice about environmental protection. It is absolutely essential and fundamental. We cannot afford not to have it. The European Community's latest environmental action programme puts it well when it states flatly that: "The resources of the environment are the basis of -- but set the limits to -- further economic and social development and the improvement of living conditions".

Our task is clear -- to devise and enforce strict environmental protection policies which will provide a healthy environment for the present and future generations, whilst at the same time facilitating and encouraging further economic growth and development.

We have all made a beginning over the last 20 years with the development of responsible environmental policies -- but only a beginning.

Too much of the environment is still treated as a waste tip, too many of our rivers are in effect sewers, too much avoidable damage is done to wildlife and to nature.

It is clear that, in order to achieve a smooth adjustment process, changes must be made and must be managed in a way aiming to adjust present instruments, where necessary, introducing new tools within the next few years. Clearly, it is not a question of "whether", but a question of "how and when".

In large measure, as far as existing environmental problems are concerned, we already know, if we are being honest, what is needed. As far as new problems are concerned, we know that we have a good chance of avoiding future environmental "time-bombs" if we build sufficiently strict environmental protection measures into the planning and execution of new developments. And we know, too, that, properly used, innovation, industrial restructuring and new developments of all kinds can be positive for the environment.

The reasons why we have not already made more rapid progress than we have are almost entirely economic. Hence the key importance of this Conference.

Actually to achieve the necessary adjustments, both vision and political will are required to achieve a proper balance of economic and environmental arguments and to persist against too short-sighted economic arguments. And it will involve making changes in structures, decision-making processes, frameworks for economic analyses and judgement. All these are matters that we shall be looking into in detail in the next few days.

Furthermore, we all believe in the efficiency of the free market system, subject to surveillance of course, but not strangled by regulations. If, in such a situation, we are to succeed in achieving our environmental goals, then I believe (in addition to using regulations to secure basic levels of protection) that we shall need more and more to find ways of using market mechanisms to serve environmental (as well as economic) goals. In other words I believe that our ultimate objective should be to find ways of adjusting the frameworks within which economic judgements are made so that decision makers, in going for what is economically attractive and profitable, will also serve environmental ends.

This would mean, in particular, that the framework within which market economies are efficient should be altered in such a way as to adjust economies to ways and means of production which take account of the scarcity of clean environment. This would be one of the foundations of a more general policy to be pursued, based on the principle of prevention rather than cure.

A large part of our task in the next few days will be to examine tools and instruments in some detail and to identify the most promising ways forward so that -- dare I say it -- by 1990 we shall no longer be asking whether we should impose tough environmental policies but only whether the tools we are using are effective to that end.

Mr. Chairman, Mr. Secretary-General, ministers, ladies and gentlemen, I believe that our goals are clear, and widely shared. Our task is to find means of attaining them.

A first step towards finding solutions for problems is to define the problems. And that is our task in Session 1.

Let me draw some conclusions from the interesting Issue Papers concerning this session. It seems to me that the problems of air pollution, as far as acid deposits are concerned, will remain with us and, according to the statistics worked out by the Secretariat, air quality is likely to deteriorate. We, in the European Commission, do not entirely share this pessimistic view. We are much more of the opinion that the European Community as a block of 270 million people in the centre of Europe, with its legislative capacity, will substantially reduce these problems.

Furthermore, water availability and the quality of water is an issue which will become of major global importance. Finally, industrial countries are likely to encounter new problems from non-conventional pollutants including concentrations in surface water and groundwater resulting from run-off from agriculture and problems associated with hazardous wastes.

As far as costs are concerned we should not be obsessed and blinkered by the undoubted cost implications (for both industries and products) of many necessary environmental measures, but we must also -- and increasingly -- pay attention to the damage costs (which can in many cases include a lot of human misery and suffering) of failing to take necessary measures as well as to the economic benefits that can be generated by at least some environmental policies.

That is our agenda for the remainder of today, and a long and challenging one it is. I can think of no one better than Professor Gerelli, who has a long and distinguished record in many fields -- not least in the work he has undertaken for the OECD's Environment Committee -- to launch us into our debate on these issues.

Without further ado therefore I should like to give the floor to our Keynote Speaker, Professor Gerelli.

THE LIMITS TO GROWTH OR GROWTH OF THE LIMITS?

Introduction by

Professor Emilio GERELLI

Chairman, Commission on Public Expenditures,
Ministry of the Treasury, Rome, and Director,
Post-Graduate School of Environmental Land-Use
Management, University of Pavia, Italy

"It is scarcely necessary to remark that a
stationary condition of capital and population implies
no stationary state of human improvement".

John Stuart Mill

"The progressive state is in reality the cheerful and
the hearty state to all the different orders of the society.
The stationary is dull; the declining, melancholy".

Adam Smith

The main conclusions to be drawn from the Issue Paper submitted to this Session are the following. Two scenarios are considered. If emissions of conventional pollutants are kept at 1978 (base-year) level, pollution control expenditures will increase by more than 100 per cent in the OECD area by the end of the 1990s. On the other hand if standards are not tightened with respect to the base-year level pollution will substantially increase, but control expenditures will increase by only 20 per cent (in real terms).

Of critical importance is the underlying assumption that technology will be constant throughout the period (certain structural changes are taken into account, however). On this basis the conclusions drawn by the study are to a degree limited to past patterns, which is quite justified by the time horizon (12 years).

We may choose between the virtue of perspiration (in case standards are tightened and costs rise) or well-earned tears due to high pollution (if the scenario "low costs, low standards" holds).

Since I shall take a rather critical view of the assumption I mentioned (with some degree of unfairness in order to be brief), let me stress at the outset that the OECD Secretariat, guided by the Group of Economic Experts, has

35

done a very useful piece of solid work by gathering and organising evidence where it was available and (what is more) by generating information through skill and imagination where data were not available at the national level (where the OECD Study could be a useful inspiration to be followed by several countries). Let me also add, on a personal basis, that 14 years ago I had the privilege of being the first to guide the group of environmental economists in the newly founded OECD Environment Directorate. It has always been a very fine group of highly skilled professionals, who have given important contributions both in assessing environmental problems and in developing policy suggestions. The development of the well-known Polluter-Pays Principle is just one example.

Since the Group of Economic Experts and the Secretariat have shown full awareness of the simplifying assumptions they used in their Issue Paper, I think it is appropriate for me to relax some of them and see what meaningful variations can be introduced, particularly when stretching out the time horizon beyond the 1990s. In other words, although nihil sub sole novi, I shall at least try to see things from a different window.

Disregarding short-term business cycles, the situation of reduced growth rates which has been a characteristic of industrialised economies in the late 1970s and in the 1980s may be interpreted (depending on the way you want to organise economic history) either as the beginning of a third industrial revolution, or as a preliminary stage before the beginning of a new long wave à la Kondratiev. All long waves (time-spans of 25 to 50 years) of the past have been linked to a technological breakthrough: the steam engine, railway construction, electricity, the motor car (1).

We are now entering the age of mass computerisation, involving all aspects of social and economic life, and are gradually leaving the industry mainly based on fossil fuels and mechanical systems.

New activities are developing which can be looked upon as a technical synthesis of industry and ecology; for example, biotechnologies, the transformation of the biomass, alternative energies, recycling and so on. Further developing sectors are of course microelectronics, materials technology and others. Assuming these technologies will produce growth (once again displacing the famous limits) (2) one cannot a priori say whether such a growth will be "clean" or "dirty", but I would contend that appropriate policies could make it fairly clean. This may be so first of all because some of the new activities (microelectronics, the information industry) do not create much pollution; they often do not conglomerate into "black spots" (3) but on the contrary require a pleasant environment (the "Silicon Valley Effect"), thus creating demand for environmental amenities.

Secondly, even new activities potentially dangerous to the environment, such as biotechnologies, are being developed in a setting which is no longer the "cowboy" economy and has experienced Minimata, Seveso, Love Canal and so on. The experience is there and it is up to us to make intelligent use of it in developing new technologies.

I have no technological breakthrough to displace the limits of time allotted to me. I must therefore already jump to conclusions. I have already said that our Issue Paper leaves us with the dismal choice between perspiration and tears. This may by and large be unavoidable in the next, say, 10 years. Even beyond that I cannot promise you anything better, but perhaps something different for which we must, however, prepare now.

Here, therefore, is my recipe:

i) Our Issue Paper rather supports the culture I called "perspiration or tears" (put up either with high costs or with a bad environment). I do not wholly disagree but I would contend that we should also spread from this Conference the culture of the management of change: technology and society do change.

ii) It is likely that our new economic development, if any, will take place particularly through the creation of economically integrated but decentralised small units. To support and provide a large number of technologically advanced units with appropriate public policies and facilities, we shall need some type of efficient federal government (that is, the appropriate distribution of government functions at local, regional, central and international level). General Motors knew and probably still know what they believe is good for them and for America, and have no difficulties in making it known. Governments, however, need more ingenuity to understand what is to be done for an efficient working of several dispersed units. The message from the author of Small is Beautiful is "to achieve smallness within large organisation". The very raw material of progress, information and knowledge, is moving faster, the world is shrinking from this view-point, and this is likely to increase the role of international organisations like the OECD and EEC in coping with the increasing number of problems which spill over national borders. This Conference is a major opportunity to think how environmental policies can be integrated into institutional change at both the national and international level.

iii) The new economic structure will probably increase a characteristic which is already with us: the separation between those who have a job in the productive system and those who are outside and cannot enter it. Job creation connected to the conservation and use of the environment (tourism will be very important) will be relevant, and will be discussed later in our Conference.

iv) Environment is mainly a non-market sector and so, in general, will be the job creation sector just mentioned. Non-market sectors give rise to the problem of inefficient use of resources because of the lack of automatic incentives and penalties. Environment has developed useful instruments of market stimulation to help solve this problem (charges and "bubble" and other policies related to the auction of pollution rights). These instruments should be further developed and transferred with imagination to other non-market sectors (it is not impossible, for example, to develop indicators even of the "productivity" of a nature park and to link related salaries to it).

v) Charité bien ordonnée commence par soi-même. I have not been following this wise saying, since, as a Mediterranean, I am only as a last topic taking up one of the points repeatedly made in the issue paper: that southern Europe is very late in tackling environmental problems. I want to declare, however, that I wholly agree with it, and I want to support the OECD warnings; therefore providean consules, because we southerners are about 20 years late in environmental policies.

Finally, lest I be accused by my ecologist friends, let me declare that I feel I am not a happy-go-lucky economist; I have never asked what future generations have done for us. I believe that Georgescu Roegen is right in saying that owing to the working of the entropy law not even the stationary state will perpetuate mankind (4). The question is that even the choice of the time horizon for relevant policies is a value judgement and a political choice. What is more, I believe we have a choice among different environmental and economic paths before doom is here. Let us at least try to choose the way which minimises our unavoidable tears and perspiration.

NOTES AND REFERENCES

1.   For a brilliant review see: J. Huber, Die verlorene Unschuld der Oekologie, Fischer, Frankfurt, 1982. This book has been stimulating in writing this note.

2.   My position with regard to the limits to growth is spelled out in detail in J. Ph. Barde, E. Gerelli, Economie et politique de l'environnement, Paris, Presses Universitaires de France, 1977, pp. 50-60.

3.   This is however maybe a mixed blessing since dispersion of activities consumes more land and may render pollution control more costly.

4.   See N. GEORGESCU ROEGEN, The Entropy Law and the Economic Process, Cambridge (Mass.), Harvard University Press, 1971.

ENVIRONMENTAL TRENDS, COSTS AND POLICY ISSUES THROUGH 1990

1. INTRODUCTION

During the late 1960s and early 1970s OECD Member countries acted to stem the rising level of "conventional" pollutants from the industrial and household sectors and to clean up the backlog of pollution resulting from previous decades of uncontrolled growth. The emphasis then was on the emissions of SO_x, NO_x, HC, CO and particulates into the air, discharges into water leading to biochemical oxygen demand, BOD and COD, and the run-off and seepage from the use of fertilizers and pesticides into surface and ground water. The precise policy responses varied between countries and reflected, among other things, the magnitude of the problem to be resolved and the ability of the economy to support the cost. But the direction of policy was the same: to put right previous environmental wrongs.

Today, the declared direction of policy is to go one stage further by adopting measures to prevent the negative and enhance the positive effects on the environment of human activities. OECD Environment Ministers, meeting in Paris in 1979, agreed that:

"... even if further economic developments were only moderate, the potential environmental consequences in many sectors could be considerable. For this reason there should be no relaxation of effort. Indeed strengthened measures, designed with a view to their economic efficiency and cost effectiveness and focussed on prevention rather than remedial action, will be needed to maintain and improve present levels of environmental quality; and to promote the concept of qualitative growth -- a partnership between environmental and economic concerns."

Reflecting on the concerns expressed in this statement made by Ministers five years ago, there are two major issues that call for discussion. The first relates to the identification of the priority problems and opportunities for environmental management presented by economic, social, and technical change through the end of this decade. This issue involves not only the conventional issues and pollutants that have been addressed in the past but also new issues that are emerging in the fields of pollution, resources, and the quality of life.

Second, an effort should be made to identify the role that government policy in other areas (such as economy, energy, agriculture, and other sectoral policies) plays in affecting the environment. The environmental and economic consequences of not examining these relationships could be great, and the interest in greater efficiency in formulating and effecting government policy requires this examination.

This paper presents the basic data for this discussion by documenting past emission levels and past pollution control costs, by projecting potential future emission levels under different scenarios and by analysing the direction of likely trends in both emission levels and control costs during the last half of this decade. The issue paper on Future Directions for Environmental Policies discusses the types of actions that could be taken to reduce the adverse effects of these trends (Session 8).

2. SUMMARY OF PROJECTED EMISSION TRENDS FOR CONVENTIONAL POLLUTANTS

To provide a basis for the formulation of anticipatory policies, the Group of Economic Experts of the OECD's Environment Committee undertook a programme of work designed to project the major emission and expenditure trends through 1990. The results of that work programme are described in the Emission Trends background paper for this session. The objective of this effort was to develop projections on a uniform basis for all OECD countries. Consequently, the projections were made, perforce, on a very aggregated level (presented here on an OECD-regional basis -- see Figure 1) based on 1978 coefficients and with assumptions that could not include detailed national considerations. Nevertheless, despite its considerable limitations such an analysis provides a useful indication of the pressures that projected economic, industrial and social changes could place on the environment by the end of this decade. It is also useful to compare the OECD's projections to those developed by a limited number of OECD countries who have been able to incorporate specific, detailed assumptions (such as age structure of industry and details of existing or planned regulations) that are impossible to include in a broader analysis. At the same time, the OECD analysis provides a benchmark for those countries that have so far not undertaken such projections.

The underlying rate of growth of polluting activities in the OECD as a whole will be substantially less in the 1980s than in the 1960s and early 1970s, but broadly on a par with the second half of the 1970s. The growth of manufacturing output is projected to be around one-third to one-half of the rates achieved in the 1960s, the car population growth will be less than half the rate of the early 1970s, and the growth in energy use in manufacturing and in electricity generation will grow at a similarly slow rate. In addition, structural changes away from the more polluting industries (such as treatment of mineral ores and metal manufacture) are expected to continue, as is the switch to the use of cleaner fuels in both the electricity generation and household sectors. All are factors that augur relatively well for a lower rate of growth in emissions of conventional pollutants.

However, more complex environmental problems are emerging, such as acid rain, whose genesis is in these conventional pollutants and the very processes designed to control them. In addition, a new group of environmental concerns have recently assumed much greater importance, including hazardous waste, toxic chemicals, the degradation of groundwater from fertilizers and

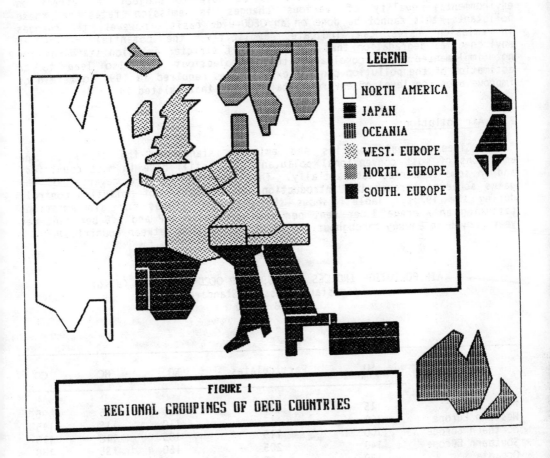

LEGEND

☐ NORTH AMERICA
■ JAPAN
▥ OCEANIA
▦ WEST. EUROPE
▨ NORTH. EUROPE
■ SOUTH. EUROPE

FIGURE 1
REGIONAL GROUPINGS OF OECD COUNTRIES

pesticides used in agriculture, and the contamination of soil by heavy metals. And the rising spectre of a much broader class of environmental concerns, those on a global scale such as rising levels of CO and CFCs in the atmosphere, is gaining more and more attention.

While it would be desirable to be able to project the effect on environmental quality of various changes in emission rates of these pollutants, this cannot be done on an OECD-wide basis. However, the changes in emission rates can indicate, implicitly, the potential damage in environmental degradation that could occur if stricter emission standards are not implemented. By corollary, these projections can also lead to an estimation of the pollution control expenditures required in 1990 to retain or improve upon the level of environmental quality that existed in 1978.

2.1. Air Pollution

Given present policies and emission standards, the trend in the emissions of most conventional pollutants will still rise in most countries, and in some countries substantially. This could represent a reversal of the gains achieved through the introduction and tightening of pollution controls during the 1970s. Table 1 shows the projected trends for air emissions (assuming an average 3 per cent per year growth in GDP and 1.8 per cent per year growth in energy throughout the OECD, but varying between countries).

Table 1

AIR POLLUTION INDICES FOR 1990 FOR OECD COUNTRIES (a)(b)
(Constant Emission Standards)
1978 = 100

	SO_x	Particulates	NO_x	HC	CO
North America	115	115	105	105	95
Western Europe	100	115	110	115	115
Northern Europe	100	115	105	110	115
Southern Europe	140	205	150	135	130
Oceania	190	190	165	105	105

a) There are no projections available for Japan at the aggregate level.

b) In recent years a number of OECD countries (US, Canada, Austria, France, Netherlands, Norway and Sweden) prepared national projections of emissions. All these projections, based largely on standards to be implemented during the 1980s and on improved technologies, show smaller increases or further declines in emissions than those given in the table. For example, for Northern America the index of SO_x emissions for 1990 is projected at 96 and for NO_x at 103 by a recent joint US/Canadian Committee.

Table 1 sets out the emission trends in the form of indices, based on 1978, for the various OECD regions. The table presents trends only. Nothing can be deduced from the table about absolute levels, which differ widely between regions, or about the absorbing capacity of the environment in these regions. For example, a very large increase in emissions in Oceania might still lead to an acceptable level of pollution while a small decline in Western Europe will leave pollution at an unacceptably high level. Although in general it is difficult to compare these figures to past emissions because of the limitation of data, such comparisons are made below where possible.

As explained above, national projections of emission trends may differ substantially from the OECD projections. For example, the OECD projections for 1990 show higher emissions for North America for all air pollutants except CO. On the other hand, projections prepared by a joint US/Canadian Committee suggest that SO_x emissions will decline slightly and NO_x emissions increase marginally. However, even at these levels, acid rain is likely to remain a serious problem, and particulate pollution could also remain severe due to the projected increase in the use of coal in the electricity generating sector. This picture is in contrast to air pollution trends during the 1970s, when emissions of all conventional pollutants, with the exception of NO_x, declined by between 20 and 50 per cent in the United States, while in Canada, SO_x, CO and HC emissions declined -- the latter two by over 30 per cent -- although NO_x and particulate emissions increased.

In Oceania, substantial increases in emissions of SO_x, NO_x, and particulates are projected, while HC and CO emissions should remain stable. The industry sector is likely to be the major source of increase in these emissions in both Australia and New Zealand. In Australia, the electricity generating sector will be an additional major source of air pollutants due to large increases in coal use; as will the household sector in the case of NO_x, due to increased use of gas. In New Zealand, the growth in the motor vehicle population will aggravate the NO_x problem. However, these increases will come on top of relatively low levels of pollution.

No projections were possible in the case of Japan. Most of the basic data available for Japan are highly disaggregated, and therefore not suitable for the type of projections presented here.

The projections for Western Europe, as a whole, reveal no particular pollutant increasing significantly. This reflects partly the low rates of growth in energy use combined with a switch away from the more polluting fossil fuels in many countries. More important than fuel switching is the move from "low-level" household emissions to "high-level", longer range SO_x emissions from electricity generation. This phenomenon, which is mirrored in North America, will result in a constant or increasing level of SO_x emissions, resulting in the continuation of the serious problems caused by acid rain.

Even though the whole picture is projected to remain relatively stable, there are differences between countries, as might be expected. The United Kingdom is likely to face the smallest increases in emission levels of the Western European region. Other countries, however, could be faced with relatively high rates of growth in particular emissions in certain sectors. For example, Ireland faces increases of up to 85 per cent in the growth of air emissions from the household sector; while Germany, Austria, the Netherlands and (again) Ireland face substantial increases in emissions from electricity generation. However, new standards such as those recently introduced in Germany to retrofit the major SO_x emitters will significantly reduce emissions.

These trends can be compared to those documented in Germany and the Netherlands during the 1970s. In Germany, particulates and CO declined substantially, SO_x remained constant, but both NO_x and HC increased between 25 and 35 per cent. In the Netherlands, emissions of all conventional air pollutants with the exception of NO_x declined between 10 and 30 per cent.

As in Western Europe, emissions of conventional air pollutants in Northern Europe should remain fairly constant. However, due to a projected switch from oil to coal, emissions of particulates by both manufacturing industry (process rather than energy-related emissions) and electricity generation are the main concern.

Southern Europe faces the most serious air pollution control problem in the OECD region -- with 30-50 per cent rates of growth in most pollutants and over 100 per cent in the case of particulates. This derives from the projected high rates of economic growth and energy use in the period to 1990. The potential environmental effect of this rapid rise in emissions is compounded by the limited nature of the control programmes in place in the base year.

2.2. Motor Vehicle Pollution

Future emissions from motor vehicles have been projected on the basis of emission standards already established. Taking these standards and schedules for implementation into account, emissions of HC, CO and NO_x are projected to be lower in 1990 in almost all areas of the OECD than they were in 1978. The principal exceptions are Northern and Western Europe, where HC emissions could experience substantial increases, and Southern Europe, where emissions of HC are projected to increase by up to 55 per cent, CO by up to 9 per cent and NO_x by up to 41 per cent. (The projections of emission trends from motor vehicles by Norway and Sweden indicate trends different from those of the OECD projections.)

While this picture for the motor vehicle sector is on the whole positive, three aspects of vehicle pollution not covered in detail in the OECD analysis could pose a serious problem for the future. The first is noise pollution. Projections for a number of countries point to an increasing proportion of their population being exposed to "unacceptable" (more than 65 decibels) levels of vehicle noise. The other two are lead (Pb) emissions and diesel emissions. Except in North America and Japan, these pollutants have only recently been recognised as major environmental concerns by OECD countries.

The projections prepared as national aggregates cannot reflect the sub-national, regional concentration of emissions. In the past, the emission concentrations seriously affecting human health or causing major nuisances occurred in and around the large population centres. Some of the projected increases in emissions will aggravate the problems of the major population centres, where emissions already exceed acceptable standards, including vehicle noise. For the future, policies should be developed and implemented with the objective of reducing in a significant way the emission loads in these areas.

2.3. Water Pollution

As a result of the unavailability of data on other conventional water pollutants, OECD's projections of water pollution discharges were limited to projections of biochemical oxygen demand (BOD and COD). On the basis of simple extrapolations (assuming a proportional relationship between BOD and COD discharges and manufacturing growth), the rate of growth of BOD and COD discharges by industry is likely to grow by 20 per cent in Western Europe, 30 per cent in North America, and 40 per cent in Southern Europe.

While industry will be the major source of growth in water discharges, those from the household sector (which are determined primarily by rates of population growth) are expected to increase as well during the period to 1990, by about 2 per cent for Northern and Western Europe, by about 6 per cent for Japan, by about 10 per cent for North America, and by around 12 per cent for Southern Europe.

Judging from information on local and regional changes in water quality (lakes, rivers, coastal waters), a substantial reduction in discharges must have occurred during the 1970s in those countries with legislation on these pollutants. Although the data do not permit a close comparison, they indicate that, unless discharge standards are tightened, this reduction in discharges is not likely to continue through the 1980s.

3. THE NEW ENVIRONMENTAL CHALLENGES

3.1. Chemical Products and Toxic Residuals

While most of the previous discussion has centred on the more "conventional" pollutants, a significant problem for the future will be the multitude of pollutants with potentially dangerous, life-threatening properties. The problems they pose can be divided into two broad categories, each of which then is further divided into two sub-categories. The two broad categories are chemicals as products and chemicals as toxic residuals. The problems of chemicals as products then divides into new chemicals and existing chemicals, while the toxic residuals problem divides into emissions/discharges and hazardous wastes.

Because new chemicals control programmes in OECD countries have been implemented at different times, the only available data on the number of new chemicals created annually are from the United States. Extrapolating these data, which are based on the US rather than EEC definition of a new chemical, the number of chemicals created in all OECD countries in 1990 is projected to be about 6 600. However, because of the differences in how a new chemical is defined for the purposes of the new chemical programmes, the total number of chemicals subject to these programmes in 1990 is projected to be only about 3 360.

45

The attention of many Member countries has recently turned to the problem of controlling existing chemicals that present unacceptable risks to human health and the environment. There are about 80 000 existing chemical products of which about 4 000 may require extensive testing.

The problems posed by the emission or discharge of toxic chemicals is often handled at the same time that conventional pollutants are controlled. For that reason, most of the industrial pollution control expenditures to be presented in this paper already include the cost of controlling these emissions and discharges to some degree. One problem not discussed above, however, is that of the accumulation of these toxic discharges in humans, animals, and the environment. Unless emissions and discharges of many toxic chemicals (such as heavy metals and PCBs) are eliminated altogether, their concentration in human tissues and the environment will be expected to increase. This severe problem has been addressed by several Member countries with respect to lead and mercury, but further action will be required in the future.

Hazardous waste problems, which became prominent only in recent years, will have to be dealt with urgently during the 1980s. There is a serious backlog of toxic chemicals inappropriately disposed as well as the accumulation of newly generated hazardous waste. The amount of waste inventory from the past is estimated at 300 to 400 million tons in OECD Europe and 2 000 million tons in the United States. Of this, 4 to 8 per cent is likely to need remedial action. The clean-up of the backlog is urgent and requires additional expenditures. Newly generated waste can be effectively disposed of with an efficient monitoring system, licensing of treatments and disposal facilities, and through international co-operation concerning the transfrontier movement of hazardous waste. It is estimated that at present 30 to 35 million tons of hazardous waste is being generated annually in OECD Europe and about 150 million tons in the United States.

3.2. Agricultural Pollution

The relatively fast growth in crop and animal production, 2 to 3 per cent per year, will continue in most OECD countries through the 1980s. The main pollution processes associated with agriculture can occur from the intensive use of nitrogenous and phosphorous fertilizers and animal waste. There are indications that nitrate concentrations in ground and surface waters, which have shown a marked increase in the last twenty years, could rapidly increase and become a health hazard. Urgent action is likely to be needed in the form of better water management, codes of good practice for farmers and economic measures (such as proper pricing of fertilizers) to minimise the risk to health.

3.3. New Technology

Through to 1990, OECD countries are expected to continue to face a wide range of new technologies emerging and a seemingly faster pace of technological change and use. These technological changes are the very engine of economic progress, and they provide new opportunities as well as new problems for the environment and environmental policy making. New opportunities emerge from the introduction of new technologies:

micro-electronics for monitoring and control of pollutants and new technologies for waste treatment, including biotechnologies, and economic recovery of residuals.

On the other hand, materials science is now leading towards an increasing degree of materials substitution driven by economics and shortage of natural materials. This will lead to the substitution of new materials for those posing environmental hazards as well as to the use of potentially damaging new materials. Similarly, biotechnologies with engineered organisms may present wholly new forms of environmental threats that will require careful monitoring.

4. THE EXPENDITURE IMPLICATIONS OF POLLUTION CONTROL PROGRAMMES

4.1. Expenditure Trends

The OECD analysis of emission trends to the 1990s also considered the cost implications of different degrees of emission controls. Two scenarios were developed: one assumed that average emission standards in 1978 would remain the same right through 1990 for existing and new sources of pollution (that is, constant standards). The other assumed that standards would be tightened as necessary to ensure that the total volume of emissions did not exceed that experienced in 1978 (that is, constant emissions). The one exception to this was motor vehicles where it was assumed, with the exception of one sub-scenario, that the standards already established for the 1980s would be implemented on schedule in both scenarios. Table 2 below sets out the likely expenditure increases under both scenarios. Column (1) shows the expenditure trends assuming that 1978 emission standards, including those for motor vehicles, are retained.

Costs are calculated for the emission of conventional pollutants into the air by industry, electricity generation and motor vehicles, for water discharges by industry affecting COD and BOD load, and for municipal wastewater treatment. Because water pollution expenditure data seldom distinguish between control costs for conventional and toxic pollutants, separate projections were not possible. Other areas where projections were not possible because of insufficient data are agricultural sources of pollution, emissions from household/commercial energy use, the collection of municipal solid waste, the testing and control of existing chemicals, the amelioration of abandoned hazardous waste sites, and the treatment, storage, and disposal of hazardous waste.

It should be noted that certain countries are omitted from the table owing to lack of information. In addition, the information available for the three Southern European countries -- Greece, Portugal and Spain -- is incomplete and extremely tenuous. For these countries no data were available for power plants and industry (except Portugal), but it is thought that increases in expenditures for pollution control in industry and power plants would be similar to increases calculated for the other polluting sectors in these countries.

47

Table 2

POLLUTION CONTROL EXPENDITURE INDICES FOR 1990
(CONSTANT 1978 PRICES, 1978 = 100)

| | Constant Standards Scenario (a) | | Constant Emissions Scenario (b) |
	1978 Auto Standards (1)	1990 Auto Standards (2)	(3)
Canada	125	180	255
United States	120	135	165
Australia	120	175	320
Austria	140	150	235
Belgium	120	135	225
France	110	120	160
Germany	110	110	130
Netherlands	125	135	185
Switzerland	125	140	180
United Kingdom	100	105	110
Denmark	120	125	260
Finland	125	130	210
Norway	100	105	125
Sweden	105	100	130
Greece	110	250	(700)
Italy	120	135	240
Portugal	150	300	(1 000)
Spain	145	175	(400)

a) Assumes 1978 emission standards and control technology. The lower end of the cost range for 1990 auto emission controls was assumed for the second column.

b) Assumes that for 1990 total emissions are kept at 1978 levels except for motor vehicles, which may be lower. The upper end of the cost range of all cost estimates was assumed.

The major point which emerges from the Table is that under the 1978 constant standards scenario with 1978 motor vehicles control cost (column 1), the projected expenditure increases over the period 1978-1990 could be well below those experienced in the 1970s. They range from 1 per cent in the case of the United Kingdom to 39 per cent in the case of Austria; over half the countries would face increases to 20 per cent. The implementation of mandated motor vehicles standards (column 2) would add substantially to the pollution control expenditure totals projected for a number of countries -- notably North America, Australia and Southern Europe. But even so, in the worst case, the expenditures expressed as a percentage of GDP rise no more than marginally.

As would be expected, the projected rise in expenditures is greatest under the constant total emissions scenario. In the majority of countries, if standards were tightened as necessary to keep the total volume of emissions down to 1978 levels (column 3), pollution control expenditures would at least double. In particular, the countries of Southern Europe would face levels of expenditure several times greater than they have experienced in the past. Even so, they would be incurred only to achieve a standstill, not an improvement, in the level of emissions. Should there be significant technological improvements, these cost increases are likely to be smaller. But even without such improvements the claims of environmental policies on the resources of the whole economy remain relatively small.

If the costs of chemical testing, hazardous waste disposal, and controlling toxic substances and run-off from the agricultural sector were fully included, the projections would show an even greater expenditure increase. Rough estimates suggest that existing controls on toxic substances account for 30-40 per cent of the costs to industry of controlling discharges into water. Further strengthening of controls could add at least 10-15 per cent to these costs.

The cost of the notification and testing programmes for new chemicals for 1990 is projected to range between $30 million and $70 million (in 1981 prices). Existing chemical controls, because of the cost of deciding which chemicals require control and then effecting the necessary control, vary so much from chemical to chemical, that it is not possible to develop an overall estimate of potential costs for 1990. However, based on past experience in the United States, the costs could be quite high: for example, control costs of CFC aerosols were about $1.2 billion and PCBs about $2.1 billion. With respect to testing existing chemicals, costs could range from $500 to $700 000 per chemical (1983 prices), depending upon which tests are required, and the number of chemicals that may require testing ranges from 4 000 to 10 000. These costs will be spread over 10 to 15 years.

Future disposal costs for hazardous waste are likely to be significantly higher, perhaps as much as 100 per cent higher than previous disposal methods such as simple landfilling. The current annual cost associated with the disposal of these wastes is about $9 billion (1983 prices). The amelioration of hazardous waste sites could cost OECD countries $300-$400 million (1983 prices) annually for the next 10 to 20 years. If the potential costs of victim compensation are added, these figures could become considerable underestimates.

Figure 2 gives pollution control expenditures as a percentage of GDP in 1990 for the constant total emissions scenario for OECD countries. These expenditures cover all costs for air pollution control including toxic emissions, all costs for water pollution control including municipal waste water and disposal of solid wastes. Comparing these percentages for 1990 with those for 1978 the ratio of pollution control expenditures to GDP rises from slightly less than 2 per cent in 1978 to slightly above 2 per cent in 1990 in

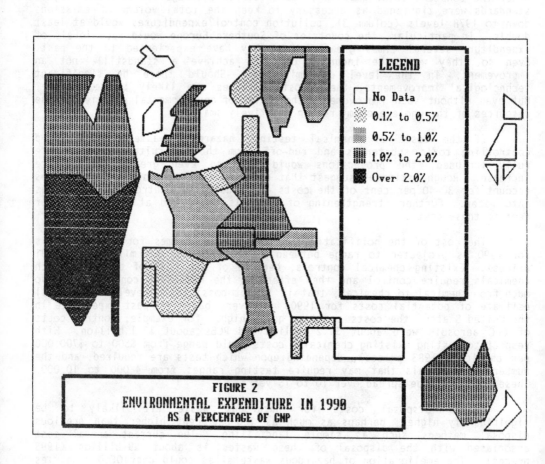

LEGEND

- ☐ No Data
- ░ 0.1% to 0.5%
- ▒ 0.5% to 1.0%
- ▤ 1.0% to 2.0%
- ■ Over 2.0%

FIGURE 2

ENVIRONMENTAL EXPENDITURE IN 1990

AS A PERCENTAGE OF GNP

only one country: the United States. The ratio in 1990 will be between 0.5 and 2 per cent of GDP for the majority of OECD countries. This is the same range as in 1978 but with some decline for the United Kingdom, Sweden and Germany. The percentage of GDP taken up in pollution control expenditure in Southern Europe will not rise above 0.5 per cent by 1990; Belgium, Denmark and Norway will also remain in this range. In comparing the percentages among countries, it should be remembered that these percentages reflect relative amounts of resources devoted to environmental protection, and that environmental quality is influenced also by the degree and type of industrialisation and by the absorbing capacity of the environment in each country.

4.2. Financing of Expenditures

Although the prospects are in general good for the majority of countries to maintain their total emissions at 1978 levels, without undue strain on the economy as a whole, each country will necessarily decide how, when, and, most importantly, by whom the total environmental burden (pollution control cost and residual damage) shall be borne in the light of their own economic, industrial and environmental circumstances. The Polluter-Pays Principle and other OECD recommendations combined with the conclusions of this analysis offer guidance for the 1980s to Member governments for developing environmental policies that are economically efficient and cost effective.

From the point of view of financing of pollution control expenditure, the relevant questions are what proportion of total expenditures are financed out of taxes and from charges and fees. While the majority of OECD countries now collect data on governmental expenditures on environmental management on a fairly consistent basis, there are still a number of OECD governments, that, on account of diffused departmental responsibilities, are not very well informed on the size of their own gross and net environmental expenditures. It would greatly assist both policy making and public understanding of the efforts of individual governments if their expenditure in the field of environment were better documented.

For the future indications are that the proportion of environmental expenditures financed by governments are not going to change significantly. However, there is still considerable scope for governments to recoup the costs of their services in the form of user charges and thereby reduce the direct tax burden on their constituants.

Similarly governments could reduce further the amount of assistance provided by them to industry for pollution control purposes, even though the present size of this assistance appears to be small. The results of the 'Notification Scheme for Financial Assistance' carried out as part of the implementation of the Polluter-Pays Principle, show that in the late '70s the financial assistance to industry was, with the exception of one country, less than 4 per cent of total industrial environmental investment. The report, prepared by the Group of Economic Experts of the Environment Committee of the OECD and adopted by the Council of the OECD, concluded that "significant distortions in trade probably would not occur at the aggregate level" on account of this financial assistance, but could draw no conclusions on the trade impacts at the sectoral or industrial level. The report also concluded that concerning the formal compliance with the Polluter-Pays Principle, only one country still provided assistance to new industry, but the conditions for specifying and terminating the transitional period, during which assistance might be provided, are not strictly followed.

Long-term economic efficiency suggests that all subsidies for environmental purposes should be phased out. The issue is how quickly OECD countries could move towards this objective. There are those who argue that the short-term environmental objectives should not be threatened by too rapid and full an implementation of the Polluter-Pays Principle. Of course, if the Positive Adjustment Policies advocated by the OECD were implemented in all fields of governmental assistance, not only in the field of environment, then overall economic efficiency would be achieved more quickly, without any threat to the achievement of the environmental objectives.

Industry, including the electricity sector, was paying in the 1970s for about 30 to 40 per cent of all environmental expenditure in most countries. In the three most industrialised OECD countries, the United States, Germany and Japan, pollution control investment by industry (excluding electricity generation) amounted to between 4 and 14 per cent of total industrial investment; for the individual industry branches they varied between just over 1 per cent for 'machinery' branches, to over 20 per cent for oil refining. Investment costs have been about half of the total environmental expenditure by industry. The other half consists of operation and maintenance costs, but there are significant variations between countries. While at the macro level the net impacts of these expenditures on industrial profits and prices were insignificant (e.g., incomes from pollution control activities about equalled expenditures in industry as a whole in Germany), impacts were probably more marked on the individual branches of industry. However, little is known about these effects: for example, to what extent were costs absorbed and profits reduced or costs passed on in increased prices which resulted in switches in demand to less expensive substitutes; did they lead to a reallocation of industrial plants within the same country or to another country?

Governments have in the past intentionally, or unintentionally in some cases, managed to deflect the cost of control from their industry. They allowed or encouraged for example high-level emission of SO_x resulting in transfrontier transfer of pollution. Similarly, there were numerous cases of discharges into international waterways and coastal areas with the implicit or explicit permission of governments resulting in environmental damage and substantial clean-up expenditures in other countries. More willingness and co-operation in the provision of information and in transparency of policies are needed in the future to overcome the backlog of pollution and to avoid other transfrontier pollution problems.

Finally, there were also cases where industry was protected from the potential cost of pollution control through very liberal emission standards in branches of industry where international competition is intense. This has been justified on the grounds of greater absorptive capacity of the environment. Sometimes, however, standards have been set in a non-transparent fashion and justified as confidentiality needed for reasons of competition. In the future, when the interdependence of OECD economies are likely to increase, there will perhaps be a greater need for transparency and even for some degree of harmonization in environmental policies if the level of international trade is to be maintained and increased even further.

5. ANALYTICAL REQUIREMENTS OF ANTICIPATORY POLICIES

Whatever the field of government activity, the informational and analytical requirements of a policy of 'management by justified objectives' are more substantial than those required in support of a policy of 'management by crisis'. It is a relatively straightforward matter to recognise when schools are overcrowded or hospital waiting lists are inordinately long or a particular environmental medium is badly polluted. The complexities begin to arise in deciding how to resolve the difficulties that are being faced (such as, to what level should the problem be ameliorated? How can the problem be resolved at least cost? How many resources should be devoted to the problem?). To answer these questions it is necessary to understand more clearly the existing environmental picture, the pressures that are likely to cause the future problem, how the problem will respond to different treatments, and whether it makes economic sense to undertake expenditures to eliminate potential, but uncertain future environmental damage.

The environmental policies of the 1970s were, of necessity, management by crisis. The declaration that the policies of the 1980s should be anticipatory reflects a desire to change the policy approach to one of management by objectives. If such anticipatory policies are to be well-founded, however, governments will need to be in a position to receive answers to such questions as:

-- What degree of control do we have already over the management of the environment and what would be the justified degree of control?

-- How can these controls be best improved upon to achieve the justified degree of control?

-- What are the expenditure implications of present policies and how would a further tightening of standards add to those expenditures and in what sectors; what would be the impacts on prices, employment, and other economic indicators?

-- What do we know about the future levels of emissions in the face of changing economic, industrial and other circumstances?

-- How far can changes in technology or existing under-utilised pollution control capacity be harnessed to minimise the costs of achieving environmental objectives?

-- How can government policy enhance and accelerate technological development to improve pollution control and reduce control costs?

-- What are the industrial, inflationary, trade and other economic implications of different levels of control in different sectors of the economy?

-- Can fiscal, trade, agricultural, and environmental policies be harmonized so that they work in concert to achieve the desired economic and environmental objectives and is such harmonization desirable?

-- To what extent is prevention of the problem a more economical proposition than curing it after the fact?

A prerequisite to answering questions of this nature is a data basis that is environmentally, technically and financially oriented. It is necessary to know where you are now as well as where you are trying to go, and at what cost. Close to 50 per cent of OECD countries compile and make public data either at the national or sectoral level on the level of emissions or on how current emissions would compare to the level of emissions in the absence of controls. In a number of countries, there is now also a systematic evaluation and collection of the costs of major control programmes in individual polluting sectors.

Other countries are in the process of developing such a data base. There are, however, countries where the philosophy prevails that such a data base at industry levels or at the national level is not required because policy is based on consultation on a plant-by-plant basis and such data need not and cannot be made public. This is a question of some importance not only from the point of view of efficient policy making but for reasons of transparency from the national and international point of view.

6. CONCLUSIONS

By the end of the 1980s, in the different OECD regions, in the absence of stricter emission standards than were in effect in 1978, and in the absence of technological advances, there is likely to be an increase in the emission of conventional pollutants into air, water and on land from the levels experienced in the late 1970s (such as, SO_x, NO_x, CO, hydrocarbons and particulates). Particularly serious problems will be encountered by Southern European countries, who, if they wish to maintain or improve their environmental quality, will have to establish environmental protection programmes similar to those that other OECD countries undertook during the late 1960s and 1970s.

Furthermore, the OECD countries are likely to encounter new problems from non-conventional pollutants including concentrations in surface and ground water resulting from run-off from agriculture, toxic air and water pollutants, and hazardous wastes. Most of these new pollution problems are of concern not only in terms of the annual flows but also because of the serious accummulation problems they could present. Moreover, the indications are that a failure to take preventive action in the near future could lead to significant environmental damages arising later on. Remedial action in these fields could prove expensive -- the costs of cleaning up abandoned hazardous waste sites and nitrate removal from ground water being two cases in point.

Even if stricter emission standards for conventional pollutants are implemented and the problems of non-conventional pollutants addressed in time, there will still remain, in most Member countries, specific regional problems to remedy. OECD countries could well be required to implement special measures to resolve these regional problems. Furthermore, the Southern European OECD countries, with relatively fast economic growth, will be confronting especially severe regional pollution problems, at the time when they are only at the establishment stage of their environmental machinery. These regional problems should be faced and tackled side by side with economic development.

The environmentally-advanced OECD countries incurred significant pollution control expenditures during the 1970s to clean up the backlog of the conventional pollutants generated during the late 1960s and early 1970s. Such a situation could well be being repeated in the case of newly emerging environmental problems unless remedial action is taken in the very near future.

By 1990, it is projected that there could be an increase of about 20 per cent in pollution control expenditures (in real terms) if constant 1978 emission standards are not made stricter, and total emissions are allowed to rise; but if standards are tightened, as appears necessary to keep the total volume of emissions down at least to the 1978 levels, then these expenditures will increase by over 100 per cent. Southern Europe will face a substantially larger increase in pollution control expenditures.

Under the second scenario, with total emissions kept to 1978 levels, pollution control expenditure as a percentage of GDP is likely to increase, especially in those countries where 1970s spending on pollution control was small. The percentages will vary from just over 2 per cent in the United States to less than 0.5 per cent in countries such as Belgium, Denmark, Greece, Norway, Portugal and Spain. The OECD countries sustained these expenditures without undue economic impacts in the past; the question is how well they can absorb them under changing economic conditions in the future and particularly if, in addition, further increasing environmental expectations will have to be successfully satisfied.

A natural consequence of the discussion of the level of expenditure on pollution control are the questions surrounding the source and nature of financing these expenditures. With respect to expenses incurred by governments at different levels, the questions to be examined are to what extent governments should recoup the cost of their services, and whether these expenses should be financed by federal, state, or local governments. With respect to pollution control expenditures by industry, governments should aim at further reducing the amount of assistance they provide to industry for pollution control purposes.

Clearly there is a need to reduce costs without damaging the environment any further. Part of the solution to cost reduction could be found in technological changes both in production processes and in control technologies. Some of these will emerge as a natural response to environmental policy but governments should also consider their role in fostering such developments. The major issues surrounding new technology include: identifying how these new technological developments can be best employed in environmental control, assessing how the impacts of technological changes on the environment can be anticipated, monitored and controlled and future risk reduced, and reviewing the need for new institutional arrangements at the national and international levels to take into account new technologies. These and other possible measures to achieve cost reductions will be discussed under Sessions 4, 6 and 7.

In assessing the alternatives available for reducing pollution and then choosing and implementing the most efficient alternative, OECD countries will need to have an adequate base of information on the environmental, technical and economic issues that are intrinsic to every such decision. These data are necessary on a national, sectoral, and individual plant basis. It is not possible to judge what actions are needed if there is no adequate characterisation of the past and current trends. This is especially true when a country wishes to use anticipatory policy making.

To counter and tackle successfully existing and future pollution problems will require the full and efficient implementation of stricter emission standards and the introduction of technological changes to help to reduce costs. In addition, there will be a need for proper anticipation of the environmental issues, and for the integration of the various policies in any one country, as well as proper co-ordination at the international level. These issues are addressed in particular in Session 8 on Future Directions of Environmental Policies.

SUMMARY OF THE DISCUSSION OF SESSION ONE

Professor Dr. Meinolf DIERKES

President, Science Centre, Berlin

Issues

The Conference participants, on the basis of the Background Papers and of the presentations by the keynote speakers and discussants, specified a number of major issues that are likely to be important for environmental policy making through 1990. These issues, and other related questions, are as follows.

-- There has been significant progress in the control of major conventional air and water pollutants (for example, SO_x, NO_x and so on) but in all OECD countries there is still a significant backlog of pollution. This is especially noticeable in the southern European Member countries. To what extent does this backlog need to be, and can it be, cleaned up by the end of this decade?

-- Emissions of conventional pollutants could rise further during this decade unless major efforts are made to constrain them; in addition there are a number of emerging pollution problems posing serious challenges both to national policy making and international co-operation. These include toxic pollution, acid rain, hazardous waste and contamination of ground water. Do governments have the capacity to anticipate the effects of economic growth on conventional and new pollutants and what is the most likely environmental scenario through 1990?

-- Major technological changes are now occurring in the OECD economies with important implications for the environment: production and materials developments; micro-electronics; bio-technologies. Do governments have the capacity to recognise these changes in time and make the best use of them?

-- Side by side with pollution problems, resource management issues have emerged as a major environmental and economic challenge in a number of OECD countries. What are the major natural resources that need a broadly based, economically rational and environmentally acceptable approach?

-- In spite of the economic difficulties experienced over the last decade, public support for environmental policies has remained steady or even increased. How can governments best assess the 'moving environmental targets' in the light of both public support for the environment and economic objectives; what type of past taboos will have to be revised (such as those surrounding nuclear energy or defence policies) in the light of this public support?

-- Environmental policies are at present pursued subject to certain economic criteria (for example, that benefits should exceed costs); how can countries reconcile policies that create conflicting interests between sectors of the economy, but are complementary in terms of environment and economics at the national level? How far are environmental and economic objectives complementary? Where do they conflict and how can they be made complementary? Should irreversible changes in the environment be prevented at all cost?

-- A number of environmental problems are international, some of them even global. The indications are that pollution problems of a transfrontier nature are increasing. What is OECD's role in contributing to the solution of these problems?

-- There are close economic ties between OECD and developing countries that have important environmental implications. How can these economic ties be further developed to the mutual benefit of all countries involved and at the same time the environment of the developing world be safeguarded?

Responses

In discussing these issues a number of suggestions and proposals emerged that could provide the appropriate solutions of these problems. While there was no unanimity on all the suggestions, there was a broad consensus on a number of them.

Concerning the question of the backlog of conventional pollutants, there was a broad agreement that most countries should aim at -- and already are aiming at -- tightening standards. Consequently, in spite of the future growth of pollution activities, emissions of these pollutants should decline from the levels that obtained at the end of 1970.

In addition, it was agreed that governments should aim at anticipating both future developments concerning conventional pollutants and emerging pollution trends. Some of the OECD countries already have this capacity for conventional pollutants. One of the possible approaches is presented in the OECD Background Document and this could form part of anticipatory policies in many countries. Such projections of future trends should take into account structural changes in the economy as well as changes in control technologies and the spatial shifts in sources of pollution.

There were various views expressed on future trends in the cost of pollution control. One view put forward was that improved technologies should lead to reduced costs of control. At the same time it was suggested that more stringent environmental standards must increase the cost of control. Overall, however, there was an agreement that if countries try at the minimum to keep total pollution to current levels, total costs of control could rise quite substantially -- and any further reduction in emissions would cost even more.

Consequently, policies should be devised that make controls more efficient and therefore less costly.

Discussion of future approaches to environmental policy making centred on the need for a capacity for early problem identification. To have policies accepted that deal with problems that will become apparent only in 5 to 10 years time (but necessitate investment now) will require clear explanation in terms of both costs and benefits. OECD countries need to join together in a common assessment of the problem, which would in turn help them to clarify the issues to their own public; on these issues the acceptance of measures aimed at reducing environmental risk 5 to 10 years ahead would help.

It was generally agreed that the pace of environmental policies should be determined not by the slowest and least environmentally developed OECD countries but rather by the forward-looking Members. Even today in relatively widely accepted problem solutions such as the use of low-lead petrol, most OECD countries are 10 years behind the lead country in introducing it.

Integrated approaches to environmental problems were advocated by a number of countries. However, the interpretation of integration varied somewhat. On one level it was argued that different sources of pollution interact and comprehensive policies will be required to deal with multi-source pollution. On another level it was suggested that for environmental policy purposes the entire production and development process should be examined and that there is a need to search for an equilibrium of resources: labour, technology, social impacts and environmental inputs.

Considerable concern was expressed at the state of the environment and future trends in the southern European Member countries, and the possibility that from the environmental point of view the differences between southern Europe and the rest of the OECD could widen. The view was expressed that the OECD Mediterranean countries are subject to considerable environmental pressure, partly from the rest of the OECD countries through tourism and partly from northern African countries. Therefore, there is some obligation on these other countries to help combat pollution in a co-operative effort. Accelerated and significantly more vigorous policies are needed to stop the further growth of pollution in southern Europe, and co-operative effort should also include technical assistance.

On a more technical level it was argued that the majority of OECD countries lack the data necessary (on pollution and on ecological and economic impacts) to carry out efficient reactive, let alone anticipatory, policies. This is true for conventional pollutants but even more so for emerging issues: hazardous waste, chemicals, acid rain, natural resources and global problems (such as carbon monoxide). Considerable additional effort is needed along the lines already indicated in various OECD countries -- and work on environmental expenditures and the state of the environment is urgently needed -- to provide the necessary policy basis for reactive and anticipatory action at both the national and the global level.

OECD Responsibilities

In the field of anticipatory policies, the OECD should continue with its leadership role in developing the necessary background data for the assessment of future problems, including possible costs and economic impacts.

A common approach within the OECD to the impact of technological developments on the environment and environmental policies should be combined with these assessments.

At the same time, in order to extend the standard economic models used in the OECD, work should take into account the economy as a physical system; that is, the main polluting production processes, the siting of economic activities, the stock of certain equipment and goods (such as the motor car population) and certain activities where the market system could fail.

The OECD should develop proposals to accelerate environmental protection in the southern European Member countries in order to bring them more in line with other OECD countries.

The OECD should assess the environmental relations between OECD and developing countries and propose ways and means by which the environments of these developing countries could be safeguarded while at the same time assuring their economic development.

OECD should assume responsibility for providing guidance on reducing the threat to the global environment in a number of areas.

SESSION TWO

THE IMPACT OF ENVIRONMENTAL MEASURES ON GROWTH,
PRODUCTIVITY, INFLATION AND TRADE

CHAIRMAN'S OPENING SPEECH

Sir Rupert MYERS

Chairman, NSW State Pollution Control Commission
and Chairman, Australian National Conservation
Strategy Committee

Good morning ladies and gentlemen. I think the best experience that I can call on for handling today's programme is running a big university during troublesome times. I hope that today will be a pleasure by comparison.

Mr. Chairman, you have kindly covered, I think adequately for the purposes of the people in today's Session, what we are about, and so I shall go straight to the business of who is going to speak and how we shall handle our affairs. It will be rather similar to yesterday: we will have the Keynote Speaker and then the two discussants will speak immediately afterwards. Just before the two discussants talk I will try to indicate to you which of those speakers will get an early call in the discussion period and I will try to keep you informed, as we proceed, about what the speaking order will be. At the moment we are trying to sort out what will be the best method of grouping people so that we won't skip from one subject to another too much. First we should proceed to the Keynote Speaker, and we are very fortunate in having Professor Andreas Boltho. He has an international reputation and much experience in the field of economics. In 1973-74 he was Head of the Economic Growth Division here at the OECD. He is now at the University of Oxford. Ladies and gentlemen, I invite Professor Boltho to address us.

Introduction by

Professor Andreas BOLTHO von HOHENBACH

University of Oxford

Thank you Mr. Chairman. I will be brief, as I gather I only have ten minutes.

Let me start with the Secretariat's documentation, which is in front of us, in which the Secretariat, I think in a rather sort of careful, almost apologetic way, seems to suggest that the macro-economic effects of the environmental control policies are minute -- very small indeed, be this on inflation, balance of payments, on gross national production or on productivity. Is this right? Is this conclusion the one which should be reached on the basis of the evidence? Surely, if one looks at the environmental policies, one's first reaction, as an economist, would be one of saying, well, these must slow down, for instance, the growth rate of productivity. After all, investment is being diverted for uses which are not directly contributing to output, labour is being used to man this equipment, and therefore again, it does not contribute directly to output. Surely there must be some slow-down here in the growth rate of our economies, because of these measures?

The figures, however, do seem to suggest that if in fact there is an effect, it is indeed very small. Now, the figures can be doubted; one can argue that the economic methods are fallible by themselves, and no doubt many would want to take this line. I do not want to personally; I think economic methods have their uses and can be very powerful. One can argue more plausibly that the particular economic models that are being used to obtain these estimates may not be the most appropriate because they do not pick up the incentive effects, for instance of increased regulations, and because they are far too aggregated to really get at the core of the problem.

But there is indirect support, I think, for the Secretariat conclusions, which come from the gross accounting exercises which Dennison has made in the USA in particular, and we reach very similar conclusions to those of the economic estimates.

Secondly, or thirdly perhaps, I would have thought that the figures receive support, even if you do not believe in econometrics and even if you do not believe in gross accounting, just from common sense. What are we talking about? We are talking about figures for environmental pollution control expenditure, which in the early 1970s must have been of the order of 0.3-0.4 per cent of GNP and which have risen, depending on country, to levels of perhaps 1.0-1.5 per cent, in a few cases 2 per cent, of GNP by the end of the decade. An increase, in other words, of 1.0 percentage points over a decade. It is highly unlikely that this sort of an increase could really have had anything but very minor effects on measured output growth. You could then ask, what is all the fuss about? Why is it that, whenever one looks again, taking productivity as the best example, at academic studies of the productivity deceleration which the OECD area has suffered from over the last decade, one finds in the list of the factors that are being advanced to explain this deceleration, oil prices, lower investment ratios, lower growth rate of output and therefore effects on productivity growth, changes in demographic structures and increased regulations and pollution control?

By association I think, pollution and environmental control policies had become part and parcel of the conventional wisdom which surrounds the whole productivity discussion. Why is it that this has happened, despite the fact that common sense, econometrics and gross accounting all suggest that this should not be the case? I think it is very largely a function of what happened in one particular country, admittedly a very important country: half of the OECD area's GNP, the United States.

The United States suffered in the 1970s from virtual productivity stagnation. There was not just lower growth, there was no growth in productivity. It had, at the same time, a very rapid growth rate of environmental expenditure, much more rapid than that of other countries; hence it is likely that in the States the effects would have been somewhat larger, and the two things are clearly linked.

They were linked, more so I think in the US academic and non-academic discussion, because the USA is a country which does not like regulations; perhaps no country likes regulations, but the US is probably a country which likes regulations even less than most of our European countries, in which government intervention is a much longer-going affair. So the dislike of regulations, the productivity fall and the admittedly much more rapid build-up of environmental control in the States did create an atmosphere in America which led to these various studies, led to these various judgements being made. As I have said before, the academic study actually shows that the figures are very small, but common wisdom has it in the States that effects were relatively large.

If we take countries such as Japan or western Europe, one would see that in fact this particular issue has never really been very much at the forefront of the debate on the productivity slowdown; it has seldom been attributed even in small part to the particular factors we are discussing, in other words environmental policies. The watchword in Europe is not excessive regulation; the watchwords in Europe are public expenditure, labour market inflexibility, wage rigidity, all things which it would seem to me are basically unrelated to environmental policies.

If this is the case about the past, if I am right, and if this theory is correct, that in the past expenditure did not contribute in any large extent to our unfavourable performance over the last decade, what about the future? Is the picture likely to change for the better or for the worse? Well, it seems to me that, barring any major ecological disasters, the picture ought to change for the better. In other words, future expenditure levels are unlikely to rise as rapidly as they have risen over the last few years, again a point which the Secretariat makes in its documentation, if only because the largest effects are behind us, so that the share of expenditure in GNP is unlikely to rise markedly at all. I would have hoped that future impacts, negative impacts, will be even less if governments tend to shift increasingly towards more market-oriented mechanisms in their control of pollution expenditure.

This is an issue that will be debated in Session 7 tomorrow afternoon, but I would just like to stress the importance and would very much wish that this Conference would strongly support an economist's plea for the use of more charges, of more market-oriented instruments, or better working price mechanisms. Let me just give you an indirect examples of how effective the price mechanism can be: the astonishing savings on energy that we have been able to achieve over the last few years, because of the price increase. A similar utilisation of the price mechanism in this area, I think, could have important consequences for saving costs in terms of abatement, in terms of enforcement and in terms of accelerating technological progress in this area.

My last point is that so far I have only talked in terms of purely macro-economic effects. At the very macro level, these effects are very very small indeed; however, at the sectoral level they are bound to be much more important. This is an issue which I hope one of the discussants will address himself to: Dr. Meissner, who in fact comes from an industry that is directly effected by environmental policies.

So I will accept that at certain levels, in sectors like pulp and paper or chemicals or iron and steel, the effects could be much larger and would of course be unfavourable on these particular sectors. At the risk of perhaps being aggressive, I would argue that these effects are desirable. If indeed we are concerned with pollution, which presumably we are, then we want these sectors in a sense to become smaller. We want the investment and output and employment in these sectors to shrink in the long run, because we want lower pollution levels, less pollution emission from these sections.

Indeed, there is a second reason, I think, why we would wish for a slowing down of growth in these sectors, which is an international reason. It is the one way, or one of the better ways, in which perhaps we can further the industrialisation of developing countries, by shifting the nature of our industries away from highly polluting sectors towards less polluting sectors, and having the comparative advantage in manufacturing activities shift towards developing countries. In other words, if sectors are indeed hit quite heavily by environmental control measures, this may well be desirable rather than not.

Let me end, Mr. Chairman, on a provocative statement, which in a sense is only trying to elicit reactions and possible negative reactions. The macro issue that we are discussing here is a non-issue: there is no macro-economic worry really about these problems. There is indeed a sectoral worry, but the sectoral worry is a desirable one in a sense: the sectoral consequences are what we actually want.

ISSUE PAPER: SESSION TWO

THE IMPACT OF ENVIRONMENTAL MEASURES ON GROWTH, PRODUCTIVITY, INFLATION AND TRADE

1. INTRODUCTION

The second half of the 1970s and early 1980s have witnessed a marked deterioration in economic performance. Economic growth faltered and in some OECD Member countries ceased; rates of inflation rose and remained high; unemployment increased to 1930s levels; and balance of payments problems became widespread. Despite these difficulties governments continued to enact and enforce -- in response to the concern of their citizens -- a wide variety of regulations designed to improve health, safety and the quality of life. Environmental measures were prominent among these regulations. While economic performance depends on a wide variety of factors -- including demographic changes, technological developments, international relationships, harvests, resource prices, monetary and fiscal management -- some observers, in particular industry representatives, claim that government regulatory control stifles decision makers, constrains labour and capital resource mobility, imposes costs on producers and delays investment, thus adversely affecting economic performance. That growth in the number of regulations coincided with "stagflation" seems to support the assertion that environmental policy contributed to poor economic performance.

Those who put forward such claims argue that environmental measures can affect economic activity in a variety of ways. Environmental measures, they assert, require increased private or public expenditures. These translate into increased costs which cause higher prices or higher taxation. This in turn is seen to have negative effects on productivity and employment, and to contribute to deterioration in the balance of payments.

This assertion of causality between the growth of environmental regulation and "stagflation" in the second half of the 1970s and the early 1980s raises a major question for environmental policy. Does the relationship have a basis in fact and analysis, or is it simply a simultaneous occurence? A number of factors have clearly had a major impact on the performance of OECD economies: the rise in energy prices; the introduction of new technologies; increased competition from newly-industrialised countries; greater social resistance to change; and declining productivity, to mention a few. How do the impacts of environmental measures compare with these factors?

In considering the relative importance of environmental policies a number of empirical questions must be addressed:

-- What, in fact, has been the net impact of environmental measures on such major macroeconomic variables as economic growth, prices, productivity, employment (1) and balance of payments?

-- How does this compare with the impacts of other major public programmes, such as health, education, or defence?

-- How does this impact compare with the impacts of such major factors as the rise in energy prices?

-- Are current methodologies and models for measuring and tracing the impact of environmental measures adequate?

-- Are there additional ways of measuring that would give a more complete picture of the economic impact of environmental policies, particularly on welfare, and thus help to guide policy?

-- Are the currently available information bases adequate enough to support analysis of the economic impact of environmental measures? What should be done to improve this information base at the national and international level?

-- Based on the experience of the past decade, what can be said about the probable future impact of environmental spending on the major macroeconomic variables?

-- Given the special impact of environmental measures on certain sectors, would it be useful to supplement assessments of the macro-impact with assessments of the micro-impact? If so, on which sectors and industries should future attention be focussed? And is there a role for international co-operation in this work?

2. ENVIRONMENTAL MEASURES AND ECONOMIC GROWTH

The relative magnitude of expenditures on health, education, defence and the environment is shown in Table 1. Expenditures on these 'public' goods have been chosen for comparison because their contribution to the economy is regarded as not directly productive, and because their magnitude is decided through political processes rather than the operation of the market.

Expenditures on pollution control (total of public and private sector) ranged from 1-2 per cent of gross domestic product (GDP) in most Western European countries and in North America in 1978. Even if all these expenditures added nothing to real measured output, which of course is not the case, they would explain no more than 0.5-2 per cent of any reduction in GDP growth in 1978.

With unemployed resources, however, not all of the expenditures represent real economic costs. Indeed, with unemployed resources, an increase in total demand for environmental purposes would be expected to increase both GDP and employment. Moreover, pollution-control expenditures generate benefits which add to GDP and to welfare. The benefits to growth of pollution

Table 1

EXPENDITURE ON PUBLIC GOODS IN OECD COUNTRIES MID 1970s

(Percentage of GDP)

		Range (b)
Defence		0.9 - 5.8
Health	- Public	1.4 - 6.7
	- Public and Private	3.5 - 7.4
Education	- Public	1.9 - 7.0
Pollution Control (a)		
	- Public and Private	0.5 - 2.0

a)   For a limited number of OECD countries with well-developed environmental programmes.

b)   Countries with the lowest and highest percentage of expenditure.

Source: Public Expenditure Trends, OECD, Paris, 1978; Public Expenditure on Health, OECD, Paris, 1977.

control are estimated to be around 1.5 per cent of GDP for the US and somewhat more for France. Macroeconomic models, however (except for additional output in the form of pollution-control equipment), either cannot take into account many of these benefits or do not attribute increased output explicitly to environmental expenditures. Cost-reducing benefits -- such as reduction in corrosion damage or in raw-material requirements for industry -- and output-increasing benefits -- such as reduction in damage to crops -- are included in GDP calculations, but are not attributed to the effects of expenditures on environmental measures. A third benefit is an increase in economic welfare. This covers such diverse impacts as reduced expenditures on medical care and aesthetic improvements. But these are not reflected anywhere in the measurement of GDP.

These benefits are significant if taken into account, and suggest a far smaller negative impact on growth than the figures on spending alone indicate. On the other hand, not all of the real costs associated with environmental measures are necessarily reflected in reported figures. The occasional delays related to mandated environmental impact studies, for example, and the possible disincentive effects of additional taxes needed to support pollution control are not reflected in figures on expenditures.

Macroeconometric modelling techniques facilitate -- at least to a certain degree -- the appraisal of net impacts of some offsetting tendencies in an economy. Such models are constructed from quantitative estimates of the primary economic relationships present in an economic system. They trace the first and some second and third round impacts of environmental expenditures through the various sectors of an economy. The net effects of a policy measure on the growth of GDP, inflation, employment, balance of payments, and other macroeconomic variables can be simulated using such models. A number of OECD-Member countries have developed such models, and have used them to evaluate the effects of environmental measures. The main results of these studies are given in Table 2.

Table 2

EFFECTS OF ADDITIONAL ENVIRONMENTAL PROGRAMMES
ON SELECTED ECONOMIC VARIABLES

(Range of differences between level with
and without environmental programmes)

	Effects on:			
	GDP First year	Final year	Consumer prices First year	Final year
	(percentage points)			
Austria	..	-0.6/0.5	..	0.4/1.7 (a)
Finland	0.3	0.6	0.2	0.2
France	–	0.1/0.4	–	0.1
Netherlands	0.1	-0.3/-0.6	0.2/0.4	0.8/4.3
Norway	..	1.5	..	0.1/0.9
United States	0.2	-0.6/-1.1	0.2	0.6/0.8
Memorandum items (b)				
Italy	..	-0.2/0.4	..	0.3/0.5
Japan	1.2/2.6	0.1/0.2 (c)	–	2.2/3.8

a)   GDP deflator.

b)   Published in earlier OECD report.

c)   For the period as a whole, suggesting negative results for final year.

..   Not available.

–   Taken to be zero.

These results suggest that the impacts of environmental measures are quite different in the short-term than in the long-term. In general, the short-term impact of environmental programmes on GDP is positive. Increased demand generated by the policy increases output in economies operating at less than full capacity. Studies available in four countries (Finland, the Netherlands, the United States and Japan) estimated that environmental programmes generated increases in GDP of between 0.1 and about 1.5 per cent in their first year.

In subsequent years, however, environmental programmes would be expected to result in small reductions in GDP, since the model assumes that environmental investment declines and that higher costs and prices are felt throughout the economy. Countries experiencing such long-term effects -- about half the countries using macroeconometric models -- find the largest negative impact in the final year of the programme. The average annual impact over the whole of the period examined is equal to a decline in GDP of between 0.1 and 0.2 per cent; this reduction could run to about 1 per cent of GDP in the final year of the programme, excluding as noted earlier measurement of the environmental benefits of the programmes. In other words, taking into account both positive and negative considerations -- but not the economic evaluation of environmental benefits -- the simulations suggest that the maximum adverse effect of environmental measures on GDP is on the order of 1 per cent in the last year of a environmental programme (using the most unfavourable assumptions). The longer-term impacts are substantially smaller for most OECD countries.

The bulk of these impacts on GDP, whatever their sign and magnitude, have already been felt by the highest-income OECD Member countries. The economies of these countries have made the adjustments required to accommodate these policies. Most of the expenditures were made to abate air and water pollution and, to a limited extent, solid waste pollution. In the European OECD countries expenditures on water-pollution control were generally substantially more than on air-pollution control. In the United States air- and water-pollution control expenditures were about equal.

Those countries which began environmental action later may yet have to confront these impacts. Their environmental problems are severe and will require strong measures involving heavy expenditures. At the same time, if they choose to do so, these countries could substantially benefit from the experience of those OECD-Member countries that have been in the forefront of environmental action. Cleaner technologies and processes now exist for most industrial sectors, certainly for the most polluting. Countries seeking industrial development can require that these technologies be built into the design of new plants. The results can be more resource and energy efficient, and more economic. And certain health, property and other damage costs can be avoided at the same time. For the same level of expenditure, therefore, countries have the opportunity to enhance the positive effects of measures and reduce the negative. The future impact of environmental measures in all countries, however, will depend on several factors: on the issues they address (for example, in the areas of hazardous and toxic wastes); on the types of regulations deployed and their degree of enforcement; on advances in control technology brought about by the regulations; on whether the country is operating at full capacity and on future shifts in the composition of outputs; and, of course, on the nature and magnitude of the expenditures required.

3. ENVIRONMENTAL MEASURES AND INFLATION

At the end of the 1970s about 50 per cent of total pollution-control expenditures in Western Europe and the United States were being made by the private sector. As a percentage of GDP they range from 0.3 to 0.9 in Western Europe to 1.2 in the United States. These environmental expenditures manifest themselves as cost increases for industry. The impacts on industrial cost vary widely depending on the nature of the industry. Some industries are low polluters. Their expenditure is practically zero. Others are heavy polluters. Their environmental expenditures can represent 10-15 per cent of production costs. By comparison, the 1979 energy price increases in crude oil added more than that percentage increase to total industrial costs over the 1979-81 period.

Even if the cost increases from environmental expenditures were fully passed on in the form of price increases, the impact on inflation measured by the consumer price index would be no more than about 1 percentage point. However, as indicated above; while the price of response to some industries would be very low, that to other industries -- those with the most serious pollution problems and which are thus subject to the most severe environmental measures -- would be more substantial.

However, two caveats should be noted. First, as the "Polluter-Pays Principle" implies, the cost of environmental measures should be reflected in the costs to the industry concerned and consequently, depending upon competitive conditions, in the prices of products. In other words, changes in relative prices inducing reductions in the output of pollution-intensive products are expected, and indeed to be desired. Second, to the extent that there is an inflation impact over and above the change in relative prices, that effect will be largely a one-time event. Once the higher level of costs has been accommodated by the average level of prices, a constant level of mandated expenditures by the private sector need not lead to additional inflationary pressure. Environmental expenditures, unlike inflation indexed wages for example, do not necessarily add to the inflationary spiral.

The effects of environmental measures on prices is an empirical matter. As in the case of impacts on growth, econometric estimates have been made of these effects in a number of OECD-Member countries. Clearly the magnitude of the effect on prices will depend on the nature and stringency of the environmental measures undertaken in the countries concerned. Econometric analyses suggest that in the United States -- with perhaps the most extensive array of environmental policies in the OECD -- environmental measures would cause the price level to increase by about 7 percentage points more than it otherwise would from 1970 to 1987. Thus, the contribution of environmental measures to inflation in the United States averages about 0.4 percentage points annually, compared to an average annual increase in consumer prices of 9.2 per cent for the period 1973-80. For other countries, the estimated effects on prices are: Austria, 0.1-0.3 percentage points per year; the Netherlands, 0.1-0.6; Japan, 0.4-0.6; France and Italy, 0.1. The average annual consumer price increases for these countries for the 1973-80 period were 6.3, 7.1, 9.7, 11.1 and 17.0 per cent respectively. As a further comparison, the 1979 crude oil price increase added over 10 per cent to consumer prices in the OECD area over the 1979-81 period.

While the different impacts on prices in various countries reflect differences in the stringency of environmental measures, they also reflect differences in the structure of economies (for example, the extent of indexation of wages and of various social payments and their consequent impacts on inflation) and different assumptions regarding monetary and fiscal policies and the way these policies deal with inflationary pressure.

Given the ability of the OECD economies to adjust to the additional costs required by environmental measures, it is quite possible that future impacts on price levels will be less than those already experienced, even with a constant level of environmental policy stringency. Moreover, if the economic climate remains depressed in the 1980's future expenditure increases are likely to occur in economies with more excess capacity (and, hence, less upward price pressure) than in previous years, and in a setting where indexation measures are less rigid than in the past.

4. ENVIRONMENTAL MEASURES AND PRODUCTIVITY

The rate of productivity growth over the long-term is in some ways a fundamental indicator of economic vitality and improvement in living standards. The labour productivity measure itself captures -- in a single indicator -- both the final output of an economy (the numerator) and the primary input, labour, which contributes to that output (the denominator). Changes in this indicator reflect advances in the transformation of labour, energy and raw materials into goods and services. With rapid productivity growth wages can rise without stimulating inflation, and economic growth can occur without increases in labour supply or other inputs.

Efforts to measure productivity have so far concentrated on the measurement of labour productivity with occasional studies of capital productivity. The reason for this is that labour input can be measured with relative ease compared to capital or other inputs. Yet, the amount of energy and resources used in production would provide the basis for a very informative productivity measure. It would be more relevant from the environmental point of view to know the ratio of the output of the economy to the energy and other raw materials used to produce that output. The smaller the ratio the greater the energy and raw material efficiency of the economy, and clearly the greater the "environmental efficiency".

Some attempts have been made to establish measures of energy and resource productivity. The former have had some success, but the latter have not because of definition and measurement problems. Nevertheless, the development of a resource productivity measure could be useful to environmental policy formulation.

Labour productivity growth declined remarkably throughout the OECD area in the 1970s. Between 1960 and 1973 labour productivity in the OECD area grew at an average of about 4 per cent per year. Since 1973, however, growth has hovered around 1-2 per cent per year. While some countries have experienced little if any slowdown, productivity growth in other OECD countries (such as the United States and Canada) has virtually ceased; in Japan it has declined from 8.5 per cent to 3.0 per cent, and in many of the European OECD countries it has been halved.

In contrast to the paucity of evidence on environmental measures and economic growth and inflation, several studies have been made of the impact of such measures on labour productivity. On one level the macroeconomic studies already referred to provide some indirect evidence of this impact. These studies indicate that environmental measures have a positive initial effect on both economic growth and employment, and hence, a presumably small impact on labour productivity. In the medium to long-term, however, environmental measures are estimated to reduce slightly economic growth while stimulating employment. The net effect of these two changes is to decrease the growth in labour productivity. Overall, however, the adverse impact of environmental policy on labour productivity is expected to be small even in the medium to long-term. In the United States, where environmental controls have been relatively severe, the decrease in labour productivity growth (relative to no environmental controls) is estimated by one prominent macroeconometric study to be less than 0.1 percentage point per year between 1977 and 1987. While no estimates of the longer-term impact are available, the progressive installation of new capital equipment designed to be less polluting suggests that the longer-term effects will be even smaller.

Other estimates are consistent with those of the macroeconomic models. The prominent "growth accounting" study by Denison for the United States concludes, for example, that from 1969 to 1978 environmental regulations decreased labour productivity in the non-residential business sector by about 0.12 percentage points per year. A survey of a large number of these studies by the OECD attempted to extract from the analyses -- all of which differ in data and method -- some estimate of the contribution of environmental policies to the slowdown. It concluded that for the United States "approximately 8-12 per cent of the slowdown [which totalled 1.5 per cent] ... for the 1960s to the 1970s was due to environmental regulations," or about a 0.15 percentage point reduction per year. In comparison, the increase in energy prices and inflation in the seven major OECD countries contributed to between 40 and 90 per cent of their decline in productivity growth. The other main contributing factor was the low level of economic activity.

Several reservations should be applied to this result. First, the estimates for the United States cannot be applied directly to other OECD countries, as the level of pollution-control spending in those countries was about one-half to two-thirds of the level in the United States. It seems unlikely that the decline in the rate of labour productivity growth in these countries which is attributable to environmental controls is in excess of 0.1 per cent per year. Second, the short-term effect of environmental policies on productivity is likely to be more strongly negative than that indicated above, as investment funds are diverted from other activities to meet initial capital requirements for environmental controls, and as adjustments are made to operate in the new regulatory environment. In the longer-term, however, the production processes required by environmental regulation can employ new technologies which can be both less polluting and more efficient users of energy and raw materials. Third, in most OECD countries the large build-up in environmental controls occured when there was far less than full employment. In this situation, the diversion of resources from activities contributing to measured GDP would be much less than under conditions of full-employment, and countries would experience a smaller adverse effect on the rate of labour productivity growth. Finally, in the medium to longer-term -- as adjustments to initial dislocations are made and the effects of environmental measures are felt -- improved health, reduced absenteeism and reduced damage to plant and equipment will begin making their positive contribution to measured productivity growth.

In sum, then, the evidence makes clear that environmental regulations have contributed only modestly to the last decade's fall-off in measured labour productivity growth, and can in no way be considered the driving force behind this reduction. The expected future negative effect of these regulations is likely to be even more modest. The initial dislocations and start-up costs have already been absorbed by the economy; higher levels of unemployment and excess capacity exist now than in the early or mid-1970s (implying less displacement); modern equipment now being installed is both more technologically advanced and less polluting than in the previous decade (that is, less retrofitting of old capital is being undertaken); and the beneficial effects of improved environmental quality on workers health and materials damage should begin to be reflected in measured output.

5. BALANCE OF PAYMENTS AND ENVIRONMENTAL POLICIES

The impact of environmental policies on the balance of payments is also an empirical question. But in this case the evidence is far less than complete. In theory, the effects of environmental policies on the balance of payments are transmitted largely through the impact on economic growth, price levels and productivity. Several channels can be identified. First, those countries with more stringent environmental measures might experience lower profits or larger average price increases than their international competitors, and so an inferior competitive position with adverse effects on their balance of payments. These effects will be minimised to the extent that countries harmonize their environmental policies. Second, favourable effects on balance of payments should be experienced by those countries that gain an early lead in the production and manufacture of pollution-control equipment, or which possess unique facilities or technologies for the disposal or recycling of waste materials. Finally, investments in new plant and equipment, especially in pollution-intensive industries, may flow towards countries with lower pollution-control costs. This effect will be reduced as countries experiencing pollution-intensive economic growth introduce environmental-control measures to protect the quality of their own environment.

Only four countries (Finland, France, the Netherlands, and the United States) have undertaken macroeconometric studies on the effects of environmental policy on the balance of payment -- as transmitted through the effects of such policies on economic growth and price levels. The results of the studies in the first three countries named are of dubious value. Each of the studies made the implausible assumption that only the country in question had undertaken any environmental measures. Given this assumption, the studies of course suggest that implementation of their programmes would cause a substantial deterioration in their trade balance. In fact, the majority of OECD-Member countries started to implement their programmes simultaneously in the first half of the 1970s, although there were differences in the standards adopted and the degree of their enforcement. In the United States study, the initial effects of environmental policies on the trade balance are estimated to be negative; but they gradually lead to an improved trade balance which reaches $1.7 billion in 1987 (1979 prices).

The varied nature of these results and their sensitivity to underlying assumptions may say something about the benefits of harmonization. But they also suggest that little can be said with confidence about the overall effects of environmental measures on trade and balance of payments. While unilateral (or early) implementation of stringent measures could have a negative effect on exports as a result of somewhat higher prices of certain products, the reduction of GDP and import demand attributable to the same policies could offset this effect. In comparison, over the 1979-81 period, the cumulative increase in import prices for the OECD countries -- following the second oil price shock -- amounted to 23 per cent; the resulting combined deficit in the current balances of the OECD countries rose from an equilibrium in 1978 to over $150 billion during the period 1979-81.

The third channel noted above -- the potential migration of industrial investment -- is not treated in the macroeconomic models. Theoretically, shifts in investment with long-term consequences would be possible -- if investments were sensitive to differences in the level and stringency of environmental controls between countries. However, while there are instances of such migration both within the OECD and between OECD-countries and non-OECD-countries, they are not widespread. This conclusion is consistent with both research indicating that environmental factors are a relatively minor consideration in the location decisions of firms, and the overall evaluation that output, cost, and price effects of environmental measures are relatively small, except in certain sectors.

6. CONCLUSIONS

Environmental protection is now a relatively mature activity in the majority of OECD-Member countries. The bulk of initial investment has been largely absorbed by the economies concerned. By the end of the last decade, OECD-Member countries were investing between 0.5 and 2.0 per cent of GDP on environmental protection. In the short-term this expenditure had a positive effect on GDP, as the increased demand it generated caused increases in the output of economies operating at less than full capacity. In the longer-term -- ignoring the benefits generated by these expenditures not reflected in current measures of GDP, and assuming a levelling-off of expenditures -- the impact on GDP may become modestly adverse (0.1 and 0.2 per cent per year on average over the whole of the programme period, and up to 1 per cent in the final year of the programme).

Looking to the future, any adverse impacts on GDP would be postponed in the more advanced OECD economies should expenditures increase. For other economies, where significant investment in environmental action mostly began later, the development of new environmental technologies and experience with the design and delivery of environmental regulation could make it possible to enhance the positive and reduce the negative effects of such investment.

Expenditure on environmental control has contributed only modestly to inflation: about 0.4 percentage points annually in the United States; between 0.1 and 0.4 percentage points annually in the European countries of the OECD; and between 0.4 to 0.6 percentage points in Japan.

Those OECD economies which have accomodated to the additional investment required by environmental measures should experience an even smaller impact on inflation in the future -- even with a higher level of spending. Indeed, to the extent that such expenditures are reflected in price levels, it is largely a one-time event. Environmental expenditures, unlike inflation-indexed wages for example, do not necessarily add to the inflationary spiral.

It should be noted that while the overall impact on inflation has been modest, the impact on costs and prices in those industries that have incurred above-average expenditures has been higher and, in some cases, substantial. As the "Polluter-Pays Principle" implies, however, the costs of environmental measures should be reflected in the costs of the industry concerned, and subsequently, depending upon competitive conditions, in the prices of its products; in other words, changes in relative prices which induce reductions in the use of pollution-intensive processes and products are both expected and desired.

Several studies have been made of the impact of environmental measures on labour productivity. While evidence suggests that environmental regulations have contributed modestly to the last decade's drop in measured labour-productivity growth, they can in no way be considered the driving force behind this reduction. A survey by the OECD of a large number of these studies concluded that for the United States "approximately 8-12 per cent of the slowdown [which totalled 1.5 per cent] .... for the 1960s and 1970s was due to environmental regulations", or an average of about 0.15 percentage points per year. While these estimates cannot be applied directly to other OECD countries -- since the level of pollution-control expenditures in those countries was about half to two-thirds the level in the United States -- it seems unlikely that the decline in the rate of labour-productivity growth in these countries attributable to environmental regulation would be in excess of 0.1 per cent per year.

These and other measurements of productivity have so far concentrated on the productivity of labour rather than the productivity of capital. Yet the capital used in production -- including the amount of energy and resources -- would provide the basis for a very useful measure. Certainly, from an environmental point of view, it is less important to know the ratio of the output of the economy per unit of labour producing that output, than it is to know the ratio of the output of the economy per unit of energy and other raw materials used. The larger the latter ratio, the greater is the energy and resource efficiency of the economy, and clearly the greater the "environmental efficiency", and perhaps the greater the economic efficiency.

It is, indeed, an open question whether the focus on labour productivity, given the nature of that measure, does not tend to favour economic and other policies that encourage the maximum use of energy and other resources, and to that extent is a "perverse" measure from an environmental viewpoint. The productivity of capital may be a more attractive measure of productivity from an environmental (and perhaps even an economic) point of view.

The evidence on the effects of environmental policies on the balance of payments is incomplete. The mixed results available and their sensitivity to underlying assumptions suggests that little can be said with confidence.

Macroeconomic measurements provide a necessarily incomplete picture of the impact of environmental expenditures on GDP, price levels, productivity and balance of payments. They neglect the benefits generated by the expenditures. They either cannot take into account these benefits or they do not explicitly attribute the benefits to environmental expenditures. Cost-reducing benefits, such as a reduction in corrosion damage or in raw material requirements for industry, and output-increasing benefits such as reduction in damage to agricultural crops, are included in GDP but are not attributed to the effects of expenditures on environmental measures. A third category of benefits, representing increases in welfare, cover such diverse cases as reductions in the costs of health care and aesthetic improvements, but they are not reflected in the estimation of GDP.

NOTE AND REFERENCE

1. The impact of environmental measures on employment is the subject of Session 3 of this Conference.

Professor Finn FORSUND

University of Oslo

Participants discussed the results presented in the OECD background document on the macro-economic impacts of environmental expenditures, which are available for six OECD countries. It was generally agreed that the data presented confirmed previous impressions of the likely magnitude of these macro-economic impacts for most OECD countries. At the end of the 1970s, OECD countries were spending between 0.5 per cent and 2.0 per cent of their GNPs on pollution control. For the majority of countries this figure is probably below 1 per cent. These expenditures have certain impacts on a number of macro-economic variables, including growth, inflation, the balance of payments and productivity.

Issues

i) Estimates show that pollution control expenditures during the 1970s caused, in the short-term, an increase of between 0.1 and 0.2 percentage points in economic growth per year, an increase of between 0.1 and 0.4 percentage points in inflation and a decline of about 0.1 percentage points in productivity growth. Are these changes significant or trivial compared with changes caused by other factors, and relative to the benefits of these policies?

ii) It has been argued in the past that environmental policies could retard economic growth and could generally have major macro-economic consequences. Clearly this has not been the case. Having demonstrated this, what are the major benefits and uses of this type of macro-economic assessment?

iii) Macro-economic assessments are based on Keynesian models and relate the impact of environmental policies to environmental expenditures. How complete and accurate is this type of assessment, given the short-term nature of the impacts?

iv) Given the stated objective of a number of countries to reduce emissions below the levels obtaining at the end of the 1970s, what will be the macro-impacts if such policies are implemented?

v) Macro-models can only capture limited impacts, given their method of assessment. They could, for example, understate long-term gains in output resulting from improved health, from improved technologies generated by environmental regulations or in general from an improved environment, which underlies the productive system of the economy. Can macro-economic measurements and assessments be improved to reflect more adequately the true macro-impact of environmental expenditures?

vi) While macro-economic assessment measures overall impacts at the national level, most of these impacts, particularly the adverse ones, are concentrated on a limited number of 'smoke-stack' industries. Macro-economic assessments cannot measure the expenditure impacts on specific industrial branches or regions; nor can they measure the income-distributional effects. What type of measurements would be appropriate for assessing impacts on individual industries, and what should governments do about these impacts? Have the regional effects been usefully measured and what were the conclusions of such assessments? If they have not been measured, can they be?

vii) The impacts of environmental measures on the balance of payments of OECD countries have generally been small when measured in terms of changes in the volume of exports or imports. Other effects not measured by macro-methods are shifts of investment to areas where the effects of environmental regulations are less severe, and the effects of non-tariff trade barriers caused by environmental regulations. Have shifts in investment been significant and are they desirable? What have been the effects, if any, of non-tariff trade barriers?

Responses

i) Most participants agreed that macro-economic assessments provide useful information for policy makers on the overall impacts of their environmental programmes. They should be carried out not only to assess the impacts of past policies but also as part of anticipatory policy formulation. A number of OECD countries have already made this an integral part of their environmental planning process. They urged the wider use of this approach.

ii) It was recognised that the models used in the background documents were designed for macro-economic policy purposes and therefore, from the point of view of the environment, could capture only the short-term first and perhaps second round direct effects. Consequently, for example, welfare benefits, which in turn can have impacts on output in the longer-term, cannot be measured. In general, it was felt that further efforts are needed to extend and specify clearly the coverage of these macro-models (for example, to broaden the coverage of environmental expenditures).

iii) At the same time it has also become evident that the extension of macro-models has only limited possibilities. An alternative is to support them with a number of specific assessments, such as separate benefit assessment of environmental policies, the impacts of economic development on national heritage, or the income distributional aspects of environmental policies. These assessments, together with the macro-assessment, should be accompanied by a careful description of their coverage in order to specify the limitations of these broad national studies and at the same time to avoid the possible double-counting of expenditures or benefits.

iv) There was a general consensus that the impacts, based on the results of the macro-studies, were small, but at the same time, as far as economic performance was concerned, they were not trivial. At the same time, the point was made that where resources are unemployed the monetary cost of environmental policies is not the same as the opportunity cost. This suggests that in some periods, such as at the present, environmental protection could be undertaken at a lower social cost than the monetary costs would imply.

v) In examining the differences between the macro-impacts and some of the sectoral effects -- in particular on heavily polluting industries -- it was suggested that public attitudes, particularly opposition from industry, were largely influenced by trade and sectoral impacts. The proper policy stance for OECD countries should be to try to minimise the trade effects, but apart from making policies more efficient, governments should not try to correct the sectoral effects. The environmentally desirable and economically correct response from industry should come in response to cost and competitive pressures.

vi) To minimise the trade effects governments should try to harmonize both the timing and the severity of standards of their environmental policies. These in turn need to be considered in the light of the absorbing capacity of the environment and the potential short- and long-term effects on health and on the environment. Governments should also closely adhere to the Polluter-Pays Principle and avoid subsidising polluters. The principle should be broadened to cover areas outside pollution control, and also to cover the transfrontier and international aspects of pollution and pollution control.

vii) There were widely differing views on the possible shifting of smokestack industries to developing countries. Such shifts are already taking place under the pressure of comparative cost advantages, although these are seldom related to the environment. Should further shifts occur, they should be accompanied by up-to-date pollution controls and should take place in areas where the absorbing capacity of the environment is greatest. Resource optimisation will be approached if both developing and developed countries are better off after the shift. Japanese resource development investment in the Pacific Basin was cited as an example. The other view was that either for reasons of national security or because of international responsibility such shifts should be kept to a minimum. A number of delegates affirmed the responsibility of industrialised OECD countries to co-operate and assist developing countries to avoid environmental deprivation and to improve environmental quality.

viii) In general, it was agreed that the macro-economic results of pollution control expenditure support the argument that environmental and economic policy objectives can be complementary. There are certain economic costs that must be accepted if the environmental benefits are judged to be desirable.

ix) Consequently, environmental policy need not be justified on the basis of positive macro-impacts, but rather on the basis of benefits, some of which are of the welfare kind and some of which are of the economic type. In considering the benefits of policies, it was pointed out that the capital productivity approach (that is, environmental expenditure adds to capital stock but not to output, and that productivity must therefore decline) is not tenable because: (1) without environmental protection the productive capacity of the economy would decline; (2) future generations would have to pay substantially more for protection; (3) environmental measures could help technological development and promote competition. It was also pointed out that benefit-cost analysis used for the assessment of individual environmental measures should cover more than marketable goods, services and costs. Indeed, benefit-cost analyses need to be extended to deal with environment-related problems. For example, forestry projects should cover not only marketable timber, but also such impacts as changes in air quality due to the disappearance of forest, or the potential impact on soil, wildlife and fauna. Benefit-cost analysis should enumerate all these effects and if they cannot be quantified and assigned a value this should be stated.

x) It was suggested that the appropriate way of looking at economic growth would be to examine whether economic and resource development objectives are not in contradiction with the laws that govern ecology and with thermodynamic principles. This is completely separate from the proposal to reconcile environmental objectives with economic growth. The environment is governed by certain physical laws. In addition, environmental goods are public goods and choices made today will affect future generations. The task is to determine to what extent a market-oriented demand for environmental public goods could and should be developed.

OECD Responsibilities

i) The OECD should further encourage macro-economic measurements of the impacts of environmental expenditures; this is particularly important in the light of the expressed intention of Member countries to reduce emission levels significantly and to devote higher proportions of GNP to protection of the environment.

ii) The OECD should endeavour to extend the measurement of macro-impacts, including use of more comprehensive models and considerably more accurate information about environmental and economic impacts.

iii) At the same time, these macro-studies should be supported by micro-assessments of the industries most affected; regional assessments combined with assessments of income-distributional effects should be encouraged.

iv) The harmonization of environmental measures, including standards, timetables and implementation, should be vigorously pursued according to the objectives and subject to the constraints stated above.

v) Strict adherence to the Polluter-Pays Principle should be promoted and monitored periodically. The impact of the various financial assistances provided should be assessed for the various industry branches.

vi) There is a need at the international level to develop avenues and mechanisms, including the extension of the Polluter-Pays Principle, for dealing with transfrontier pollution movements.

vii) The extension of benefit-cost studies to make them more appropriate for environment-related projects should be promoted and their use re-examined.

SESSION THREE

ENVIRONMENTAL POLICIES: A SOURCE OF JOBS?

CHAIRMAN'S OPENING SPEECH

Hon. Antonis TRITSIS

Minister of Physical Planning,
Housing and Environment, Greece

Three points are of particular importance in relation to "jobs":

-- Stability of employment: secure existing jobs.

-- New employment opportunities: expansion of the economy to create more jobs.

-- Quality of life: The "job" as the key to a meaningful life.

1. <u>Stability of employment</u>: presupposes a stable -- sustainable -- pattern of development, which means:

   i) Conservation and renewal of basic renewable natural resources on which the specific economic activity depends: water, soils, flora, fauna;

   ii) Optimisation of use of non-renewable natural resources: minerals, tourist resources (landscape, historic sites) and so on;

   iii) Efficiency of operation: preventing waste of resources, especially energy and raw materials.

2. <u>Expansion of Economy</u>: presupposes existence of development potential, investment and so on, which to a considerable degree can be secured by: conservation, optimisation of use and efficiency of performance of existing economic activity (above-mentioned points).

3. <u>Quality of life</u> means the quality of the natural/physical environment, conducive to the healthy overall development of the individual and society, including preservation of the historic and cultural environment (heritage).

All the above points and considerations re-set the question of environment in relation to development, or better, the question of development in relation to environment. From a "residual to development", environment becomes "a parameter proper to development": the very quintessence of development as process and as outcome.

Additional points

i) Environment sets the foundation but also the limits to development. Here an underlying conflict between "enterprise" -- private or public -- and "society" is unveiled.

ii) The "market mechanism" is not an appropriate framework for environmental policies and actions. Basic environmental parameters such as energy costs or health standards either do not enter the "market" or are set -- exogenously to the market -- by government.

iii) The concept of "costs", "damage costs", is not the same for enterprises and for government. The cost to the enterprise is inevitably restricted to economic input-output considerations within the artificially restricted -- in this respect -- domain of the market.

iv) Conservation of resources; economising overall development potential and diverting it to other sectors (for example, diverting emissions of power plants to another economic activity) cannot or perhaps should not be the concern of the single enterprise. It should however, be the concern of society, through overall development planning.

v) "Environmental technology" should be conceived more as a fundamental reconsideration of the production process and not simply as an "add-on".

vi) Environment, like peace and disarmament, is one of the historic priorities of our era set by our people. Unless we stand up politically to the challenge, more and more people in our societies, especially the youth, will lose confidence in the political process, a phenomenon already observed in the West which undermines the very process of democracy.

Conclusions

The environmental dimension brings to the foreground again the general development question and resets more clearly the axiom: development means socially controlled economic activity, for the purpose of securing the proper process as well as the proper aims of development.

INTRODUCTION BY

Mr. Michel de GRAVE

Advisor to the Belgian Christian Labour Federation

Since this Session on employment is to be one of the shortest of the Conference, I shall not spend too much time talking about the linkages between the environmental policies so far conducted and employment.

The Background Paper provides useful and reassuring -- albeit incomplete and tentative -- information on this subject. Most of you are aware of other papers on the issue, and here I am thinking in particular of the contributions made by Michel Potier and Rolf-Ulrich Sprenger to the Colloquy on "Environment and Employment" organised in Barcelona by the Parliamentary Assembly of the Council of Europe.

There is one small comment I should like to make in passing, and that is that we could turn the question on its head and ask ourselves what the employment situation might be like in the absence of any environmental policy. For example, how many fishermen would be left in the year 2000 if there were no marine resource management policy? And how many jobs in the Black Forest would be under threat if the woodland environment were destroyed?

I want to concentrate on the essential: the future, asking the question "What is to be done?" and begging your pardon in advance if my thinking draws more on my own familiar environment than on that of countries whose industrial revolution came later.

The environment I know is one of derelict factories, queues of unemployed people in a region where there has been no redeployment, and railway lines disused for years. And there is not even any policy to improve this desolate industrial landscape, this environment which in itself is enough to drive away investors and jobs.

So what is to be done? The first thing that strikes me is the scale of the schemes under way in some countries and the apparent apathy in others. Perhaps this may be due to the fact that it is not easy to set up new schemes in areas where responsibility is divided among several ministries. But I believe there is another reason. Some people still think of environment policy as being a luxury which we may be able to afford in times of prosperity but which today has to give way to matters of more immediate concern.

And yet Marc Ambroise-Rendu, writing in "Le Monde" of 25th February 1982, said that "If statistics -- which always have to be handled carefully -- are to be believed, pollution is costing France FF80 billion a year: as much as unemployment". And at the Barcelona colloquy the Spanish Minister, Julian Campo, told us that the lack of pure water and air is a factor that curbs and limits growth.

Nevertheless, many people continue to see the present crisis as an untimely interruption of rapid growth which will soon begin again, aided by the new technologies. While this side of the question cannot be disregarded, can we really believe in a recovery bringing a sufficient number of jobs in industry in our countries, when we look at the trend in the sector well before the crisis and see how domestic demand for so many product categories is reaching saturation point?

We have even had to revise our thinking about development in the tertiary sector, to the extent of wondering whether our post-industrial societies may not have to be described, straightaway, as post-tertiary. And I wonder whether we are bearing this sufficiently in mind in our reasoning.

While the changes affecting our societies are often mentioned, we sometimes fail to draw the conclusion that new requirements call for new employment structures, a new conception of economic and social questions and even a new approach to the work/leisure relationship. Traditional opinion has probably paid too little attention to these developments. In any case, we are bound to admit that for a long time no heed was taken of environmental protection, so much so that new political movements were born and thrived for that very reason.

Not all environmental policies lead to job creation, but ways of killing two birds with one stone can be found. How can we draw up a plan of action which will promote employment and at the same time meet new requirements with respect to the environment and the quality of life? First let me quote one of a number of suggestions from the macroeconomic standpoint, but one worth mentioning as having been endorsed by all sides in a recent Opinion of the EEC Economic and Social Committee:

"For example, one should test the overall impact on the economy of an improvement in quality and an increase in product durability, and of a policy favouring repairs or restoration (housing, cars, and so on) rather than discarding or destroying and replacing (favourable effect on the level of imports and the trade deficit, on employment in services and building, which are highly labour-intensive and less exposed to international competition, on the reduction of waste and the cost of its disposal, on savings in foreign exchange and raw materials and so on). If economic models and national experience suggest that favourable results can be hoped for, one should consider the most appropriate ways of achieving these objectives and propose their introduction.

"The absence of any comparative analysis makes it difficult to establish whether the policies being pursued are the best. However, the restoration of old buildings, beauty spots and so on offers almost unlimited employment potential. Many jobs in all regions could also be created if repairs were carried out by small local firms on semi-durable goods such as cars which are only partly built in the Community (with fewer and fewer jobs)."

Because time is short, I shall mention only briefly the possibility of strengthening the position of enterprises in the environmental sector. Here it must be remembered that countries where pollution control policy has been longest and most firmly established have become net exporters of the techniques concerned (for example, water treatment in France), whereas they have remained net importers where stricter laws abroad have led other countries to develop processes.

I would also allude to the example of forest products, the second most important cause of the EEC trade deficit. While deforestation in the Third World is giving cause for concern, since forest resources can be renewed only slowly, internal divisions within the EEC have so far prevented the adoption of a common forestry policy, and we remain passively dependent on the use of land for costly types of cultivation, even though this is not the result of a deliberate choice.

I now come to the micro-economic level. I am aware that some countries have national programmes -- and other countries non-programmes -- but I have to admit that I am not sufficiently conversant with all existing situations to be able to summarise them properly. But I am struck by the targeting and quality of some national schemes, and I believe that in this Conference, like all those which enable policy-makers and administrators to compare notes on their experience, successes and difficulties in this relatively new area are in themselves much more of a stimulus than anything I could say in 10 minutes. So I advise you to look at those schemes in detail.

I shall mention only a single example, with apologies for this perhaps arbitrary choice. According to the provisional report dated 27 September 1983 on the French scheme, "Innovation -- Employment -- Environment", the average cost of creating one job under the scheme (FF131 000) is particularly low in comparison with that in other sectors.

The report lists many projects in widely different areas, such as:

-- "Soft" techniques for the maintenance of the Mediterranean coastline (beach-cleaning machines);

-- Small-scale agricultural activities, either new ones or old ones that have fallen into disuse -- for instance, those not included in the framework of national or EEC agricultural policies (edible sweet chestnuts, pleurotus mushrooms, snails, herbs and medicinal plants, silkworms and so on);

-- Development of alternative tourism;

-- Rural group activities;

-- Utilisation of difficult land (marshland, arid land, mountain land);

-- Rational production and use of compost;

-- Restoration of old buildings and vocational training adapted for that purpose;

-- Rehabilitation of disused industrial sites;

-- Alternative energy sources (mobile exhibitions providing

information, support for projects producing methane from pig slurry, compost);

-- Recycling (tyres, waste paper, plastic, wrecked cars);

-- Water treatment stations;

-- Ecological control of rivers (upkeep and so on).

Such a policy, of course, goes further than one concerned with environment alone, dealing with the environment in the broadest sense and not merely with pollution control. But environmental concerns are inseparable from the general aspiration toward a higher quality of life.

The multiplier effect of this type of environmental project seems to be at least as great as in other fields where it has traditionally been sought. I should like to stress two other important advantages to be gained from this kind of programme:

-- First, many economic activities related to improvement of the environment mean not only more jobs but jobs in all geographical areas and based on a very considerable potential for drive, initiative and inventiveness;

-- Second -- and this is a point that cannot be overemphasised -- many such schemes might also contribute to the reinsertion of delinquents into working life or the integration of young people (or adults) in difficulty.

In Berlin, for instance, I visited a number of "alternative" enterprises providing vocational training for young people who in the normal educational system had been misfits. Such enterprises constitute a haven, catering for vulnerable people whose cost to the taxpayer might have been much higher than it is today if they had been allowed to drop out of society in one way or another. Significantly, many psychologists and social workers are to be found in these alternative groups. Investment in human resources is certainly not the least worthwhile form of investment in today's destabilising world. Here I am thinking of education and vocational training, but also of clubs offering leisure pursuits (where young people may, for instance, amuse themselves and at the same time learn computer techniques or where many other activities for young people and adults are provided). Or, as another concrete example, I might mention the group of French graphologists specialising in the early detection, through the study of children's handwriting, of various personality problems which might have an adverse effect on the future life of the child concerned (not only on his personal welfare but also on his social behaviour and his capacity to work and thus his usefulness to society). What a small investment for potentially substantial returns!

In addition to its human and social content, a policy that aims to improve the quality of life may often be considered to be an investment with a positive economic impact:

-- Less absenteeism, fewer nervous or occupational diseases, fewer accidents;

-- Greater job satisfaction and thus more incentive to work or learn new skills;

-- A reduction in the costs induced by pollution for certain enterprises, for damage to housing stock, to health or in other sectors;

-- Preservation of cultural assets which may be turned to account for industrial or tourism purposes;

-- Lower costs of all kinds related to social maladjustment (relegation in all its forms, alcoholism, drug addiction, incapacity to work);

-- Lower insurance costs (damage, premiums).

So it would be a mistake to think that a policy aimed at improving the quality of life is a luxury that can be assigned second place at times of crisis. As in other sectors (defence, education, research, investment in facilities) money spent on improving the quality of life may show a return only in the long run, and only in macroeconomic terms -- though this does not mean that financing such spending in the short term may not frequently be far from easy. And this is not to speak of the consequences of unemployment. Can we be sure that the exclusion from society of increasing numbers of young people may not one day lead to situations for which we are unprepared?

You may say, perhaps these expenditures are well worth while -- but where are we to find the money? True enough, it is not possible to say, "We all have to do so...", even if we do wonder whether there would not be some better use for the money that is poured into gambling, spent on keeping up with the Joneses or on consumerism brought to fever pitch by television advertising, or wasted in ways that fuel inflation.

But the results achieved in certain countries show that not all policy-makers are resigned to failure and that there are ministers who, like do-it-yourself enthusiasts, achieve a great deal with little money, a few ideas, good back-up workers and, above all, willingness to listen to groups which are prepared to take initiatives. Certainly money is scarce -- but this is not always the case when it comes to other policies.

The European Community has a research programme -- admittedly a modest one, spread over several years, on housing conditions; but the houses concerned are henhouses. One day I upset a member of the Commission by suggesting that part of that money might be allocated to studies on housing conditions for human beings or on overcrowding in peak-hour buses.

While I admit that this suggestion was largely intended to be provocative, is there not some truth here which our over-mercenary conception of economic policy prevents us from discerning?

I hope that this Conference will inspire new do-it-yourself adepts, because we can no longer tolerate that the present unacceptable level of unemployment should continue, while at the same time essential needs are not being met. We must aim to broaden the range of the politically possible, simply because it is politically necessary.

ENVIRONMENTAL POLICIES: A SOURCE OF JOBS?

1. INTRODUCTION

The primary objective of environmental policies is improvement in the quality of the environment.' However, at a time when OECD Member countries have the highest rates of unemployment in recent years (an average of 9 per cent of the total working population in 1983 compared to 5 per cent in 1977 and an average of 2.81 per cent for 1962-1973), and when unemployment for 1984 is projected to be 34.75 million, there is understandably considerable interest in and concern about the impact of environmental policies on employment.

In an attempt to clarify the debate on this topic, this paper will address the following questions:

-- What are the channels through which environmental policy can affect employment levels -- either positively or adversely?

-- What empirical evidence exists regarding the total number of people permanently employed in the environment sector?

-- What empirical evidence exists regarding the net impact on employment of environmental policy? To what extent does this evidence consider both direct and indirect effects, multiplier effects, displacement effects, and long- versus short-term effects of environmental policy?

-- Have environmental measures been included in direct job-creation programmes adopted by OECD Member countries? And to what extent were such environmentally-related job-creation schemes able to effectively increase employment? What characteristics should environmental programmes have to provide the maximum employment impact and environmental improvement for a given level of expenditure?

2. THE EMPLOYMENT EFFECTS OF ENVIRONMENTAL POLICY: CHANNELS OF IMPACT

Environmental regulations require enterprises both to invest in emission control equipment, and to operate and maintain it. The resulting increase in the cost of production leads to higher prices of the products of affected industries and, the argument goes, could result in job reductions. Either whole plants which were marginally profitable before environmental controls will have to be closed, or production will have to be reduced, with some loss of employment, when there is a gradual shift to lower priced substitutes. It is also argued that the overall impact on employment is likely to be more severe if the switch is to imported goods, or if investment is moved to a country with lower levels of environmental control. There could be losses of jobs -- mostly on a regional basis -- when for reasons of conservation (for example, of native forests) certain economic activities are curtailed and jobs are either lost or not created.

While these adverse effects on employment of environmental policies no doubt exist, environmental measures are also likely to have favourable offsetting impacts on employment. Looking first at the gross employment generated in observing controls, regulations on emission levels create a demand for equipment and manpower to operate it which otherwise would not have existed. Indeed, environmental policy will likely stimulate an entirely new industrial sector -- the pollution control industry -- which could lead to substantial job creation. Government expenditure in support of pollution control could have positive or negative impacts depending on the area of public expenditure from which the funds have been drawn, and the impact on taxes and borrowing.

Any full appraisal of the effects on employment of environmental policies must consider both the employment-stimulating and employment-depressing effects of such policy. The net impact is relevant. Such an appraisal must take into account indirect impacts, displacement effects and general equilibrium wage and price effects. Furthermore, the impact of environmental measures on employment over the long-term should be considered; focusing only on short-term effects -- which are the most visible -- can be seriously misleading. Finally, any appraisal of impacts must consider whether the demand for pollution control equipment is met by domestic production or by imports from countries specialising in production of this equipment.

The net effect on employment of environmental policies will differ depending on the level and structure of unemployment and idle capacity in an economy. For example, an increase in spending for pollution-control equipment will directly increase employment if the skill mix of workers required by the pollution-control equipment industry to increase output is concentrated in labour markets with substantial unemployment. On the other hand, if employment demands of the pollution-control equipment industry are focused on labour markets characterised by full employment -- or on fully employed occupations where there is little possible substitution with other occupations experiencing high unemployment -- any employment increases will be smaller, wage and price increases larger, and lags in implementing control longer.

3. THE EMPLOYMENT EFFECTS OF ENVIRONMENTAL POLICY: THE EVIDENCE

Substantial empirical work has been carried out both at the macro and micro level on the effect of air and water pollution control policies on employment. Several countries have carried out macroeconometric studies (consistent with the considerations noted above) to evaluate the full impact of air and water pollution control programmes. These studies suggest that in the short-term the net employment effects of air and water pollution control measures tend to be positive. But in the long-term negative effects on employment of those measures, resulting from an increase in the costs and prices of the products of the polluting industries, outweigh the positive effects. In every case those effects, whether positive or negative, appear to be a very small percentage of total employment.

Available micro studies indicate that public sector environmental expenditures are relatively labour-intensive. The primary beneficiaries of employment induced by environmental expenditure in the pollution equipment industry tend to be highly skilled workers.

Evidence on the adverse effects on employment of closing marginal plants because of environmental measures indicates that those effects are miniscule. The most recent report prepared in the United States as part of the Economic Dislocation Early Warning System and published in October 1983 identified 155 plant closures since 1971 involving 32 899 job losses as a result of pollution-control regulations. The few plants which have been closed were high cost, older facilities whose phase-out was perhaps accelerated by environmental policy. Moreover, the output which would have been produced in these facilities tends to be shifted to new lower-cost facilities. Plant closure is, of course, only part of the story: impacts may have been greater on plants which did not expand, or new plants which were not built, because of pollution-control regulation.

Various efforts have been made in a number of OECD countries to evaluate the impact of environmental programmes on employment by estimating the number of jobs created as a result of specific environmental protection programmes, or by conducting surveys of specific sectors, such as various levels of government. However, the results of the surveys given in the following paragraphs do not include any displacement effects.

The United States Environmental Protection Agency estimates that the Federal Pollution Control Programme created 42 000 jobs on construction sites and 63 000 jobs elsewhere within the building industry in 1980 as a result of purification plant projects which the Agency helped to finance. Moreover, according to a study by A.D. Little, employment in the pollution-control equipment industry (water, air pollution) was estimated at 36 000 jobs for the same year and at 43 900 jobs for 1983.

A paper prepared for the Federal Republic of Germany assessed the average annual impact on employment of environmental expenditure at 218 000 man-years for 1975-1979. These figures represent about 0.8 per cent of the working population. A subsequent 1979 IFO study reached the same conclusions. On the basis of more detailed statistics, the average annual impact on employment was estimated at 200 000 man-years for 1972-77 and at 250 000 for 1978-80.

Three surveys were carried out in France -- in 1976, 1979 and 1981 -- to estimate the number of jobs directly and indirectly linked to environmental policies. In 1976 environment-related activity accounted for an estimated

290 000 jobs. However, the French survey was based on a different definition of activities than that used in the United States or Germany. It included, for example, jobs connected with water supply and distribution and with household refuse collection and waste recovery.

The 1979 French survey extended the activities covered even further. In addition to jobs such as water supply and distribution mentioned above (80 000 jobs), it included jobs related to the protection of wildlife and the countryside, for example national parks, hunting and fishing reserves (18 000 jobs), and jobs connected with improvement in the quality of life, for example regional parks and public open spaces (29 000 jobs). In all some 370 000 jobs were created. The 1981 survey covering the same field as the 1979 survey -- but incorporating indirect jobs related to environmental policies -- gave an estimate of 390 000 jobs. Aside from household refuse collection and cleansing about 100 000 persons, or about 0.43 per cent of the working population, are employed on programmes combatting water and air pollution.

While data on the sectoral -- industrial, occupational, and regional -- impacts of environmental policy would be helpful in framing an overall appraisal of employment effects, little detailed information on such impacts is available. The most reliable information comes from studies done in the Federal Republic of Germany. These studies indicate that: (i) those industries adversely affected by environmental policy are the chemical, petroleum, non-ferrous metal, pulp and paper, iron and steel, and electric power industries; (ii) medium-size firms within these industries bear the largest burden of cost and employment losses; (iii) the relationship between the burden of environmental policies on industry and industry unemployment rates is very small. But those industries most adversely affected appear to have somewhat lower unemployment rates than average; and (iv) the industries which benefit from environmental policies are those most closely related to the pollution-control industry.

4. THE ROLE OF ENVIRONMENTAL MEASURES IN EMPLOYMENT AND DIRECT JOB CREATION POLICY

In some Member countries environmental projects have been explicitly included in job creation schemes. Often these projects have been part of larger or accelerated public works schemes. Both the objectives and structure of these environmental projects is quite different from the emission-control efforts emphasized in the 1970s. Whereas the efforts to control emissions aimed to improve air and water quality, more recent public works measures involve landscape beautification projects, reforestation, park and recreation area construction, and urban structure rehabilitation. Only in some exceptional cases were sewer construction and landfill improvement, wastewater treatment plant construction, and more traditional water resources investments also included. The impact on employment of these measures depends on both their labour-intensiveness and the extent to which they are targetted at either low-skill or high-skill workers, as well as the particular region of implementation and the speed at which they can be implemented. Any overall evaluation of employment effects would have to take into account the particular characteristics of any specific measure.

Evaluation of proposed job-creation schemes in general, and

environmentally-related schemes in particular, should be undertaken prior to implementation to determine if such programmes yield net economic benefits. Moreover, in designing and implementing such programmes, the need for conservation or environmental improvements should be adequately demonstrated. Such projects should be implemented only if projected outputs justify costs, particularly of increased taxation, reduced public spending on alternative programmes, or displaced private activities. The self-sustaining character of the projects should also be assessed. In addition, environment-related schemes should be compared with other job-creation projects, in particular those designed to facilitate general economic development. It must be recognised however, that although desirable, evaluation of environmentally-related job-creation schemes prior to implementation is not always performed in OECD Member countries.

5. THE EFFECTIVENESS OF ENVIRONMENTAL MEASURES IN EMPLOYMENT AND DIRECT JOB CREATION POLICY

Among the various types of public expenditure for special direct employment projects, environmental measures (for example, the construction of water and wastewater treatment facilities) appear to create as many jobs per unit of expenditure as other construction or building-oriented expenditures (such as highway construction). But they do not have a significantly higher employment generation potential than these other measures. Again, these findings are fairly aggregate, and do not consider the specific characteristics of various environmental projects.

Among the various types of environmental projects which could serve as the focus of special employment-generating public works projects, some have substantially larger employment generation effects than others. Those with the largest impact on employment per dollar of cost are the labour intensive, direct job creation measures which emphasize conservation and landscaping. Studies in the Federal Republic of Germany and Sweden, for example, indicate that environmental relief works which emphasize labour-intensive reforestations, parks and open spaces, nature and recreation, and river control have much greater job-creation potential per unit of public expenditure than investments in sewage works, drainage facilities, or noise protection. A recent survey of these direct environment-related job creation measures, however, indicates that the jobs they created represented less than 0.05 per cent of employment in all of the countries studied.

Several OECD Member countries -- Sweden, Finland, the Netherlands, France, Denmark, Norway, the Federal Republic of Germany, and Austria -- have recently undertaken special public works programmes with environmental components. Studies of the impacts of these programmes verify that: (i) programmes oriented towards environmental construction do not have a significantly higher employment generation potential than other programmes in terms of job creation per unit of expenditure; (ii) labour-intensive environmental measures, largely involving management of the natural environment, have superior job creation performance relative to those emphasizing the construction of facilities; and (iii) substantial employment multiplier effects amounting to 50 per cent of the direct employment effects are associated with labour-intensive environmental projects. These multiplier

~~ects stem from incremental expenditures by project workers who would
~~herwise be unemployed, and exist despite the fact that these projects
produce no marketable output. However, there may be cases where new
environment-related jobs are not self-sustaining, and may not be in areas
important to long-term employment creation.

6. CONCLUSIONS

The primary objective of environmental policies has been in the past
-- and should be in the future -- improvement in the quality of the
environment. The environmental measures instituted during the .1970s
-- largely air and water pollution-control measures -- had both positive and
negative employment effects. Evidence from past and present experience
suggests that so far those effects are positive, while over the longer-term
the measures may result in some minor reduction in aggregate employment, as
the emission control activities resulted in somewhat higher costs and prices.

The evidence presented on these employment impacts is based largely on
results from macroeconomic model simulations complemented by results from
sectoral studies. Results from the macroeconomic model simulation may be
considered inconclusive because of the small number of studies involved.
Available sectoral studies point to positive effects. But they consider, by
their very nature, only past and present impacts.

In the presence of high and growing unemployment, direct labour market
interventions of a targetted nature have been implemented in many Member
countries in recent years. Direct job creation programmes have been an
important component of these employment-generating measures. Environmentally
related projects, often of a public works nature, have occasionally been
included among these direct job-creation efforts.

Although environmentally-related construction activities appear to be
no more effective in generating employment than other construction activities
(such as highways), labour-intensive projects such as measures undertaken to
manage the natural environment proved to be especially effective in generating
employment.

If Member countries want to use environmentally-related projects in
direct job creation programmes they should compare not only the cost and
amount of employment generated by such programmes with alternative programmes,
but also assess the potential benefits for the environment of such
job-creation programmes.

SUMMARY OF THE DISCUSSION OF SESSION THREE

Mr. Maurice Bommensath

Director, General Commission for
Scientific Organisation (CEGOS), Paris

Issues

i) The total number of unemployed in OECD countries is approaching 35 million and there is considerable concern about future prospects for employment. The major causes of unemployment have been well identified, including the various branches of industry where there has been a significant decline in employment; a number of these industries, such as the iron and steel industry, are also the worst polluters. Given this background, it is legitimate to ask what have been the overall net impacts of environmental policies on employment; to what extent have they been negative or positive? Which sectors have experienced these impacts and what were the regional consequences? If there were negative effects, should environmental measures be postponed or curtailed?

ii) In almost all OECD countries there are now various job-creation programmes to provide jobs for new job seekers coming onto the market and also to reduce the number of unemployed. These job creation schemes take many forms: subsidised retraining facilities, subsidised apprenticeship schemes, regional development programmes to attract domestic and foreign capital to depressed regions and public expenditure programmes directly for public works. In a number of countries environmental measures have been included in these job creation schemes, sometimes in the form of public expenditure programmes in pollution control or conservation and occasionally as regulations to speed up and also to provide financial support for pollution control investment in the private sector. Were these programmes effective both for job creation and for environmental protection? What was the relative significance of these programmes as a percentage of the total number of new jobs or as a percentage of the total number unemployed?

iii) There are a number of industries where economically and environmentally efficient management of resources is needed to maintain long-term employment. Examples include agriculture, fisheries, forestry and tourism. There have been cases where medium- and longer-term economic and social objectives have been

sacrificed for the sake of short-term profitability (and
employment) with the permanent loss of jobs. What type of
environmental policies are needed and how could economic and
environmental objectives be constructively combined to ensure the
maintenance of job opportunities and the creation of new jobs in
the medium and longer term?

iv) There have been unjustified fears in the past, accentuated by the
present high level of unemployment, that jobs could be lost to
other countries because environmental control costs will reduce
the international competitiveness of a country, or that non-tariff
barriers would be created by environmental legislation (for
example, through standards for motor cars or specified designs for
pollution control equipment). There is little factual evidence
that a significant number of jobs have been lost through
international competition owing to environmental measures.
Nevertheless, the question remains: what could be done through
international measures and co-operation to minimise unjustifiable
shifts in employment between countries that might be caused by
environmental measures?

Responses

Discussion showed that the issue of environment and employment will
remain a lively one for the rest of the decade, and a number of proposals were
made on how to deal with these problems in environmentally and economically
acceptable ways.

i) There was a broad consensus that the net direct employment impacts
of environmental expenditures in the short term were positive but
very slight. Views vary about the reliability of the longer-run
estimates, which appear to show a slight negative direct impact.
At the same time, however, it was pointed out that these estimates
ignore certain indirect effects that reduced environmental and
health damage could have on employment and which are likely to be
positive.

ii) The net employment effects clearly have both positive and negative
aspects. The negative impacts were concentrated in industries
employing old technologies and in highly polluting industries, and
jobs were lost owing to the combined effect of these and other
economic forces. These job losses were also concentrated in
certain regions. However, it was pointed out that in a number of
countries efforts have been made, often at the cost of
environmental protection, to prevent or minimise job losses. Such
solutions can be regarded as inefficient from both the economic
and the environmental point of view. Measures aimed
simultaneously at both environmental and employment improvements
should be carefully evaluated in order to avoid inefficient
solutions in both areas.

iii) In order to avoid sudden regional rises in unemployment due to the
shutdown of old plants, anticipatory policies are needed to phase
out old industries gradually and possibly to replace them with new

clean industries. Some form of government intervention in this structural readjustment will be essential, at least through some retraining and also through more environmentally based new jobs. It was agreed that in these cases there is a need for a graduated stance on environmental policy implementation.

iv) The majority of speakers strongly supported government actions, already taken in a number of countries, to include environmental measures in their overall policy of job creation. The general view was that at a time of high unemployment, such as today, the opportunity cost of environmental policies was low, while benefits could be very substantial. Given overall governmental objectives for reducing unemployment and improving the environment, such policies should be promoted. At the same time a number of qualifications were made:

-- It is desirable that jobs of long-term duration be created. It is relatively easy and inexpensive to introduce projects, say in nature conservation, with a high employment content, but they are usually of short duration; job creation in accordance with the changing industrial structure should be sought.

-- Job creation needs some pre-planning; properly planned environmental programmes introduced at the right period of the business cycle would create jobs and bring about positive adjustments by industry. There have been cases where environmental programmes designed with the intention of saving or creating jobs have been extremely expensive per job created. The view was put forward that in many cases environmental measures should be designed for their environmental objectives alone, and that job creation requires appropriate measures of its own.

-- Another view was that all environmental expenditures should be treated as investment to bring out their impact on assets and resources (water, forests and so on) and hence in the preservation of a number of lasting jobs.

-- In connection with urban environmental projects, many of them particularly labour intensive, the view was expressed that preference should be given to jobs of longer duration. It should also be recognised that a good urban environment has many side benefits, including social and economic benefits.

v) Under the broader definition of environment, apart from pollution control and conservation, the importance of quality of employment should be recognised: there is already a trend away from employment in heavy and dirty industries towards service industries, and environmental policies could encourage this trend towards smaller and cleaner industrial service establishments.

OECD Responsibilities

i) The relationship between environment and employment has been

99

examined only so far as the direct effects of environmental expenditures are concerned. Some countries also make estimates of the total number of people working in environmental protection and conservation, amounting to between 1 per cent and 2 per cent of the active work force. However, the relationship appears to be more complex than the first direct employment impacts of environmental expenditures suggest, and this should be explored in detail by the OECD.

ii) OECD should also examine future employment trends and see how consistent they are with future environmental objectives. This could be undertaken in the broader international context, taking into account also the possible shifts in employment in response to environmental regulations and examining how far these shifts are desirable and to what extent harmonization of environmental policies is needed to counteract these trends.

SESSION FOUR

THE IMPACT OF ENVIRONMENTAL POLICIES ON INDUSTRIAL INNOVATION

CHAIRMAN'S OPENING SPEECH

Mr. Koji KAKIZAWA

Vice-Minister, Japanese Environment Agency

The key role played by innovation in today's dynamic economy cannot be over-emphasized. The post-war period of strong economic growth in the industrialised nations of OECD has been ensured by an unprecedented advance in research and development (R&D) activities.

The fundamental question presented to us is twofold. The first is the relationship between environmental regulation and innovation; more specifically, the question of whether the impact of environmental regulation upon industrial innovation is positive or negative. The second is the question of what types of environmental measures can induce innovation, and how and under what conditions such environmental policies can be formulated and implemented in an economically effective and efficient manner.

In order to give some hints for our discussion, I would like to make some observations on the Japanese experience which I think are very relevant to the subjects before us.

1. Intensive Economic Activity on a Limited Land Area

The fundamental reality behind Japan's environmental problems has been the rapid formation of a high-density economy and society on this country's limited land area.

According to OECD statistics, the ratio of habitable area to total land area in Japan is only 22 per cent, compared with 91 per cent in the United Kingdom, 69 per cent in France and 52 per cent in the United States. If we examine production density by the yardstick of gross national product (GNP) per unit habitable area, Japan's is about four times that of West Germany, about 14 times that of France, and about 30 times that of the United States. These figures suggest that the same level of environmental effort has not been enough for Japan to enjoy the same level of economic prosperity in comparison with other industrialised nations of the OECD.

Japan's conspicuously high concentration of economic and social activities in comparison with other industrialised countries has placed a heavy burden on the environment owing to the excessive concentration in some regions.

2. Industrial Innovation -- A Prerequisite for Survival

Under such conditions, the role of industrial innovation and the development of technology has been of extreme importance for Japanese firms in order to conform with the stringent environmental requirements and at the same time to survive in the competitive domestic and international market.

Japanese firms have been put under extremely severe environmental, resource and other conditions. Generally speaking, such hardship has ensured an innovative response by Japanese firms to environmental regulations.

This is my personal observation and I hope it will provoke argument about the relationship between environmental regulation and industrial innovation.

INTRODUCTION BY

Dr. Joe T. LING

Vice-President, 3M Company, St. Paul, Minnesota, USA

It is an honour for me to have been asked to make the Keynote Speech at this Session. I bring with me today an environmental management career that includes academic life, government service, and work as an independent consultant and as a vice-president of a major corporation. My experience in these positions gives me broad insight on the policy issues of this Session, which are described in the accompanying Issue Paper.

The goal of this Session is to improve our understanding and perceptions so that we can develop efficient, productive environmental management policies and encourage industrial innovation at the same time. Achievement of this goal will require open discussions and exchange of views between representatives of all concerned. This Conference offers us such an opportunity.

We start with the premise that the nations and the people of the world require environmental management to avoid the dangers of air, water and land pollution, and also require economic growth to improve and sustain their standard and quality of living.

We recognise that the environmental cycle -- involving air, water and land -- exists as a delicate balance that can be disrupted by external factors. But industrial innovation, which is a major component of sustained economic growth, also operates on a delicate balance of internal forces within the private sector.

The policies of government represent one of these external influences that can affect the balance of both the environmental cycle and industrial innovation. In fact, government action in one of these two areas may impact the other.

For example, environmental policies and regulations can stifle industrial innovation by increasing production costs, by decreasing profitability and by blunting the ability to innovate. However, environmental policies can also be a positive force in encouraging new technologies that are not only more environmentally efficient but more economical and profitable. In other words, industrial innovation can be both regulation-driven and market-driven.

Concern over such positive and negative effects prompted a number of investigations by both the public and private sectors in the United States.

As part of a 1978 domestic policy review, President Carter established an Advisory Committee on Environment, Health and Safety Regulations on Industrial Innovations. The committee was chaired by the Secretary of Commerce and a report was published in April 1979.

A year later, the Office of Technology Assessment of the US Congress established an Advisory Committee on Technological Innovations and Health, Safety and Environmental Regulations. The results were reported in December 1981. Both committees included leaders from all sectors of society -- and I had the honour of serving on both committees.

There have been a number of similar studies on this subject in other countries. Some of these are mentioned in the Conference documents. It is difficult to reach definite conclusions because different approaches were taken in each investigation; however, the following general observations can be made:

    i) While many factors affect industrial innovation, governmental environmental policy and regulation have a major influence. These policies and regulations have a profound impact on certain industrial sectors but only a minor impact on others. Therefore, macro-economic studies in terms of gross national product do not reflect the real impact. For example, heavily impacted sectors such as steel and the pulp and paper industry that must spend more than 15 per cent of their capital expenditures on pollution control must divert funds from investment in new facilities and enterprises that generate innovation.

    ii) A study by the US Office of Technology Assessment in 1981 revealed that US environmental policies have not significantly affected the overall level of innovative effort in terms of research and development expenditures. But they have affected the pattern of industrial innovation. Today, there is much less industrial emphasis on the development of high risk potential products -- even if the need is urgent. Rather, industrial innovation is concentrated on high volume, large market products with secure and predictable profit potential. In short, efforts are spent on "the sure thing".

    iii) Based on general observations in the United States, environmental policies and regulations have increased the cost of product development. They have lengthened the product development process and increased uncertainty, which raises the risk in innovative venture investment.

    iv) It has been found that regulatory mechanisms and the manner of governmental intervention have more effect than the stringency of an environmental policy or regulation. For example, use of a policy such as the "bubble concept" to control the air emission discharges from an entire factory rather than from each individual discharge stack has stimulated industrial innovation in the United States. Such a policy allows for flexibility and thus the development of innovative technologies to achieve the environmental goal at a lower cost.

v) It has been observed that pollution control equipment manufacturers have developed new and sometimes lower cost control technologies and equipment to meet the technology-oriented environmental requirements.

In addition, a number of industries have also responded to the environmental regulatory demand through the development of innovative solutions. For example, the Pollution Prevention Pays (3P) programme in the 3M Company has applied an innovative approach since 1975 to reformulate products and redesign processes to eliminate and reduce rather than control pollution. As a result, this programme each year has eliminated over 90 000 tonnes of air pollutants, 10 000 tonnes of water pollutants, 1 000 million gallons of wastewater and 150 000 tonnes of solid wastes.

At this writing, 3P has also generated a total saving of about US$200 million, of which about 60 per cent represents annual operating and maintenance costs. In spite of these selected accomplishments, current governmental policies and regulations, in general, do not encourage industrial innovation of this kind.

vi) Environmental regulations have produced more impact on smaller companies with less financial and human resources than on larger firms. For example, the US Chemical Speciality Manufacturers Association estimated that after implementation of the Toxic Substances Control Act new substance development fell an average of 26 per cent for 1979-1981 in comparison with the period 1976-1978 on the basis of available data at that time. Furthermore, 98 per cent of that decline occurred in companies with less than $100 million of annual sales. Since small enterprises have historically generated more innovation than larger industry, this could have serious policy implications.

These six general observations, based on the findings of studies by various public and private groups, return us to our central theme: what policies should governments pursue in order to enhance both environmental management practices and industrial innovations. To stimulate our thinking and discussion today, I offer the following six suggestions that are based on my environmental career experiences:

i) Environmental policy should foster a multimedia approach that emphasizes the interrelationships between air, land and water. Environmental policy should also be closely related to overall long-range natural resource management activities that include minerals, forests, and so on.

ii) Environmental policies should shift from end-of-production controls to promote broader management concepts, including preventive approaches that address the entire business cycle -- from product design to production, to use, to disposal. Such policies will not only encourage the development of innovative approaches, such as the 3P programme, but can also promote environmentally safer products and cleaner manufacturing processes.

iii) If and when end-of-production controls are necessary, regulatory policy should stress environmental objectives or performance standards rather than technology standards. This would provide incentive for industry to develop innovative technologies in order to increase efficiency and reduce the cost of controls.

iv) Better and more careful analysis is needed of risk versus cost versus benefit in the establishment of government policies and regulations that affect both the environment and industrial innovation.

v) Special policy considerations should be given to localised environmental problems and to small industries and other industries that face severe regulatory hardship. This does not suggest use of different standards; rather it suggests flexibility in the process of achieving compliance with the standards.

vi) Early co-operation between government and industry in the decision-making process should be encouraged so that environmental policies and regulations provide requirements and compliance schedules compatible with the innovative capacity of industry.

About 600 BC, the famous Chinese philosopher Lao Tze alluded to today's topic with these freely translated words of ancient wisdom: "As restrictions and prohibitions multiply, the people grow poorer and poorer. When they are subjected to too much government, the land is thrown into confusion."

Unfortunately, Lao Tze didn't tell us how to cope with "too much government", especially those governmental interventions that interfere with innovation. So today, I would like to pose several additional questions for further consideration.

i) What are the inhibitors of innovation in present environmental policies and regulations? How can their effects be reversed?

ii) What economic instruments can be incorporated into environmental policy to help induce industrial innovation?

iii) What kind of special consideration should be given to small industries or those industries severely impacted by environmental policies so that their innovative capacity will not be impaired?

iv) How can governments develop anticipatory policies that address emerging environmental problems and -- at the same time -- encourage industrial innovation?

v) What techniques might be used by environmental authorities working in conjunction with other government authorities in non-environmental areas to integrate industrial innovation considerations into other domestic policies and regulations?

vi) How can environmental policy be co-ordinated among individual nations to encourage industrial innovation without affecting international competition?

These suggestions and questions are intended only as thought provokers for our discussion. I hope our discussion will lead to harmonious steps towards the universal goal of environmental improvement and greater industrial innovation throughout the world.

Working together -- as we are today -- with patience, understanding and co-operation, I believe we can make an important contribution. And the world will be the better off for it.

THE IMPACT OF ENVIRONMENTAL POLICIES ON INDUSTRIAL INNOVATION

1. INTRODUCTION

Innovation has always been recognised as a spur to growth and a critical characteristic of a dynamic economy (1). The postwar period of strong economic growth was accompanied by an unprecedented advance in technical innovation, supported by a sustained increase in research and development (R&D) activities. Since the mid-1960s, however, there has been a decline in the growth of labour productivity, making even more critical the issue of technical change.

The key role played by innovation has been re-emphasized recently by OECD Member countries. In a Declaration on Policies for Science and Technology, Ministers stressed the need to do everything possible to encourage innovation and, in particular, they mentioned the need to assign priority to R&D activities, to develop market conditions favourable to innovation, to encourage risk taking in the public and private sectors, to develop the innovative potential of small and medium-sized firms and to promote the diffusion of technical information (2).

1.1.   The Issues

In a market economy, innovation is inherent in entrepreneurship, stemming from a creative response to changes in the economic, social and political environment. The changes stimulating innovation may come from the market (e.g., new products and competitors, domestic and foreign) and from government laws, policies and regulations.

Although many factors influence a country's capacity to innovate (3), government intervention has attracted particular attention. The relationship between environmental policy and innovation has become particularly contentious, with strongly conflicting claims being made. On the one hand, environmental policy, especially in the form of regulation, is seen to stifle innovation by increasing production costs, decreasing profitability and reducing the propensity to innovate. On the other hand, environmental regulations are seen as a source of change that have had a positive effect on innovation, forcing the development and introduction of new technologies that are often not only more resource- and energy- efficient and hence generally more environmentally efficient, but also more economic.

In the light of these conflicting claims, it is clearly important to assess the relationships between environmental regulation and innovation. Looking to the future, while most Member countries will continue to address "first generation" issues where an emphasis on curative responses to existing problems is the order of the day, many will increasingly need to confront "second generation" issues for which policies of anticipation and prevention are the overriding concern. In this context, consideration should also be given to the criteria that should guide the development and application of regulations in the future.

The following questions emerge as basic issues:

-- What characteristics of environmental regulation can influence innovation?

-- What characteristics of an industry or firm enable it to respond innovatively to environmental regulation?

-- What criteria should guide the development and application of regulations in order to stimulate an innovative response by industry?

-- What should be done to overcome the dearth of theory, data and empirical research on the relationship between environmental policy generally, including regulation, and innovation?

2. BACKGROUND

In considering these questions, two broad types of innovations should be distinguished: those whose development and introduction are prompted by market or commercial forces, (i.e., business innovations), and those prompted by the need to comply with environmental regulations (compliance innovations). Regulations can give rise to several forms of compliance, but they fall essentially under three categories: "add-on" technologies which abate pollution at the end of a production process without changing the process (for example, an "end-of-pipe" treatment facility); "integrated" techniques involving the development of new less polluting production processes (e.g., recycling) and/or using different raw material inputs; and redesigning the product so as to use less polluting components. The first usually entails the use of conventional "best available" techniques, although some innovative and advanced "end-of-pipe" treatment technologies have been developed (4). The second may result from a reassessment of a production process or may involve the development of new "clean" or "low-waste" technologies. Usually, it stems from a deliberate attempt to find an innovative, efficient and low-cost response to compliance. The third and to some extent the second also are more typical of the type of response needed to deal with "second generation" problems, involving prevention rather than cure.

The impacts of a policy on compliance and business innovations are of course related. New technologies, processes and products prompted by environmental regulations may well reduce the costs of energy and raw materials and improve both labour and capital productivity. The relationship may also be negative. It is argued that the resources required to develop or apply innovations needed to comply with environmental regulations reduce the resources available to the firm to develop innovative products, processes and technologies for strictly commercial and profit-enhancing purposes. In short, the question is not whether the two are related but whether, on a net basis, the relationship is positive or negative.

There is little information available on the way in which firms in various sectors affected by environmental regulation decide on the allocation of their R&D budgets. Information is equally scarce on the process of innovation and empirical analyses are even scarcer. Moreover, the theory to guide such analyses is not well developed.

Recent OECD studies on the chemical industry considered mainly pharmaceuticals and pesticides (5,6), and they focussed in particular on regulations requiring the testing and assessment of a chemical or product before it is put on the market. Such regulations are typical of those designed to address "second generation" problems with policies of prevention. These studies could not identify any significant negative effects of regulations on business innovation. The lack of a body of theory and of analytical tools made the studies particularly complex. However, they established that while it is difficult to disentangle the relative roles of the various factors, it is probable that the regulations have had only a limited impact compared with other factors such as the size and maturity of the firms involved and the structure of the market.

Other OECD work documents a number of cases where environmental policies have stimulated the implementation of more effective pollution control techniques. In addition, they show that environmental policies have in certain cases prompted the development of more efficient cleaner technologies which have enabled the more effective attainment of desired environmental objectives.

The application of cleaner technologies by firms remains limited at present, however. Thus in the United States it would appear that, during the period 1973-1980, changes in production processes constituted on average only about 20 per cent of industry's air and water pollution control expenditures. This indicates a rather low level of penetration of clean technologies. The penetration rate is also low in France where in 1979 less than 7 per cent of industrial establishments had installed such technologies. Since 1979, however, this penetration has probably increased. In Denmark, over the period 1975-1980, 35 per cent of pollution control investments took the form of process changes.

This method of "measuring" technical change is not entirely satisfactory (cleaner technology is not a synonym for innovation) but it does underline the fact that there exists a significant potential for a greater diffusion of such cleaner technologies. Governments should consider how best to undertake further in-depth work in co-operation with those industries that have been most subject to regulation, with specific attention to the issue of how far clean technology is also cost-reducing for the firm.

3. INDUSTRIES' CAPACITY TO RESPOND INNOVATIVELY TO REGULATION

Experience shows that an industry's strategy and capacity to respond innovatively to environmental regulation is the result of many interacting factors. Some of these concern overall political and economic conditions and certain characteristics of the industry or firm. Others concern the nature of the regulations and the way in which they are applied.

Among the former, the most important are the firms' customary strategies of technical change and their openness and access to technical information. Additional significant factors appear to be the overall economic conditions, the financial position of the firm, the size of the firm and the burden of environmental costs. The possibility of the firm's marketing any new processes and products developed (for example, to patent and sell new pollution control technologies) can also be important. Among the latter, the prescription of the technology to be used, the targetting of the regulation, the time for compliance, the provision of technical information, and the support for R&D appear to be the most critical.

3.1. Customary Strategy of the Firm

The impact of environmental regulation on innovation by a firm can be influenced to a significant extent by the firm's customary strategy concerning technical change. It has been the more forward looking and technologically dynamic firms that have responded to environmental policies with efficient production and pollution control techniques. A sugar manufacturer in the Netherlands, for example, and an aluminium producer in Norway had customarily encouraged a high level of technical changes. During the 1970s, they adopted a positive attitude to environmental policies and incorporated pollution control considerations into their R&D programmes, which were expanding at that time. As a result, they implemented a series of financially beneficial changes in their production processes and developed more effective and efficient pollution control techniques. Likewise, many Canadian pulp and paper firms have strong R&D departments and responded dynamically to environmental regulation by continuously developing and/or applying changes in their production and pollution control techniques.

In contrast, those French pulp and paper firms that have traditionally followed a passive strategy towards technical change have shown little innovation in compliance. Similarly, the rigid reluctance of the Netherlands leather tanning firms to implement changes in their basic production process was a major reason for the limited adoption by this industry of recently developed processing technologies that are more efficient and less polluting (for example, chromium recycling).

In fact, industry should have an integrated approach to general business and compliance innovations so that pollution control considerations are treated as a normal part of product or process innovation, and not as a constraint to be added on at the end that thereby entails trade-offs between environmental and other types of innovation. Such an integrated approach has been successfully followed by the sugar industry in the Netherlands.

3.2. Economic Conditions

Economic conditions clearly play an important role in enabling an innovative response by industry to environmental regulation. Depressed economic conditions may give rise to a social and political climate marked by conflict and uncertainty, in which firms are inhibited from investing in innovation of any kind, let alone environmental innovation. They may also lead to a tight financial situation in which only short-term measures to survive find a place on the firm's agenda. The poor economic position of the leather tanning industry in the Netherlands has been a major obstacle to the introduction of improved pollution control measures; the same applies since 1980 to the metal-plating industry in the United Kingdom, which has generally retreated into the installation of conventional "end-of-line" technologies instead of applying more innovative changes in production processes.

On the other hand, a promising if not buoyant economic situation can alter the social and political climate for innovation. A rising demand for a firm's products can make it less reluctant to invest in R&D and experiment with new processes, equipment and products. Several examples can be cited. Sustained growth during the 1970s enabled the Japanese automobile industry to expand a strong R&D potential, and to respond innovatively and effectively to environmental requirements by developing new emission control techniques and also new, less polluting and at the same time more efficient engines.

Equally important, a healthy economy accelerates the retirement of older processes, plant and equipment and their replacement with newer and usually cleaner ones. Accelerated capital replacement may be further forced by competition from new products, domestic or imported, or from new firms whose entry is made easier by buoyant conditions. Capital replacement provides an unparalleled opportunity to innovate in the design of production processes and equipment that are less polluting, less consumptive of energy and resources per unit of output and more economic. Thus, the Norwegian aluminium industry incorporated environmental considerations in the plant modernisation and expansion programme that it undertook during the 1970s. This led to its developing and applying control techniques that achieved a greater reduction in air pollution at lower cost than the conventional techniques. It is essential to ensure that environmental considerations are incorporated at an early stage in firms' plans for the construction of new plant and for the alteration of their existing facilities.

3.3. The Financial Position of the Firm

The financial position of a firm is clearly an important determinant of its capacity to respond innovatively to environmental regulation. Firms in a weak financial position will be at least reluctant and, perhaps, unable to assign resources to finding new and better ways to reduce emissions or otherwise conform with environmental regulations. Where an industry is made up largely of financially weak firms, special measures may be necessary, at least on a temporary basis, including technical assistance, jointly financed R&D and perhaps some form of publicly supported provision of technical information to ensure that the industry is aware of the options available to bring their plants into conformity. An important issue is the availability of finance for innovation: banking institutions are often reluctant to lend money for research in technologies of uncertain profitability. Public authorities have an important role to play in making available such so-called "venture capital".

It is also possible that a tight economic position may oblige an industry to rationalise its production process in order to reduce costs; necessity is a law unto itself, and technical change becomes even more imperative in these circumstances. The government could, of course, promote this through a variety of financial, tax and other measures designed also to induce firms to integrate environmental considerations into their plans for plant modernisation. Rationalisation assistance programmes have been successfully employed in this way in a number of cases. One example is in the pulp and paper industry in Canada, where such a programme contributed to the design and operation of more efficient plants into which less polluting processes were built.

3.4. The Size of the Firm

Although small and medium-sized firms can have a significant capacity to innovate (7), big firms appear to constitute the major source of innovation related to environmental protection. The industry case studies show that, in the field of environmental technology, small firms have in most cases proved to be less open to change than larger ones. Indeed, the structure of the industry is of special importance in this regard. When the industry is highly fragmented, containing many smaller units, change penetrates only with great difficulty and at a slow rate. This has been the case for the leather industry in the Netherlands for example, and for the metal plating industry in the United Kingdom and in the Federal Republic of Germany. The small size of firms involved in these industries prevented any large-scale R&D, and the fragmented structure of these industries proved to be a special hindrance to the diffusion of technical information to each firm. The organisation of R&D and information channels on a collective basis therefore becomes necessary and can be successful, as the experience of the French metal plating industry points out.

When an industry comprises only a few large units, however, its potential for innovation is necessarily concentrated and can be easily rationalised. This point is illustrated by the Netherlands' sugar industry, which is made up of two well-structured and well-organised groups. Similarly, the large pulp and paper firms in Canada, Norway and Sweden were able to benefit from R&D activities performed by their central research laboratories and from the technical changes developed by their industry research institutes. In France, a more innovative and efficient technological response to the environmental regulations was made by those pulp and paper firms that were part of a larger industrial corporation.

3.5. The Burden of Environmental Costs

The macroeconomic cost of environmental protection ranges between one and two per cent of GDP, while investment by the private sector in pollution control has, on the average, stood around three to five per cent of total investment, except for a few years in Japan. These macro figures, however, tend to mask the impact of environmental regulation on certain industries. Firms making iron and steel, non-ferrous metals, pulp and paper and chemicals, and electric utilities have been major polluters, and they have borne a significant proportion of total pollution control investment in industry. In the United States, for example, pollution control investment in 1977 represented over 16 per cent of total plant and equipment investment in the iron and steel industry; 17 per cent in non-ferrous metals; and over 10 per cent for the electric utilities. Generally similar figures have been reported from other Member countries.

These costs are not negligible. The important question, however, is whether they have induced innovation or inhibited it.

A definitive answer does not appear possible. Representatives of some firms argue, however, that environmental regulations force a "diversion" of available resources from "productive" and, hence, potentially profitable investment to "non-productive" and essentially non-profitable investment. In the same vein, they argue that resources that would normally go into R&D for productive and profitable objectives are diverted to R&D for pollution control. While this position strikes a credible note, it presumes that a firm's budget is relatively fixed and rigidly allocated.

The burden of pollution control expenditures appears to vary over time. Initially when the environmental policies are implemented, some firms have to make a special effort in investing in pollution control equipment to meet the regulations. The level of these investments then later diminishes. A similar picture is apparent for the effect of pollution control expenditures on R&D. Some firms have allocated up to 20 to 45 per cent of their R&D budget to finding better control techniques, but this peak is sustained for only a short time and expenditures on pollution control R&D then decline. However, the evidence on this is scanty.

There is ample evidence, on the other hand, that in the case of the automobile, pulp and paper, food processing, chemicals and other industries, many firms have responded to environmental regulation with a broad range of innovations. These have not been restricted to new and improved forms of "end-of-pipe" treatment. They have involved new or modified forms of production equipment that reduce energy consumption, processes that recover raw materials for re-use, and products redesigned to employ materials that are both less expensive and easier to manage environmentally. Moreover, an analysis of German environmental policy indicates that the industries most affected by environmental regulation, defined as those for which regulation imposed a net cost burden, enjoyed a labour productivity increase 1.6 per cent higher than other industries. While this productivity improvement cannot be attributed directly to regulation, it does suggest that the impact of regulation has not been negative.

In the case of the automobile industry, of course, the impact of environmental regulations on innovation between 1970 and 1972 was reinforced by the oil shocks of 1974 and 1979. In the chemicals industry, as in the automobile and other industries, certain firms have taken the lead, such as a major American company which, under its "Pollution Prevention Pays" programme, has been registering savings in energy and raw materials valued at $195 million since 1975.

Certain companies that were able to or chose to respond innovatively to environmental regulation have benefitted in terms of plant that is more resource efficient, more energy efficient and often more economic and competitive. A survey of 200 clean technologies in France showed that almost half have favourable effects in terms of energy saving (51 per cent of cases), raw material saving (47 per cent of cases) and improved working conditions

(40 per cent of cases). In Denmark, the implementation of cleaner production processes yielded a financial benefit in 44 per cent of the cases. Many companies have also found new opportunities for investment, sales and exports. It has been estimated, for example, that, by 1978, world trade in environmental technology had grown to the order of $11 billion per year. At present, exports of pollution control equipment and expertise from Denmark alone are running at one billion Danish crowns per year. The German pollution control industry exported 25 per cent of its production in 1980.

4. DESIGNING ENVIRONMENTAL POLICIES TO STIMULATE INNOVATION

The experience of the past decade demonstrates that in many industries innovation and technical change have been an essential part of complying with environmental regulation in an efficient and cost-effective manner. For the shift from first to second generation problems, innovation and technical change will be even more critical. Environmental policies will need increasingly to consider how they may influence the introduction of technologies, processes and even products that are energy- and resource-efficient and therefore more "environmentally efficient" and, at the same time, more economic and cost-effective.

Among the characteristics to be considered in improving the relationship between environmental policies and innovation, the following stand out: prescription of technology to be used; targetting of regulation; time for compliance; provision of technical information; and support for environmental R&D.

4.1. Prescribing the Means

In addition to establishing performance standards (ambient or emission standards), environmental regulations in many cases prescribe the existing processes and technologies that are to be employed to achieve the standards. Often, they prescribe the "best available" technology. This approach may have merit in dealing with "first generation" problems. In other cases, however, this approach has no doubt served to inhibit innovation. Without wishing to be paradoxical, it may be said that the less regulations impose techniques, the more they encourage innovation. In other words, there is no surer way to inhibit innovation than to impose ready-made solutions on industry.

What might be termed "technological flexibility" should be a fundamental rule of environmental policy. In the majority of cases, innovation springs from a combination of necessity (for example, a requirement to reduce emissions) and of freedom of action in selecting the means. Regulations may and, in respect of certain industries, increasingly should stipulate performance standards without mandating the process or technology to be employed. Even where the performance standard reflects existing technology, not mandating it can spur industry to innovate and employ the most cost-effective method of achieving it.

Performance standards, however, may also anticipate development of the means to achieve them and, where they do, they are clearly intended to force

116

innovation. Such standards can constitute a challenge to industry. Examples abound, but the innovative response of the Japanese automobile industry to the performance standards for nitrogen oxide emissions mandated in the early 1970s is perhaps the best known.

Performance standards may also be supplemented by economic instruments of various kinds, such as marketable pollution rights (e.g., the US "Emission Trading Programme") and emission charges. These instruments leave industry complete freedom of choice with regard to compliance techniques. In principle, a system of emission charges provides a stronger incentive to innovate, since the more effective the compliance measures adopted by the firm, the more savings are realised in the emission charges paid. In fact, of course, short of a provision for the automatic indexing of the charges, it is difficult to maintain the incentive in the face of inflation.

4.2. Targetting Regulations

During the past decade, regulations have often been "targetted" on the end of an industrial process. In a number of cases, for example, regulations to reduce sulphur emissions from power plants have focussed on releases after the fuel has been burned rather than on the quality of the fuel used or on points upstream in the process at which the quality of the fuel might be upgraded. Again, this end-of-process targetting is no longer sufficient as the focus of policy shifts increasingly to "second generation" issues and the overriding concern becomes prevention rather than cure.

Prevention policies aim at reducing or eliminating the sources of a pollution problem rather than spending money and resources to clean it up afterwards. They consider the complete cycle of a product, be it wheat, energy or automobiles, from raw materials used and their sources, through design, development, marketing, use and disposal. They address the proposition that it is more effective environmentally, technologically and economically to eliminate the sources of pollution than to clean up the consequences afterwards.

The reshaping of environmental policies for the second generation of pollution problems raises questions that go beyond regulation and innovation. However, ensuring that regulations -- and other measures -- support rather than inhibit innovation and change is a crucial component of this reshaping. Without affecting the necessary freedom of choice of industry, environmental regulations should be designed in order to cope most efficiently with these second generation issues, without inducing industry, directly or indirectly, to rely upon "first generation" types of solutions. It would appear that regulations designed to address "second generation" problems and facilitate prevention should meet at least three criteria: they should enable a search for the most effective points in the total cycle of a product at which to address the pollutant in question; they should provide performance standards at the earliest possible point in the product cycle, including its design; and they should induce and support the innovation of better methods to cope with it.

Conventional regulations fail to meet these criteria to the extent that they assume that the most effective point is at the "end of a pipe" and, usually, at the end of a product cycle, and where they prescribe existing, and normally, the "best available" technology.

"Second generation" environment problems become apparent much earlier in the development cycle concerned (whether it is primary production, manufacturing, energy or housing) than those of the "first generation". In the case of pollution, they tend to focus on products and their components.

If the user is another producer or manufacturer, he may try to deal with the pollutant at the end of his product cycle. However, that may not be the most effective point at which to deal with it. In the case of sulphur oxide emissions, for example, it is often more economically efficient and cost-effective to reduce emissions through choice of fuel, or through fuel treatment in the case of coal, than through emission control technologies. In the case of industrial processes, it has often been found more effective environmentally and economically to reduce emissions through substitution and recycling than through treatment.

If the user lacks the means to deal with the problem, it must either be passed back to the manufacturer or passed on to the public authorities. In many cases, firms have completely redesigned products to eliminate an environmentally unacceptable component rather than face the task of developing a safer means of handling and disposal. Detergents are a notable example, as are automobiles. Many more, including fertilizers and pesticides, remain to be addressed satisfactorily.

4.3. Time for Compliance

Performance standards, targetted at the most appropriate points of the product cycle, are necessary but not sufficient conditions for an innovative response to be encouraged. In addition, it is important that the industry or firm concerned be given a reasonable time in which to comply.

Establishing reasonable deadlines and a firm timetable for compliance could involve consultations with the firm and with experts knowledgeable about conditions in the industry. It will depend on many things, including the age of the plant and the economics of the firm. It will also depend on whether a new technology has to be invented, as in the case of controls on automobile emissions in the early 1970s, on whether a new substitute needs to be found and tested, as in the case of bio-degradable detergents, or whether it is a question of redesigning processes or products, or some combination of all of these.

However difficult, establishing a definite deadline and timetable for compliance is clearly essential; without it, indeterminate time limits or the prospect of influencing their continual change and postponement would simply foster inaction and uncertainty.

4.4. A Strengthened R&D Capacity

Many firms lack a strong R&D capacity. Indeed, many lack simple awareness about and access to information on environmentally effective processes, technologies and products, even within their own industries.

R&D promotion can be, and has been, approached in various ways by the private and public sectors working separately and together. Strong firms, for example, may be encouraged to organise and support an industry-wide R&D capacity. The US electrical power industry has done this through a common research institute. Trade organisations may also perform this function and many do; for example the Pulp and Paper Associations in Canada, Scandinavia and France.

Industries marked by weaker, small and medium-sized firms might find it more effective to establish a liaison with an existing R&D institution, private, public or university-based. As a matter of policy, governments might wish to encourage joint R&D among companies. Indeed, government support is an important means of promoting R&D in the private sectors and of directing it to work on clean and low-waste processes and technologies. Such measures have been successfully adopted in a number of cases, notably in the Netherlands.

In general, however, government support for R&D has fallen off since the mid-1960s. Public R&D in the environmental field is at a very low level in most countries, ranging from one to three per cent of total public R&D expenditures.

In addition to supporting R&D by the private sector, government can develop strong publicly owned and operated research institutions and most OECD Member countries currently do this.

4.5. Provision of Technical Information

In this regard, relevant institutes might also be encouraged to provide specific firms and industries with information on recent developments in clean production processes and technologies and in pollution control techniques. This is particularly valuable for small or medium-sized firms.

Environmental agencies might also establish their own, more general, technical information services. In France, a special department of the Ministry for the Quality of Life ("Mission des Technologies Propres") collects and disseminates information on clean processes and technologies in a variety of industrial sectors. In the Netherlands, the "Environmental Production Plan" involves, among other things, a strong technical information network. International efforts to promote awareness in industry of new clean and low-waste technologies have included the compilation of a compendium on these technologies by the UN Economic Commission for Europe in Geneva, Switzerland.

4.6. Coherent and Streamlined Regulations

Environmental regulations can be more effective if they are coherent and not contradicted by other requirements. The automobile industry, for example, has been faced with contradictory requirements to reduce the energy consumption of vehicles through adoption of diesel engines, while at the same time reducing noise emissions (the diesel engine and in particular the direct injection diesel being intrinsically noisier than the petrol engine), and improving the structural safety of cars (which means increased weight and energy consumption).

The situation is made more complex when regulations go beyond stipulating performance standards and set out the means of compliance.

119

Indeed, in those cases where it can be done, removing references to the means of compliance can be the most direct way of reducing the level of incoherence and contradiction in regulations.

Beyond that, it would appear useful and increasingly necessary to set up mechanisms for regulatory review within and between agencies of government, punctuated perhaps with periodic overall reviews by a special body or commission. The problem may take on new dimensions as second generation problems become more dominant. A notable case is that of inter-media transfers of pollution, where an innovative response to air emission standards, for example, could give rise to violations of standards for water discharges and solid wastes. The lack of coordination between regulations on water and solid waste has in fact been a considerable problem for the Dutch leather tanning industry. The Netherlands authorities are taking steps to "streamline" environmental regulations by implementing an integrated licensing procedure, under which a firm would be subject to a single permit covering all pollutants emitted into the various environmental media. Several other examples could be drawn from the interrelated areas of health, safety and the environment. In areas like toxic substances and hazardous wastes, for example, it will be increasingly important for the one hand of government to know what the other intends to do, and why.

4.7. Government-Industry Co-operation

It is evident from the above that environmental regulations, both in their design and in their delivery, require consultation with the industry concerned, and will probably become even more vital as second generation problems come to the fore.

Such consultations can help to ensure that regulations and performance standards are reasonable and well targetted and that the time frames for compliance are within the reach of the R&D capacity of the industry, and are short enough to induce action but not so long as to induce lethargy. Consultations can also serve to inform industry of the rationale for the intended regulations, their scope and the means available for compliance. In addition, these consultations should result in a reasonable predictability of standards and regulations which could help to generate the confidence required for making long term R&D investments.

Consultation can also reduce the adversary character of regulation design and enforcement. In Sweden, a hundred-year-old tradition of co-operation has made a considerable contribution to the cost-effective solution of environmental problems. In the United States, where government-industry relations often tend to be adversarial, the Environmental Protection Agency is endeavouring to increase co-operation and consultation with industry.

5. CONCLUSIONS

Innovation has played a key role in the dynamic growth of the world's economies, and OECD Member governments are again stressing measures to encourage it.

Innovation has also been an important feature of successful responses to environmental problems, involving changes in products, processes and control technologies that are not only more resource- and energy-efficient but also more environmentally efficient and, hence, often more economic. Looking to the future and, in particular, the shift from first to second generation problems for which anticipation and prevention are the overriding concern, innovation and technical change will be even more critical.

The relationship between environmental regulation and innovation can be positive or negative. Experience shows, however, that the capacity of an industry or firm to respond innovatively to environmental regulation depends upon two broad categories of interrelated factors.

The first concerns economic conditions and certain characteristics of the firm such as its size, the age and structure of its equipment, its financial situation and its customary strategy towards technical change.

The second is the appropriate design and application of regulations. In particular:

-- Regulations should as far as possible stipulate performance standards without mandating the process or technology to be used, as is often the case today;

-- Establishing reasonable deadlines and a timetable for compliance with performance standards is essential;

-- Economic instruments of various kinds, including marketable pollution rights and emission charges, can be used effectively to supplement performance standards since they leave industry with complete freedom of choice of compliance techniques and build into the market an incentive to innovate;

-- Regulations designed to address "second generation" problems and to facilitate prevention should enable a search, in consultation with industry, of the most effective points in the cycle of a product (which may not be the end of this cycle) at which to tackle the problem in question;

-- Environmental regulations will have a more positive impact on innovation if they are coherent and not contradicted by other requirements. It would appear useful to set up mechanisms or provisions for regulatory review within and between agencies of government, punctuated with overall reviews by a special body or commission.

NOTES AND REFERENCES

1. Innovation can be defined as the development, application and introduction on the market of a new product or process. Innovation may have its origin inside or outside the firm (i.e., the firm may develop the innovation itself or may adopt and apply a technique developed by others).

2. OECD, "Ministerial Declaration on Policies for Science and Technology", Science and Technology Policy for the 1980s, Paris, 1981.

3. For example, the level of R&D activity and the existence of suitable sources of finance for this, the quality and intensity of individual technical training, and the efficient functioning of mechanisms for disseminating innovation through the economy (see the background report Environmental Policy and Technical Change).

4. It must be noted too that, in some instances, an "end-of-pipe" technique may be the only feasible solution.

5. OECD, Regulation and Innovation in the Chemical Industry, Paris, 1982.

6. OECD, The Impact of Chemicals Control upon Trade, Innovation and the Small Firm, Paris, 1982.

7. OECD, Innovation in Small and Medium Firms, Paris, 1982.

122

SUMMARY OF THE DISCUSSION OF SESSION FOUR

Dr. Roy Rothwell

Senior Fellow, Science Policy Research Unit

Evidence has been cited to demonstrate that environmental controls can effect both the rate and the direction of "business" technological innovation at the level of the firm. Their influence can be either positive or negative. The magnitude of the influence vary with such factors as the industry sector, the size of the firm, the response of the firm to regulations and, of course, the nature of the regulations themselves, as well as the relationship between them. There are also significant differences between countries.

Main Issues Raised during the Debate

i) The main issue here seems to be the apparent conflict between the need to protect the environment through regulations while at the same time maintaining a climate for industry that is conducive to the development and diffusion of business innovations. The essential task for governments is to minimise this tension and also, of course, to promote advanced technology and the development of new and more efficient and effective pollution control technologies.

ii) Evidence has been presented to show that governments can, given the appropriate response from industry, stimulate the adoption of clean technologies that protect the environment while at the same time offering industry certain benefits in, for example, energy saving and productivity increases. It remains true, however, that in most countries the level of diffusion of clean technologies is relatively low. What could be done to promote a greater diffusion of these technologies?

iii) The process of technological innovation is highly complex. The complexity of the interactions between innovation and environmental regulations is probably even greater. How can this complex web of interactions be disentangled? Indeed, many of the most important influences of regulations on innovation are indirect rather than direct. How can regulations be formulated and implemented in order to reduce potential negative (innovation inhibiting) and to induce positive (innovation permitting or stimulating) influences? There are a number of useful pointers that can be grouped under four general headings:

123

-- The nature of the regulations;

-- The nature of the regulatory system;

-- The characteristics of the firm or industry;

-- Governmental support measures.

Responses

Turning to the nature of the regulations themselves, there are a number of points here:

i) There is a need to shift, where possible, from "first generation" measures to "second or third generation" measures: in other words, to place the emphasis more on prevention rather than cure -- to move from a "responsive" to an "anticipative" or "proactive" approach.

ii) It is desirable to adopt performance standards rather than specification standards, where possible, since the former are generally more flexible and conducive to technological innovation.

iii) On balance, pollution charges would appear to offer greater incentives than emission standards for compliance innovation.

iv) Regulations should be clear, consistent and unambiguous in order to minimise uncertainty for the regulated firm.

v) Forward-looking regulations that anticipate technological developments might be employed in some cases to stimulate compliance innovation.

vi) Regulations should, where practicable, be aimed at those points in the production cycle that offer maximum leverage in reducing pollution at the minimum cost, rather than concentrating solely on the output stage of the cycle. This means that we should be concerned with stimulating innovations right through the production cycle -- or even the complete business system.

Turning now to the nature of the regulatory system, a number of significant points have emerged:

i) Perhaps the most important is the degree and nature of the interaction between industry and the regulatory authorities. An adverserial approach generally elicits a hostile and uncooperative response. Establishing a system of effective consultation and cooperation, on the other hand, can be beneficial to both parties. For maximum effectiveness it seems that consultation on new regulations should begin at as early a stage as possible.

ii) Time-to-compliance can be an important factor influencing the nature of the compliance technology: if the time is too short, non-optimal stop-gap solutions might be implemented. On the other hand, in certain cases, if the time is too long the regulations might lag behind the state of the art in compliance technology, thus retarding technological change.

iii) Uncertainties induced by regulations and having an adverse effect on innovation have often arisen because of a lack of coordination between different regulatory bodies. Clearly greater inter-agency coordination is desirable.

iv) Where regulatory initiatives are linked to other public sector initiatives, most notably investment or modernisation schemes, they can be especially effective. Thus, coordination between regulatory agencies and other public sector bodies is to be actively encouraged. Certainly, there should be a greater degree of integration between economic policy, technology policy and policies for environmental protection.

As we might expect, the characteristics of firms and industries can significantly influence their innovatory (or non-innovatory) response to regulations:

i) Not suprisingly, firms that are technically progressive in the business sense also generally respond innovatively to regulations. They achieve this best when environmental control considerations are an integrated part of product or process development. A proactive approach by firms is by far the most effective and yields the greatest benefit. Similarly, it is preferable that environmental considerations are integrated as part of a firm's investment programme for the construction of new plant and equipment and the modernisation of existing facilities. Also, it often turns out that technically advanced industries are cleaner and thus more responsive to environmental protection needs.

ii) Again, not surprisingly, firms that operate in a poor economic environment, those operating at low profitability and those that lack technical capacity tend to adopt a non-innovative approach to compliance. With such firms, even relatively small negative regulatory impacts can be significant.

iii) The structure of an industry appears to have a special influence on its propensity to develop and adopt compliance innovations. In highly fragmented sectors with many small firms, compliance technological change penetrates only slowly and with difficulty. The reverse is true in the case of industries consisting of only a few large units.

iv) In fragmented industries information flow is a major problem, and industrial associations and chamber of commerce can help greatly in this respect. Many small firms appear simply to be unaware of the range of new and improved clean technologies available to them.

Turning finally to government support measures, the following instruments are used with some success in various countries.

i) Information services;

ii) Subsidies for expenditure on compliance-related R&D or equipment. Where capital grants are available, they may be used, where possible, to promote the purchase of clean technologies rather than end-of-pipe treatment systems. Special provision might also be made for small firms.

iii) Government support of expenditure related to environmental control by collective industrial research institutes. This is especially important in the case of fragmented industries. Such organisations can play a particularly important role when they adopt a proactive approach to R&D and information dissemination.

iv) While government R&D expenditure on environmental issues has in general been relatively small, it does appear to have had an important "locomotive" effect in complementing and stimulating private sector R&D. Calls for increased expenditure, of course, are unlikely to sit well with governments that are currently involved in cutting public sector expenditure. It is also worth recognising that environmental control decisions, like those pertaining to other aspects of national life, are often political as well as being economic and technological. Finally, as for industrial firms, governments should adopt a proactive -- and not a crisis response -- approach to environmental issues.

OECD Responsibilities

In present economic circumstances it is more than ever necessary to promote greater efficiency in environmental control technologies. The OECD should investigate the ways and means of ensuring a greater promotion and diffusion of cleaner technologies in industry; that is, the factors influencing the adoption of clean technologies by industry and the policy options that public authorities can deploy to promote a wider diffusion of these technologies. The OECD should also act as a forum for policy analysis and the exchange of information.

SESSION FIVE

THE BENEFITS OF ENVIRONMENTAL POLICIES

CHAIRMAN'S OPENING SPEECH

Mrs. Huguette BOUCHARDEAU

Secretary of State for the Environment and the Quality of Life, France

Mr. Chairman, ladies and gentlemen, I should like first of all to take my turn in congratulating the OECD on its initiative in organising this Conference on Environment and Economics, which comes at a time of profound change that is of decisive importance for the future of environmental policies.

I also want to thank the Organisation for giving me the chance to discuss with you the essential question of the benefits of environmental policies, even though that question is really rather a strange one. We are going to ask ourselves "What is the purpose of environmental policies?" Few policies for the community are questioned in such a radical manner: in our countries we often wonder, for example, about the kind of health policies we should have, seldom about whether we need health policies.

Basically, though, I feel it is a very good thing for this question to be asked, both because we are responsible for managing limited resources and must be able at all times to make sure that we are using them judiciously, and because we must fight against the tendency to maintain or increase the number of regulations and public offices without always knowing whether we are really meeting the needs of our countries.

The Economic Burden of Damage: Damage is Costlier than Pollution Prevention

Protecting the environment costs money. In France more than FF 50 billion in all is spent each year on environmental protection. That is a lot of money, even if it represents less than 4 per cent of expenditure on welfare, education, culture and defence.

However, this amount must be set against the cost of pollution damage. That cost is very real: human beings have to suffer the ill effects on their health and welfare; the natural environment likewise suffers, because the ability of flora and fauna to reproduce and maintain their diversity is impaired; economic activity is also a victim, with production losses and extra costs.

It has been calculated in France that the cost to the community of chronic pollution damage is equivalent to between 3 and 4 per cent of GDP, which is twice what we spend on anti-pollution measures. This in itself is a good reason for having an environmental policy, but there are others.

A Broader Conception of Environmental Policy Benefits

Because studies to date have favoured an approach in terms of preferences, evaluating gains and losses in consumption, they seem to me to underestimate greatly the benefits that safeguarding the environment brings.

Much of the reasoning is concerned with social demand for environmental protection leading to public expenditure and legislative action. But this social demand also has supply-side effects in that, for example, it "pushes up" the quality of products and contributes to technological progress. Also, concern for the environment is at one with the need to conserve energy, raw materials and even renewable resources.

There is also the role played by the environment:

-- As a factor of production: the environment supports forestry, fishing and tourism among other activities;

-- As a factor in maintaining human "labour power", to use an expression I do not care for much (lower absenteeism, higher productivity and so on);

-- Lastly, as one of the main determinants of the public's perception of industry and technological progress.

I should like to stress the importance of this last aspect, more often than not overlooked, in the light of what we know in France. As a result of the French people's concern about the environment, which continues to grow in spite of the crisis, industry has very clearly been put on trial: fears of pollution very often lead to the rejection of proposals for certain new industrial sites. For a business enterprise, being on good terms with the environment is, like good industrial relations, often essential to an effective industrial strategy. There are some other benefits arising from an environmental policy that should, I think, be mentioned.

By reducing uncertainty, forestalling the irreversible and preventing the worst (ecological disasters, major accidents), environmental policies help to leave us free to choose as we think right now and in the future and to keep our strategy options intact.

I would also venture to add that, on an international level this time, environmental policies help to reduce tension between states (acid rain, pollution of the River Rhine and so on) and are one of the best means of expressing our solidarity with the countries that are poorest and most environmentally at risk.

Some Methods of Assessing Damage are Open to Criticism

While it would be wrong to underestimate some of the benefits of environmental policies, the decision-making aid provided by an assessment of damage in money terms must not be overestimated either. Of course, for a politician or a businessman there can be no "right decision" without allowance for the economic parameters. But by the same token, whenever the general interest is concerned, there can be no "right decision" that results simply from a reckoning of financial costs and benefits. In all Member countries, the tools of economic science have become extraordinarily sophisticated over the past 20 years; yet at the same time we have discovered that we can no longer dream of a world in which all decisions can be taken by a computer and some economists. Dream or nightmare? It matters little: everyone acknowledges today that the basic responsibility of ministers, businessmen and trade unionists is to reconcile multiple needs, propose strategies and generate discussion.

This does not mean that we should cast out economics when dealing with environmental problems and return to a purely moralistic approach -- quite the contrary. The same applies here as in relations between a firm's management and the workers. There can be no question of ignoring economics: in fact both sides must take economics into account if they are to work out realistic solutions.

That is why it seems to me essential to make a considerable effort, particularly at international level, to improve our approach to environmental economics. Such an effort is all the more necessary, I feel, in that the validity of many financial evaluations is debatable. Direct evaluation methods, based on what is termed people's "willingness to pay", are often simply a reflection of income inequalities, social and cultural differences and so on. What is one to make of the current kind of reasoning that runs as follows: "Since they are less willing to pay, the poor presumably do not attach the same value to improving the environment as do the rich"?

As for indirect methods (putting a money value on damage assessed in physical terms), they are based on an intrinsically debatable decision about what can and what cannot be regarded as damage. It is essentially these differences of definition that explain why the figure put on damage can be anywhere on a scale from one to ten.

I hope we shall be able here to discuss fully the different technical, economic, social and political aspects of these questions.

Conclusion: New Ideas for Consideration

Before finally giving the floor to Mr. Kampmann, our Keynote Speaker, allow me to say that despite all the importance that some people, and I myself am one of them, attach to assessments of damages and benefits for a country as a whole, these are not enough.

Two questions seem to me fundamental today, and I hope we can discuss them also:

-- How is damage distributed? Over social groups, regions?

-- Who benefits from environmental policies and who bears their cost?

In other words, we must consider "ecological inequality" and the implicit redistributive effects of environmental policies.

INTRODUCTION BY

Mr. Jens KAMPMANN

Director General, Environment Agency of Denmark

In my speech I want to discuss the economic valuation of benefits, and how valuations are used in the decision-making process.

Environmental policy, like other policy areas, must be seen in a social perspective. This means that there is a great need to set the order of priority of the environment and other sectors. In this process the valuation of benefits from environmental measures in comparison with the benefits gained in connection with efforts in other areas will play a dominant role. A big problem in this regard is the order of priority of the various environmental areas where benefits are particularly great.

Therefore it is only natural that the debate on the assessment and economic evaluation of benefits has presented itself so vigorously, and that, especially in a soft area like environmental policy, it is considered to be so important. This again has resulted in a wish to be able to weigh both costs and benefits together by a simple method, and the natural idea has been to try to find a monetary measurement unit.

It is no wonder that the valuation of benefits has become so crucial to the decision makers and politicians in the broad sense of the word. If benefits could be measured in a simple way, in terms of money, the political decisions would be quite simple.

The main point in the Issue Paper is that cost-benefit analyses have not been used as much as they ought to have been. For instance, the paper argues that it must be admitted that cost-benefit analysis is not used in the decision-making process as much as desirable.

As a matter of fact, however, the valuation of costs and benefits constitutes only part of the basis for decisions. In the final part of my speech I want to comment on some more dynamic aspects which are not integrated in the cost-benefit analysis, but which are necessary in order to make what we understand as a social evaluation of the measures taken.

There are a large number of theoretical and practical problems in connection with the economic valuation of benefits, as you all know. But the question is: Are the problems of such a nature that they constitute a real threat to the use of cost-benefit analysis, or are we only talking about minor problems which in the political decision-making process have no decisive effect on the final results? In other words, do the theoretical/practical problems of evaluating benefits have the effect that the result depends more on the person making the analyses/valuation than on the actual situation? This is a problem which we ought to discuss in this forum.

But let us have a look at some of the problems in connection with evaluation:

First the relation between a given pollution and its effects. One of the major problems within the area of environment is that in practice the relation between pollution and its impact on man and on flora, fauna and materials is very often either very uncertain or in fact unknown. A few examples:

-- The use of fertilizers, the resulting nitrate in groundwater and the consequences for the health of man;

-- CO pollution and its consequences for the climate.

However, we not only have to know how many people are affected by a given case of pollution. To make an evaluation of benefits, we also have to consider who is affected: I will come back to this point later.

The economic analyses is tied up with for instance the distribution of income at the moment in question, with the level of knowledge of the population at the moment in question, with the level of education of the population and with the technological possibilities of reducing the pollution.

These points may seem trivial, but in fact they very much reduce the utility of evaluating benefits. If, for instance, the debate on measures in a given area increases the information level, the results obtained from the benefit evaluation before the decision-making process started will not actually reflect the attitudes of the population at the moment the decision is to be taken. An example -- witnessed in many countries in recent years-- is the consequences of sulphur oxides pollution from the energy system. Other areas may be the attitude towards chemical substances and their long-term effects.

Another point where we meet great problems is the measuring of the economic value of benefits. First, who is going to make this measurement? Is it the politician? Is it the government officials? Is it the researchers? Or is it the individual consumer who may be exposed to pollution? In accordance with welfare economics it is the individual person who must measure the benefit value to him and thus decide how much he is willing to pay in order to avoid the pollution in question. This theory lies behind many of the analyses of this type made, for instance, in the USA today.

But at the same time, this attitude -- that it is the individual consumer's measurement of benefits that should be used -- implies some results which from a political point of view are hardly valid.

It is generally recognised that the price consumers are willing to pay to protect themselves against pollution rises significantly with rising income: not always because of a different evaluation of the pollution, but rather because of different abilities to pay. Therefore, in government-made analyses, should pollution affecting high-income groups be given a higher economic value than pollution affecting consumers with lower incomes?

These aspects are reflected in the population's choice of living space. In most towns we have areas inhabited by senior officials and independent businessmen where pollution is less serious and the recreational values higher than they are in other areas of the town. Furthermore, the prices of real property are higher, as an expression of these groups' economic valuation of the environment. If the public authorities follow the results of the "willingness-to-pay" analyses, the result would very often be that pollution has not to be reduced but to be moved elsewhere to affect consumers not willing to pay so much to avoid it; that is, the lower income groups.

A special problem is the types of pollution that have long-term effects. Should the preferences of the present population be used as a basis for cost-benefit analyses? It is very difficult for the individual to estimate the value of reducing some future pollution damages which are going to affect future generations.

-- How much will you pay to avoid the ozone layer being halved in 70 years; or

-- How much will you pay to ensure that the genetic resources of the rain forests exist in 90 years' time?

A question of particular interest in this forum is of course the question of transfrontier pollution. In connection with national analyses of benefits, there are no economic arguments in favour of evaluation of the effects the pollution damages have in other countries. As an example, I can tell you that in Denmark, in connection with the evaluation of the consequences of SO_2 pollution, some economists were of the opinion that only the damage effects in Denmark were to be measured, and that the measurement of the damage effects in, for instance, the other Nordic countries was only relevant in so far as it could form the basis for negotiations with these countries about, for instance, the supply of power to Denmark.

The question still remains to be answered: how do we actually include the damaging effects in other countries in our own economic evaluations?

In view of the remarks I have made above, my conclusion is that great care and discretion is needed when using the economic evaluation of benefits in a political decision-making process. As I have pointed out, the results may lead both to absurdities and also to results which from a political point of view cannot be accepted.

Let me give you an idea of the problems of particular importance:

-- The measurement of the economic value of human life and diseases;

-- The economic valuation of long-term effects;

-- The economic valuation of benefits which cannot be measured in terms of market prices but which are considered merely from the point of view of attitudes;

-- Valuation of benefits where the dose-response relationship is not sufficiently clear.

In practice, cost-benefit analysis will therefore often result in more or less accidental evaluations of the economic value of benefits. Analyses can be used to point out the importance of the benefit side of the matter, but they can never be used as a scientific "proof" that no measures should be taken against pollution.

Dynamic Aspects

As I mentioned in my introduction, there are also a number of dynamic aspects which, by tradition, are not included in cost-benefit analysis. They are very important to consider, however, because they form part of the definition of the future basis for production, and thus for the welfare of the population.

The aspects I have in my mind are:

i) Evaluation of the flow of materials. The analyses of the flow of materials, together with the economic analysis, will illustrate both the consumption and the waste of physical materials and substances in the process. This analyses is of particular importance in connection with non-renewable resources, dangerous substances and imports from the developing countries of renewable resources manufactured by processes that are harmful to nature.

ii) Technology assessment. Assessment of technological changes in production processes and in products.

iii) Evaluation of the traditional macro-economic consequences. A description of the consequences to the balance of payments, the rate of employment and the income distribution policy in the country.

Final Remarks

It may be difficult to recognise that it is often impossible to describe the consequences of pollution so simply that the results can be given in figures. On the other side it is very important to present the economic and physical element included in an analysis in a clear and well-arranged way. In this case it will be possible for the people to discuss the problems. We will also have a clear basis for the decisions we have to make.

But the idea is not to enable governments -- under the cover of cost-benefit analyses for instance -- to hide some political aspects of a given measure.

ISSUE PAPER: SESSION 5

BENEFITS OF ENVIRONMENTAL POLICIES

1. DEFINING BENEFITS

Over the last decade, environmental policies followed in OECD countries have yielded significant improvements in environmental quality. Emissions of SO_x have decreased or stabilized in most countries since the mid-1970s despite increased economic activity and increased energy use. Large cities have witnessed significant improvements in air quality: for instance, over the period 1970-1980, concentration of sulphur oxides decreased by 55 per cent in Tokyo and London, by 27 per cent in Paris and by 70 per cent in Montreal. Emissions of carbon monoxide have also decreased or stabilized, especially since 1979. Emissions of nitrogen oxides have stabilized and even decreased in Japan during recent years. Water pollution by organic matter has also decreased in a number of rivers and lakes.

These improvements have yielded significant benefits to society. Better air quality has brought about lower mortality and morbidity rates, reduced material and building corrosion, increased crops yield, less damage to ecosystems and better visibility. Increasing the quality of waters has provided improved recreational amenities, improved fisheries, better water for municipalities and industry. Generally speaking, pollution abatement provides a great number of benefits which can be defined as the damage avoided as a result of the prevention and control measures; Table 1 gives an overview of the main categories of damages avoided.

While the concept of benefit as damage avoided is the primary concept in evaluating the benefits of environmental policies, it does not encompass the full set of advantages provided by environmental policies.

For instance, environmental policies not only reduce pollution but also provide amenities accruing from, for example, nature protection or the improvement of urban parks.

Also, other categories of benefits, wider in scope than those which accrue directly to users, have been identified. They include both present and future impacts. These benefit concepts include option value -- the willingness to pay for the preservation of a facility or the existence of an amenity; and bequest value -- the willingness to pay for the preservation of a facility for future generations. For instance, Greenley (1) and Strand (2) suggest that such benefits may equal or exceed the direct value of a recreational benefit.

Table 1

TYPOLOGY OF ENVIRONMENTAL DAMAGE (a)

Medium of Pollution	Type of Pollutant	Human Health	Built Environment and Non-Food Real Costs	Natural and Food Environment	Aesthetic Environment
AIR	SO_x	+ (1)	Corrosion	Acid rain	-
	TSP	+ (2)	Soiling/cleaning	-	-
	NO_x	- (3)	-	-	Visibility
	HC+Ph. Oxidants (4)	-	-	Crop damage	Visibility
	Toxics: Lead	+	-	Soil contamination	-
	Cadmium	+	-	Soil contamination	-
	Benzene	+	-	Concentrations in fish and plants	-
	Asbestos	+	-	-	-
	PAH	+	-	-	-
	CFC	+	-	Climatic change	-
	CO_2	-	-	Climatic change	-
FRESH WATER	Acidification	+ (6)	+	Forests and fish	+ Recreational
	BOD/COD (5)	-	-	Fish loss / Wildlife loss / Ecosystem damage / Crop losses	Fish loss / Boating / Swimming / Wildlife loss / (Option value) (7)
	TRM (8)	+	Treatment costs	Agriculture	-
	Salt	-	Household and industry	-	-
OCEANS	Oil	-	Clean-up costs / Tourism losses (9)	Fish loss / Wildlife loss / Ecosystem Damage	Fish loss / Amenity loss / Wildlife loss
RADIATION		+	Property contamination (10)	Crop and animal food Contamination (10)	-
NOISE		+ (11)			

Comment:

(1) Geographical variation US positive. UK zero
(2) Ditto
(3) Inconclusive studies
(4) Arising from NO_x interactions etc.
(5) Plus nitrates etc.
(6) In severe cases
(7) Accruing to users and non-users
(8) Trihalomethane in potable water
(9) Net of transfers between regions
(10) Significant nuclear plant accidents only
(11) Annoyance plus possible physiological effects (auditory and non-auditory)

a) This typology is only indicative and not exhaustive. The numbers in brackets refer to the column "Comment".

136

Other indirect benefits -- over and above direct user benefits (including damages avoided) and the non-user benefits -- can also enter into calculations of the effects of environmental regulations. For example, when pollution control devices are required to be installed, new markets are created for their production and sale. In an economic situation in which there is less than full employment, the development of these new markets leads to net job creation, and the output of otherwise unemployed workers is an economic benefit. In addition, industry is stimulated to find innovative ways to reduce the cost of compliance with new regulations. In so far as the technological advances are the result of this innovative activity, the ensuing benefit to society must also be counted. It must be stressed, however, that these types of benefits can be attributed to the environmental policy only if it can be ascertained that they would not have occurred otherwise, that is, that they are the sole reflection of a benefit; failing this, there would .be double counting.

1.1. The Issues

If the benefits, especially some, of environmental policies are not easy to identify, they are even more difficult to measure. This measurement, though, is crucial for decision-making and to monitor the achievements of environmental policies. In this context, four main issues need to be addressed:

-- How to measure the benefits of environmental policies?

-- Why is it necessary to make an economic valuation?

-- How to interpret available estimates?

-- How to assist decision-making when economic valuations are lacking?

2. MEASURING BENEFITS

2.1. The Physical Measurement of Benefits

Benefits can be measured in "physical" terms by a series of indicators such as mortality and morbidity elasticities (3), number of people exposed to various levels of pollution and noise, corrosion of materials, or indicators of water quality. These types of measurement are the keystone of environmental assessment and in fact constitute an element of monitoring the state of the environment (4).

These "physical" measurements enable the achievement, and hence the effectiveness, of environmental policies, such as improved health, better visibility, better outdoor recreation, to be assessed. Furthermore, these measurements are the prerequisite for an economic evaluation; decreased morbidity or corrosion must be measured before a monetary value can be put on them.

2.2. The Economic Measurement of Benefits

a)   Why An Economic Measurement?

The physical measurements of benefits have two major shortcomings: first they do not lend themselves to a meaningful -- that is, in a common monetary unit -- comparison with costs, and second, they do not permit the aggregation of the various types of benefits into a common unit. This is why the economic valuation of benefits is required as an indispensable guide for action.

One of the most widely accepted techniques for evaluating the impact of environmental policy on well-being is known as benefit cost analysis. Considered most simply, this procedure takes the preferences of members of society at a given point in time and seeks to value the gains and losses in their consumption in terms of what they would be willing to pay for them. Hence money is used as a yardstick. Consumption includes the use and enjoyment of both conventional goods and services and less tangible environmental amenities.

Benefit cost analysis is comprehensive and objective and avoids double counting; it includes the effects of an activity on all members of society. The goal is to guide decision-makers so as to achieve an efficient allocation of society's resources. Moreover, comprehensive benefit evaluation studies must take into account the implications of risk and uncertainty, the fact that many benefits and costs do not occur until far into the future and the impacts on future generations, and they may also incorporate the income distributional effects of activities.

b)   Valuation Techniques

Two basic techniques one indirect and the other direct, are used to measure benefits in monetary terms.

The indirect method consists of evaluating damage in physical (non-monetary) terms and then putting a money value on each type of damage recorded. The benefit of a policy equals the value of the damage avoided. Thus, in the case of air pollution (SO_x), epidemiological studies are used to evaluate mortality and morbidity impacts and a money value is then applied for the costs of illness (medical and pharmaceutical costs, working days lost, and so on) and for human life (for example, valuations of reduced risk of mortality as revealed by studies of wage premiums in risky occupations). As regards damage to material, a similar procedure is followed; that is, an evaluation is made of corrosion effects of a pollutant on the stock of materials exposed to pollution (especially buildings and metallic structures) and then the effects of this corrosion are valued. In this case, the conversion into monetary terms is less difficult, since the replacement value or repair costs can be evaluated.

The second approach is to measure the benefits directly. This bases the value of a benefit on consumers' "willingness to pay" for improvements in environmental quality (5). Several techniques can be used. Property price (or "hedonic price") valuation assumes that ability and willingness of individuals to pay for improved environmental quality are reflected in rental rates or capitalised values for housing. The idea is that the market price of two pieces of residential property which differ only in the level of pollution to which they are exposed will reflect the willingness of property owners to pay for reduced pollution levels. Wage differentials are taken to reflect the willingness to pay for reduced probability of health damage associated with the workplace. This method uses wage differential information from occupations that require similar skills but carry different occupational risks; it is presumed that individuals will be prepared to pay a sum equal to the differential for the reduction of health risks from environmental pollution. Aversion costs measure the cost of isolating the individual from the adverse effects of pollutants, either temporarily or permanently, for example by insulating housing against noise from nearby airports or highways. Travel time evaluation is used primarily to determine the willingness to pay for recreational amenities by using the costs of the time (and other resources) spent on travelling to and from the particular site and the likelihood of attending. In effect, the response of the probability of attending is observed to vary in response to different levels of travel cost, and an implicit demand curve for a site is derived. The survey or questionnaire (also called the "bidding game") approach involves interviewing consumers directly, or surveying them by means of a postal questionnaire, to determine their willingness to pay for improvements in environmental quality or for the avoidance of environmental deterioration. Such surveys usually control for inconsistencies or response bias.

c)   Results Obtained from Previous Studies

A number of studies have been carried out in various countries, most of them in the United States. They are discussed in the background paper and summarised in Tables 2 and 3. Only a few salient results are presented here.

With regard to air pollution, the benefits of the 20 per cent reduction in SO_x concentration realised in 1978 in the United States have been estimated at $21.4 billion (1 per cent of GDP). This is $4.8 billion more than the $16.6 billion spent on SO_x abatement in the same year (6). Estimates in Norway also indicate that the benefits of air pollution control outweigh the cost. Estimates of damage cost show that pollution reduction can yield substantial benefits to society. For instance, the damage caused by SO_x pollution is estimated at between 0.6 per cent and 2.2 per cent of GDP for several OECD countries (see Table 2).

Damage caused by water pollution in France was estimated at FF 13 to 16 billion in 1978 (0.6-0.7 per cent of GDP), and the benefit of water pollution control in 1978 in the United States was estimated at 0.3 per cent of GDP (6).

For noise abatement, there are no comparable aggregate benefit estimates; the studies that exist have been of specific locations. The general approach they have used is based on estimates of housing price differences associated with noise levels, or hedonic price studies. Analyses of airport and traffic noise control have been undertaken in Australia, Canada, France, the United Kingdom, and the United States. The consensus of the studies is that an average reduction in housing value of 0.4 to 1 per cent can be expected per decibel of noise increase. The best point estimate is a 0.5 per cent depreciation per decibel over a threshold of 55 decibels.

Benefit estimates have also been carried out for the effects of

Table 2

COMPARISON OF AIR POLLUTION BENEFITS AND DAMAGES (a)
(Billion US dollars, 1978, per annum)

COUNTRY/ AUTHOR	Health (a) $	(% of total)	Soiling-cleaning $	(% of total)	Vegetation $	(% of total)	Materials $	(% of total)	Others $	(% of total)	TOTAL $	$ per inhabitant	Percentage of GDP
UNITED STATES (1978 - benefit) (b) (Freeman)	17	(80)	2.0	(9)	0.7	(3)	0.9	(4)	0.8	(4)	21.4	90	1
FRANCE (1978 - benefit) (b) (Barré)	1.29	(53)	0.4	(16)	n.a.		0.18	(7)	0.55	(23)	2.42	45	0.6
FRANCE (1978 - damage) (Ministry of the Environment)											3.3-4.1	61-76	0.8-1.0
NORWAY (1979 - benefit) (c) (Ministry of the Environment)	0.007						0.003				0.01	4.7	0.02 (d)
NETHERLANDS (1970 - damage) (University of Amsterdam)	0.87	(38)			0.07	(3)	0.09	(4)	1.2	(55)	2.3	176	2.26

a) Excludes damage from toxic substances.

b) Benefits of a 20 per cent reduction in SO_x and TSP.

c) Benefits for a reduction in sulphur content of fuels.

d) GDP for southern Norway.

Table 3

OVERVIEW OF BENEFIT SURVEY

Medium	Pollutant	Country	Damage	Conclusion on Damage	Comments
AIR	SO_x + TSP	US	Health	0.2-0.8% GNP	Estimate for 1978 based on 20% reduction compared with 1970.
	SO_2 + smoke	UK	Health	Minimal	Probable indication that damage is zero or very low in countries with low dose levels. Note the implications for dose-response functions and the danger of "borrowing" elasticities.
	SO_x + TSP	Norway	Health and Materials	0.02% of GDP	Study for southern Norway using Freeman's morbidity and mortality elasticities.
	SO_x + TSP	France/Greece	Health	0.3-0.4% GNP	Within range for US but French study has unknown bias.
	SO_x + TSP	US/FRG	Soiling	Positive	"Per capita" estimates are consistent.
	SO_x + TSP	US/Norway/ Netherlands	Corrosion etc.	Positive	Strong evidence of damage. Norway and United States studies consistent.
	SO_2	Various	Vegetation	Positive	Forest and crop damage but of lower priority than soiling and materials damage.
	SO_x + TSP	US	Property values	Positive	More research needed on what part of losses is additional to other impacts (health etc.). On current information this "aesthetic damage" is not of high priority compared to materials and "physical" damage (and health in the United States).
AIR	Oxidants	US	Health	Probably small	
	Oxidants	US	Crops	Positive	Damage is possibly 3% of crop value.
	Oxidants	US	Visibility	Positive	Possibly very significant damage.
	Toxic substances	Various	Health	Unknown	Recorded substances are very toxic at high concentration levels; but lack of epidemiological data for exposure at lower levels in the environment - potential hazard.
WATER	Various	US/Norway	Recreation	Significant	Recreational effects almost certainly dominate surface water pollution damage.
	Various	US	Health	Unknown	Specific pollutants could be a very significant hazard.
	Various	FRG (Lake Tegel)	Recreation	Significant	Recreational benefit dominant; benefit-cost ratios from 1.7 to 2.9
	Salt	Netherlands	Materials) Agricultural)	Significant	
		Australia	Materials) Agriculture) Industry)	Significant	Annual damage of A$64 million (A$4.4 per inhabitant)
NOISE	-	US/UK/ Australia/ etc.	Annoyance	Positive	House price studies converge on values of 0.5% of house price per NEF (aircraft noise) and 0.4% per dB (traffic noise).
	-	US	Health	Unknown	Relationship to cardiovascular disease under investigation.
	NUCLEAR RADIATION	US/UK/etc.	Health	Positive but probably insignificant for "routine" releases	Dose-response function disputed.
GLOBAL	CFC/CFM	US	Health	Positive: skin cancers	
	CFC/CFM	US	Materials	Positive	Probably of greater significance than health damage.
	CFC/CFM	US	Climate (hence crops etc.)	Positive	Preliminary studies suggest climatic change impacts would dominate.
	CO_2	Various	Climate	Positive	See above.

reducing oil spills and the improvement of hazardous waste dumps. There are problems in comparing the results, however, because relatively few such studies have been undertaken and because each case has its own special features. An overview of benefits survey is given in Table 3.

3. SCOPE AND USE OF BENEFITS ESTIMATES FOR DECISION-MAKING

Do the available estimates provide sufficient guidance for action? There is no doubt that the existing information is quite useful as it gives orders of magnitude, sheds light on important areas of concern and, not least, raises a number of key issues for environmental policies. This kind of information also has an important educational value for the general public as well as for policy-makers. It must be recognised, however, that although significant progress has been made over the last decade, benefits estimates remain scarce, especially outside the United States, where the vast majority of studies has been done.

It must be admitted that cost-benefit analysis has not been used in the decision-making process as much as desirable. This might be due to the fact that in the face of all the present technical difficulties, cost-benefit analysis is often perceived as being costly, burdensome and time-consuming. Hence, some conclude that the exercise is not worth the effort, although it can be asserted that cost-benefit studies consume only a tiny fraction of the resources used up in any significant investment decision. Others infer that a never-ending cost-benefit analysis can be used as an alibi for inaction. Others dispute the legitimacy of putting a price tag on "intangibles" or on human life. Without entering into this controversy, it must be stressed that implicit valuations of intangibles and human life are made continually and inevitably when decisions involving environmental protection, health and safety are taken. Clearly such decisions imply that the expected benefits are worth the costs. The need and usefulness of benefit assessment can be gauged by the fact that, in the United States, regulatory procedures require that any major proposed regulation must be subject to a cost-benefit analysis. It remains the case, however, that a number of shortcomings and difficulties have to be overcome.

First, background scientific data about the diffusion and effects of pollutants are badly lacking. For instance, epidemiological data on the health effects of various air and water pollutants, where they exist, are scarce and subject to controversy. The main problems are those of synergism, multi-media exposure, multiple determinants of effects, uncertainty, lack of reliable information on dose-response relationships, and transfer effects from one medium to another.

Second, the benefits of the control of certain pollutants are by and large ignored. It has to be stressed that, to a considerable extent, we appear to know little about issues that it is suspected will be of great importance in the future. The range of uncertainty about the effects of widely dispersed and diffuse toxic pollutants in the atmosphere and in surface waters, for example, contrasts with a fairly extensive programme of work on dose-response relationships for "traditional" pollutants. This state of knowledge may simply reflect the "changeover" period in which awareness of the problems raised by toxic pollutants is growing.

Third, the evidence remains that noise is one of the most dominant pollutants in the public perception. Damage studies indicate that the benefit to be achieved by reductions of noise levels from aircraft and road traffic is likely to be very large. But little is known about the health effects of environmental noise and global estimates of the benefits of noise abatement are still lacking.

Fourth, in some cases we can identify certain thresholds, which means that further benefits of certain types from greater control may not be significant. The evidence suggests, for example, that in the area of SO_x and particulates, further benefits to human health from additional control measures could be substantial in the United States, but that they are less important in certain parts of Europe than other benefits such as reduced metal and building corrosion, reduced damage to historic monuments and vegetation and aesthetic gains through improved visibility. That is, while for some countries further control of SO_x and particulates will be justified in terms of improved morbidity, for others the dominant gains will be in the form of non-health benefits. For still others, the gains will be in the form of both health and non-health benefits. This shows that environmental policy yields joint benefits and that due regard to non-health benefits should be exercised with respect to future environmental policy.

Fifth, benefit estimates from one country have often been applied to another. This practice of "borrowing" estimates can be misleading if the relationship between emissions or discharges and ambient concentrations, or of concentrations and damages avoided, varies considerably across countries. Moreover, the policy context differs substantially across countries, and this could affect the extent to which benefit estimates can be extrapolated across national boundaries.

Sixth, in the area of water pollution, existing national damage studies have tended to demonstrate that the dominant benefit from cleaning up internal waterways and lakes comes from increased recreational use. But some evidence tends to indicate that these benefits to users may be equalled and possibly exceeded by non-user benefits in the form of option and bequest values. The principle can be extended to wildlife and other natural resources where actual "value in use" may be small, but where value revealed in a market in options for use could be substantial.

Seventh, while some of the benefits of environmental policies are registered in national accounts, others affect the welfare of people without being recorded in accounts or markets. Indeed GNP is a measure of output and not a measure of welfare. Hence, some of the benefits increase welfare or "utility", but are not reflected in GNP accounts as they do not lead to marketable output. Other benefits result in cost reductions (such as reduced expenditures in materials replacement, health, and so on) which imply the release of resources; when these freed resources are re-employed elsewhere in the economy, an increase in GNP is recorded. Other benefits such as increased fisheries and crops result in a direct increase in GNP. It is not yet clear which categories of benefits are the most significant. Freeman, for example, argues that for the United States, welfare benefits would represent about 90 per cent of the total benefit. But no other data permits the establishment of a meaningful breakdown. The fact that option and bequest values, as mentioned above, tend to be significant would give even more importance to welfare benefits. This conclusion emphasizes the serious problems of using measured GNP as an indicator of economic welfare; it excludes many important welfare effects. This does not, however, mean that output-increasing or cost-reducing benefits are negligible: corrosion, soiling, acid rain and crop and fisheries yields remain significant benefits from environmental measures.

Eighth, what is the appropriate level of aggregation of benefits and the representativeness of estimates made at particular levels, such as the local, regional, or national level? The estimation of benefits at the local level characterises noise control studies undertaken in Member countries. The estimation of benefits from air or water pollution control measures has usually been undertaken at the regional level (an airshed, a watershed, or regional recreation area). While these studies often follow the approaches used for local benefit estimation, other methods more appropriate to a regional framework -- including regional input-output analysis -- have been used for assessing the impacts of environmental regulations. While the purpose of benefit estimation at the local or regional level is to determine the net benefits of specific environmental policies, estimates of national or international benefits focus on environmental impacts which are relevant to all of a nations' citizens, or which cross national boundaries. National benefit estimates, such as those for the United States and France, tend to aggregate benefits of all environmental regulations undertaken in a country; international estimates address the results of attempting to control a particular pollutant having global effects, such as halocarbon aerosol propellants or carbon dioxide. Both the national and the international studies rely upon a considerable amount of extrapolation from a limited number of empirical studies to arrive at damage estimates, and then attempt to calculate the benefits of avoiding such damages. Using more restricted empirical studies as a basis for extrapolation to large populations presumes that the estimated relationships and impacts are robust over samples, and that the original sample on which the estimate is based is representative of the larger population.

Yet some form of aggregation at the national level, even if tenuous, is necessary, if the erroneous picture of the effect of environmental regulation as recorded in the national income accounts is to be corrected. As noted above, a significant, perhaps dominant, share of the total benefits of environmental measures is not reflected in national accounts.

There is a risk, however, that aggregate national estimates may tend to overvalue the benefits, since these global estimates are being extrapolated from sectoral, regional studies where pollution problems are particularly significant. For instance, mortality and morbidity elasticites are bound to vary within a country and cannot be applied to the entire territory. Also, the per capita national willingness to pay for a given environmental improvement may be less than that recorded at the level of a given region or locality where a particular problem is serious.

4. CONCLUSIONS

Few countries have made economic evaluations of the benefits of their environmental policies. Where information is available, it indicates that the benefits outweigh the costs.

This review of the state of the art of benefits estimates shows that a significant number of issues remain to be solved. Yet decisions must be, and are, taken on environmental policies which need to be based on a reliable set of data on the benefits expected or achieved.

The main issue to be resolved concerns the extent to which the physical bases of benefit estimates are satisfactory. Benefit estimates usually focus on single pollutants; dose-response relationships usually concern only one pathway of exposure. Problems of multiple exposure and multiple factor relationships need to be examined in detail. More attention to determining the relationship between the control of emissions and the eventual manifestation of damage reduction is also required.

The question of which benefits to include in such estimates is an important issue requiring further investigation. Most studies to date have focussed on the concept of benefits as avoided damage. More recent analyses have found, however, that other evaluation methods, such as those designed to evaluate option value, may point to a significant benefit associated with a policy. Other indirect benefits have also been excluded in most benefit estimates made thus far, although it is possible that they may have considerable weight.

The approaches that have been used to estimate benefits are a combination of relatively simple and traditional procedures (as in valuing physical damage) or relatively recent and sophisticated ones (as in the property price or questionnaire methods). There has been a tendency for particular pollution problems to be associated with particular approaches. Only further experience can tell us whether this is the best strategy for benefit estimation, or whether alternative approaches to a particular problem would yield improved estimates and whether emerging problems such as hazardous waste management need new techniques or significant modifications of existing approaches.

The level of aggregation of benefits and, more particularly, the wider applicability of estimates that were originally made for specific situations are of importance. There is clearly a need to clarify the purpose of benefit estimation; that is, whether it is needed to aid in the assessment of particular controls, or the evaluation of a regional improvement scheme, or accounting for the national benefit of a set of regulations. If the need is to assess the effects of a set of regulations, it may not be appropriate to base the national estimates on extrapolations from a small number of local and possibly unrepresentative estimates. They should instead be based upon a wider representative survey, or on some approach designed to yield the aggregate measures directly.

When benefits cannot be monetised, they can be quantified in "physical" units and embodied in a cost effectiveness analysis of various alternatives. Also, decision-making can be aided by a listing of unquantifiable benefits and/or by risk assessment procedures. In any case, having several forms of benefit assessment, though imperfect, is better than having none. The decision-making process generally involves both analysis and judgement. Judgements need to be explicitly recognised and, as far as possible, enlightened by quantified data.

Finally, it should be emphasized that whether or not to attempt benefit measurement is not an issue. Only through the use of benefit estimates, even though imperfect, can insight into the appropriate level of control be gained or can the cost effectiveness of particular regulatory approaches be assessed. Even though particular techniques may be subject to controversy, totally neglecting benefit estimation may lead to regulations which are either too lax or too stringent. Imperfect, though objective, estimates can both inform the political process and constrain the most extreme judgement forthcoming from it in the absence of such estimates.

NOTES AND REFERENCES

1.   Greenley, J., et al., "Option Value: Empirical Evidence from a Case Study of Recreation and Water Quality", Quarterly Journal of Economics, November 1981, pp. 657-673.

2.   Strand, J., "Evaluation of Freshwater Fish as a Public Good in Norway", mimeo, Oslo University, 1981; and "Economic Evaluation of Damage to Freshwater Fish in Norway due to Acid Precipitation", mimeo, Oslo University, 1982.

3.   Elasticities are the percentage variation of mortality or morbidity corresponding to a 1 per cent variation in pollution. For example, with a morbidity elasticity of 0.05, a 1.0 per cent reduction in morbidity would result from a 20 per cent reduction in pollution.

4.   See OECD, The State of the Environment in OECD Countries, Paris 1979.

5.   The concept of "willingness to pay" does not imply that the individual will have to pay.

6.   Freeman, A.M., The Benefits of Air and Water Pollution Control: a Review and Survey of Recent Estimates, United States Presidential Council on Environmental Quality, Washington, D.C., 1979.

SUMMARY OF THE DISCUSSION OF SESSION FIVE

Professor David W. Pearce

University College, London

The reliability of the methods used to make a monetary evaluation of the benefits of environmental policies and of the results obtained was discussed. To a large extent, the debate focussed on the relevance of Cost Benefit Analysis (CBA) for decision making. As of yet, very few countries have used this technique as an aid for policy making in the field of environmental protection. This, together with the methodological difficulties, explains the paucity of available data.

Main Issues Raised During the Debate

     i) Is the monetary evaluation of environmental benefits feasible and justifiable in every instance?

    ii) Is CBA an appropriate tool for decision making? Does it provide the ultimate criterion or should other criteria be taken into account? Are there other complementary on substitutable techniques?

   iii) How can CBA be improved? Are present evaluation techniques reliable?

   iv) How does CBA fit into the political process and how does it interact with public opinion and public participation? Does CBA help to make policy decisions explicit or is there a risk of rejection or misunderstanding by public opinion?

    v) Should the social incidence of environmental policies (that is, the distribution of cost and benefits) be assessed and how could this be done?

Responses

Benefit estimation was seen as an integral part of the application of cost-benefit analysis to environmental policy. CBA has some importance in assessing significant ("non-marginal") changes in policy, but the view was also expressed that it has a similar significance for "fine-tuning" environmental policy once major changes have been made. While the prospects for cost-benefit analysis (CBA) varied, there was a general expression of faith in the technique and hence that it was worth attempting to estimate the monetary value of benefits. There was also general recognition that the very conceptual basis of cost-benefit analysis requires that the gains and losses of activities to all citizens, as these citizens themselves value these gains and losses, be assessed in a comprehensive social framework that allows the effects on any relevant group to be identified. CBA is at least an indicative process, a reasonable guide to the issues of net gains or losses in such a way as to guide our thinking on policy. Moreover, it is the responsibility of the analyst and policy advisor at least to try to estimate the monetary value of benefits.

CBA cannot be the sole input into decision making on environmental matters, nor is it free from problems. There is uncertainty about physical dose-response relationships, about how to handle detrimental effects that occur with very long time lags, about how the underlying value judgement of consumer sovereignty can be made compatible with the political context in which decisions are made and about the geographical boundaries that limit any analysis.

Nonetheless, however reticent we may be to place money values on benefits, two factors emphasize the need to make the effort.

First, with finite resources all decisions imply monetary evaluations even if those evaluations are not made explicit. This is as true of human life and suffering as it is for material damage, crop losses, forestry damage and so on.

Second, if CBA is not used, something else must be. The alternatives are no better than CBA and share many of the same problems. Possibly some techniques can be developed to overcome these problems; CBA may be integrated into a multi-objective approach; it may be supplemented with physical measures of impact; or it may be linked formally to environmental impact assessments.

Distributional issues can be tackled and have been in a number of CBAs in the USA. Explicit consideration can and should be given to different social groups of great political importance in given countries.

There are opposing views. Some may feel that the problems of quantification are too daunting for CBA to be reliable in some instances. Some feel that CBA obscures rather than clarifies the underlying and varied impacts. But environmental policy is not costless and hence the effort to monetise benefits so as to secure a sound basis for comparison, supplemented by other considerations, is very important. While the search for precision is illusory and, indeed, excessive sophistication may be avoided, approximation is better than no attempt at all.

The evidence from benefit studies is that they show the gains from environmental policy to be significant and substantial; thus benefit measurement is a major source of intellectual and politicial support for the environment.

OECD Responsibilities

The OECD should continue to collect, review and disseminate data on the benefits of environmental policies. In particular, the "physical" data base for benefit assessment (for example dose-response relationships and epidemiological data) should be considerably developed.

The OECD should also contribute to the improvement of evaluation techniques. Not only is it necessary further to improve and develop CBA but also to combine CBA with other techniques. In particular, decision making can be considerably improved by developing non-monetary indicators, combined as appropriate with economic evaluations. In this respect, risk assessment can be a useful tool and should be further studied by OECD.

SESSION SIX

MORE EFFECTIVE AND EFFICIENT ENVIRONMENTAL POLICIES

CHAIRMAN'S OPENING SPEECH

Mr. Charles CACCIA

Minister of Environment, Canada

Thank you Mr. President and Ladies and Gentlemen. I don't know whether I will guide you through but if I don't you will guide me and we will get the Session rolling very quickly. There are three issues, as you know, and each one of them, of course, carries considerable weight. I will briefly warm up and advance for discussion issue number one, which I will interpret very briefly from a governmental point of view.

As you know, it reads that integration of environmental considerations in the policies of other sectors, from the viewpoint of any Minister of the Environment who is a member of a cabinet and therefore has to advance environmentalist goals, is a desirable objective. It seems to me that what we are engaged in today is a competitive situation whereby in the modern state in the early 1980s we are desperately trying to compete with interests of other departments and we even try to ensure that our departments, some more than others (like transport or defence or agriculture or forestry), do understand and accept and integrate in their policy-making environmental considerations.

That battle has either begun or is well advanced depending on each of the Member nations of the OECD; I would hope that this phase, however, will be followed by another which we are just beginning to tackle in Canada and which I will put to you very succinctly. Namely, that as we begin to realise that, whether or not an economy is based on natural resources, the economy of a nation depends on the health of the public, on the availability of water and fisheries and forests and other resources that are well managed; and that at the centre of the decision-making policy process, which has a different name depending on the structure of each government, the environment becomes a central concern and not just a competitive concern. If we succeed in convincing those who work with us that the economy flows from the environment, this concept is one that is just in its early stages of acceptance as far as the Canadian experience is concerned; I don't know about the experience of others.

I am going to conclude (because my three minutes are up and we want to have a good exchange) by expressing the hope that pehaps at the next OECD-sponsored meeting on the Environment we might have a session on this particular aspect of competitiveness versus a central role for the environment and an assessment as to where each nation finds itself as part of the various themes.

In introducing our distinguished Keynote Speaker, William K. Reilly, I will briefly report to you that he is President of the Conservation Foundation, which is a non-government Environmental Policy Research Organisation in Washington. Under his leadership the Conservation Foundation, I am told, has taken a major role in attempting to bring industry and environmentalists together to agree on more efficient environmental programmes and to improve the quality of information and analysis upon which policies are based. A recent example of the Foundation's activities is its sponsorship of a private corporation established to clean up hazardous waste sites and financially supported by funds provided by chemical companies and other private firms. Another example is the publication last week of a pretty heavy report on the "State of the Environment" and on page 470 of it I've found a paragraph which sounds like music to Canadian ears; I will read it to you:

> "Through most of '70s the Federal government was the principle focus of interest group efforts to shape national environmental policy and through national policy to shape state and local policies. The Federal government's retreat in the 1980s from its commitment to environmental protection leaves a void that state and local governments have yet to fill satisfactorily. These governments will have to play a larger role in the future but they will need federal support, both financial and political, to succeed."

I agree with you Sir and I give you the floor.

INTRODUCTION BY

INTRODUCTION BY

Mr. William K. REILLY

President, Conservation Foundation, Washington DC

The previous Sessions of this Conference have focussed on the accomplishments and costs of the environmental programmes that the OECD countries have adopted over the past 10 years or so. The evidence presented at this Conference indicates that the programmes are succeeding, and the economic impacts are not excessive.

These are encouraging conclusions, but they do not obviate the need for considering the subject of this Session -- the need for more effective and efficient environmental policies. The search for such policies ought to be a continuing part of any environmental programme, and indeed of any government programme. But there are a number of reasons why the search is of particular importance now to the nations gathered here today. I might list a few of the reasons I see as most important.

First, we still have a long way to go to ensure that environmental programmes do in fact achieve the ambitious goals we have set for them. Realising environmental objectives has proven more time-consuming and more expensive than had been expected.

Second, we are discovering additional environmental problems -- some of them new, some not previously recognised -- that require attention. Some examples of such problems include acid rain, cleaning up abandoned hazardous waste disposal sites and protecting our groundwater supplies. These newly perceived threats will require additional resources. Moreover, dealing effectively with this new generation of environmental problems will probably be more difficult or expensive than the original set of conventional air, water and toxic problems.

A third reason why we will need to focus on more efficient approaches is that we are in a period in which our environmental programmes must contend with severe economic constraints. None of the OECD economies is as robust as in the 1960s and early 1970s, when the decade of major environmental commitments began.

Even as economic growth in our countries begins to return, we are left with the realisation that our economic capacities are limited and under stress. We cannot afford to burden our economies excessively or to initiate programmes which do not accomplish their goals in the most efficient manner.

Experience over the past 10 to 15 years has also demonstrated to us some of the weaknesses and inefficiencies in our existing programmes. We might not have been able to foresee these when we began, but we can see them now, and seeing them we cannot afford to ignore them.

These, then, are some of the reasons why we have to be interested in more efficient and effective environmental programmes. The need for environmental programmes themselves is still indisputable. Postponing action may be false economy. Environmental programmes are important both to the economic health and the environmental health of our countries. In the long run a healthy economy depends upon a healthy environment.

We may, I trust, at this point in the Conference assume general agreement that we need more effective and efficient environmental programmes. But getting agreement on the need is a far cry from getting agreement on the means.

Some of the ingredients of a recipe for efficiency and effectiveness in environmental programmes have been outlined in the Background and Issue Papers for this conference -- both for this particular session and for those that have already passed or are to come. I will not attempt to list and discuss all of these. To attempt to do so would have me here far into the night, and I am conscious of a higher obligation than that of presenting a comprehensive recipe; that is, the obligation to confine the duration of my remarks to ten minutes.

I would, however, like to mention two or three issues that I consider very important, but which are often given less consideration than some others. One of these is the need to integrate environmental concerns with other programmes and activities in both the public and private sectors. Environmental protection should not be pasted on as an afterthought. It should not just be treated by governments or enterprises as a series of externally imposed requirements to be responded to -- or avoided -- after everything else has been taken care of.

Government programmes, whether they be for economic development, more equitable income distribution or natural resource management, should incorporate environmental concerns from the beginning of the programme planning. This, of course, was the purpose of adopting the environmental impact statement process in many countries. But this process and the philosophy behind it seem to have been faltering in the last few years. Very few countries have advanced the concept and some have apparently attempted to retreat from the degree of integration they had achieved in the past. This is discouraging because the most effective and efficient way to deal with environmental problems is to anticipate and avoid them in the first place.

Another example of the need for more integrated policies can be found within the environmental programmes themselves. Recent data in the United States suggest that 60 to 90 per cent of the PCBs in Lakes Michigan and Superior got there as a result of air transport. More recent research indicates that some of the largest sources of volatile organic air pollution in some of our major metropolitan areas, such as Philadelphia, are wastewater treatment plants. Too often, it appears, our existing programmes just move pollutants around, taking them out of the water and releasing them to the air, or taking them out of the air and dumping them on the ground where they may wash off into the streams or be picked up by the wind. The risks that these pollutants pose may actually be increased by these "cross-media" transfers. As environmentalists we would appear to be in a weak position for arguing for the closer integration of environmental concerns with those of other government programmes if we cannot integrate the environmental programmes among ourselves. Understanding and adapting to the cross-media nature of pollution, I believe, is likely to be a major environmental issue in the years ahead.

There are essentially four ways to respond more effectively to cross-media problems: by focussing on the totality of pollutants coming from a single source, as the bubble policy does; by focussing on a geographic area; by focussing on a single pollutant and seeking the most efficient point of control as it passes through several media; or by co-ordinating with other media regulators. When considering a water pollution effluent permit, for example, concern for cross-media problems would require an effort to be sure that limiting a water release would not simply add to air pollution or land disposal. Given the enormous political, legal and institutional revisions required by many of these approaches, in the short run informal co-ordination of specific permits, together with more research attention to cross-media issues, is probably the most practical way to begin. I should add that combining many or all pollution control authorities in one agency clearly does not ensure a cross-media approach.

Business should similarly be attempting to integrate environmental concerns into their normal corporate planning and management. In the long run a clean enterprise is an economically viable enterprise, because it usually is much cheaper to prevent problems from occurring in the first place than to spend the substantial amounts necessary to clean them up afterwards. One encouraging example of this approach is the adoption of environmental auditing by some particularly forward-looking firms in many OECD countries. Under an environmental auditing scheme, the company itself accepts the responsibility for determining whether its actions are causing potential health or other environmental problems and whether it is in compliance with all of its permits and with other requirements. These firms are taking the initiative to act as good corporate citizens, and are not waiting until their problems are discovered by someone else. I am familiar with a corporation that recently acquired a company and then learned that the new subsidiary had a huge potential liability for cleaning up several derelict hazardous waste sites. The economics of the acquisition were discovered to be negative and a public disclosure of the contingent liability was required by law in the public statements of the acquiring company, which promptly sold its acquisition at a loss. In this instance an environmental audit would have saved a corporation millions of dollars.

Another example of a progressive private sector effort to take the initiative in confronting environmental problems is the recently announced decision by a group of chemical and other companies along with environmental organisations in the United States to form a private corporation for the purpose of cleaning up derelict hazardous waste sites that may be posing significant health and environmental problems. The corporations involved believe they can assist the government in this important task and that they may be able to do the job more quickly and cheaply than the government can. The companies have taken what I consider to be a very constructive step to act as good corporate citizens, a step that will entail contributed clean-up costs of several hundred million dollars a year, a step that reflects the manner in which the senior officials in these firms are integrating environmental concerns into their decision-making process. In doing so the chemical industry particularly is addressing the issue that has been principally associated with its negative public image: derelict hazardous waste dumps.

Such efforts to improve integration are definitely one important ingredient in the recipe for more effective and efficient environmental programmes. A second is shifting more of our attention to anticipating and preventing future problems rather than looking only at how past problems can be cleaned up. It is often difficult to keep our attention on the future when we have so many problems in the present, but it is necessary to do so if we are to have truly effective programmes. As I have said, it is almost always cheaper to avoid the problems before they occur than to attempt to clean them up afterwards.

But in order to be able to anticipate better, we need much better information about the ways in which our environment operates, how chemicals behave after they are released to the environment, and about environmental conditions and trends. This, then, is the third ingredient -- better information. My own organisation has attempted to contribute toward meeting this need for better data by publishing a comprehensive report last week: State of the Environment: An Assessment at Mid-Decade. I am very concerned that often the first governmental programmes to be cut in periods of economic constraints are exactly those -- data gathering, research and analysis -- required to make environmental programmes more effective and more efficient. We cannot, in the long run, afford these false savings.

A fourth ingredient in the recipe is improved tools for decision making in both the public and private sectors. We have some very difficult decisions ahead of us, and we will need the best tools and the best data we can obtain in order to make them correctly. Two of the primary tools were discussed in the background papers for this Session -- benefit-cost analysis and risk analysis. There is no question but that we would have more efficient programmes if we were to improve our ability to use both of these tools. But we also have to realise that these are only tools to aid the decision maker, not rules for making a decision. Our ability to carry out these analyses is still, and will remain for many years, very imperfect and they will never be better than the information they use.

We also have to recognise that, no matter how sophisticated these tools become, their use will still require a substantial amount of policy judgement. They are not scientific techniques that reflect universally accepted scientific principles. There will always be judgements to be made, and these judgements ought to be made openly by senior policy officials. There is no greater abuse of such decision-making tools than to pretend that they somehow give scientifically correct answers behind which the decision-makers can hide.

The wider use of these tools would certainly improve decision. But I also think that these improvements are relatively minor compared to those that result from having an open decision-making process that includes all of the elements of the society that have an interest in the decision. By this I mean unions, citizen groups and others that are knowledgeable about the issues and have a strong interest in the decisions being made. I am told that in many OECD countries there are considered to be no responsible citizen groups that could be included in the decision-making process in this way. I respond that if no responsible groups now exist, that is because the decision-makers have not treated those groups that do exist responsibly. If the OECD countries are to have coherent, stable, environmental policies, these policies must have coherent, stable support from an informed population. The best insurance for this support is to be sure that the population is truly informed about the issues and has not been excluded from participation in decisions regarding them.

All of these ingredients would, I believe contribute substantially to producing more efficient and effective environmental programmes. But other changes are needed as well. We have to look very carefully at the incentives the programmes create. We should be looking for policies that reward good actors and penalise the bad. Too often, our current programmes may do just the opposite -- penalising the good actors.

We have to search for policies that make it more profitable to protect the environment than to destroy it. We have to search for policies that place realistic prices on environmental commodities to ensure that people making use of these resources realise the full costs of their actions. But these are subjects for the next Session to address, and I would like to end my comments here, with only the observations that we still have very difficult tasks ahead of us, that we need to make many improvements in our programmes if we are to deal with these tasks effectively and efficiently, and that accomplishing our environmental goals will require substantial co-operation among all the parties of interest -- government, enterprises, unions and the public.

Fernand Bradel, the French historian who stood the study of history on its head by discounting treaties, battles and dynastic events while emphasizing what he referred to as "the structures of everyday life" -- the price of bread, the productivity of a peasant -- concluded his major life's work with an observation directly relevant to the subject of this Conference: "In the end I am persuaded that more than any other factor, or any human intervention, what determines the prosperity and endurance of a civilization is the productivity of its soil, the dependability and management of good fresh water, the fertility of nature and natural systems": another way of expressing the thought that all our activities, including economic activities, depend upon healthy natural systems and a productive environment.

MORE EFFECTIVE AND EFFICIENT ENVIRONMENTAL POLICIES

1. INTRODUCTION

1.1. Background

During the late 1960s and 1970s an increasing emphasis was being placed on environmental protection. In most OECD countries, many existing regulations were strengthened or enforced with greater vigour and new legislation was implemented to reduce the amounts of industrial emissions into the air, water or soil. In addition, new regulatory agencies were created. Such government action is needed on account of the environmental damages imposed on third parties as a result of the abuse of common property environmental resources, such as air and water, and also the unhindered access to common resources, such as game and fish stocks. In the absence of government regulations, such environmental damages would lead to a socially inefficient allocation of resources. These governmental measures have resulted in substantial environmental quality improvements being achieved in almost every country, in the form of cleaner air, less polluted water and less exposure to hazardous or toxic substances (see Session 5) (1).

The realisation of these environmental improvements has resulted, however, in costs being imposed on industrial producers, especially in the highly polluting sectors such as mining, pulp and paper processing, metals smelting and refining, petroleum extraction and refining, automobile production and coal-fired electrical utilities. The slowing of economic growth and the serious rise in unemployment in OECD countries have brought into question these economic impacts of certain forms of environmental regulations. Moreover, the adverse economic conditions currently experienced by most OECD countries and the recent increases in the levels of government expenditures and regulations have prompted a call for a reduction in the amount of bureaucratic intervention by the government.

Nevertheless, public concern about environmental damages has remained at a high level and there has been widespread sustained support for government action to tackle these environmental problems. Therefore, in the specific context of environmental policies, the current economic pressures are being translated into a call for regulatory reform rather than de-regulation per se. This has included demands for a streamlining and simplification of the regulations and a greater integration of environmental considerations in other government policies (such as agriculture).

Consequently, there is a growing need for more effective and efficient environmental policies. To be effective they must be complied with and achieve the desired outcome; to be economically efficient they must not only be justified in terms of generating benefits that outweigh costs but they must also ensure that the regulated firms meet the environmental requirements in the least-cost manner. A further condition of economic efficiency is that polluters should bear the costs imposed on second and third parties and incorporate these costs in their output prices.

1.2. Issues to Be Addressed

The central issue addressed in this paper is "how can the efficiency and effectiveness of environmental policies be increased?". This can usefully be subdivided into the following specific issues relating to particular components of the environmental policy-making process:

-- How can the authorities develop appropriate anticipatory policies to tackle more efficiently emerging environmental problems?

-- How can techniques, such as economic analyses of costs and benefits and risk assessments, be used more effectively so as to improve the decision-making process on environmental problems?

-- Which levels of government are most appropriate for implementing policies to tackle which types of environmental problems?

-- Should there be a greater integration between the policies affecting different environmental media and between environmental policies and other government policies? If so, how could this be achieved in practice?

-- How can the authorities ensure that environmental considerations are taken into account at an early stage in the planning of major investment projects?

-- How can environmental policies be implemented more efficiently?

-- What measures could be taken to enhance the efficiency and effectiveness with which environmental policies are monitored and enforced?

2. IMPORTANT UNDERLYING NATIONAL CHARACTERISTICS DETERMINING THE EFFICIENCY AND EFFECTIVENESS OF ENVIRONMENTAL POLICIES

There are various underlying national characteristics that have had a significant effect in shaping the environmental policy system that has developed in individual countries, and hence have an important influence on the determination of the appropriate measures for improving the efficiency and effectiveness of an individual country's environmental policies. Therefore, it is useful to view the issues outlined above in the context of these fundamental characteristics.

These underlying national characteristics include a country's size, prevailing socio-economic conditions, institutional arrangements (e.g., a tradition of open government), legal traditions and the traditional relationships between the public authorities and the private sector.

Thus these characteristics affect the extent to which a country adopts a centralised system of detailed legislative mandates and environmental standards based upon specific criteria (e.g., health impacts or availability of control technologies) or uses broad enabling legislation and more flexible regulations based upon various local environmental, economic and technological factors. Moreover, these characteristics determine the complexity and formality of the procedures customarily followed for the formulation and implementation of the regulations. In particular, they influence the extent to which there is public access to information and opportunities for intervention by private groups and individuals in vigorous public debates. Similarly, these underlying characteristics can affect the extent to which scientific and economic analysis are used during the formulation of policies.

The resulting regulatory systems have their own respective advantages and disadvantages. A regulatory system built on rigid standards, extensive technical requirements and opportunities for explicit administrative procedures has the advantage of being visible, subject to public participation and enabling a widespread articulation of rigorous analyses of benefits and costs. It can entail excessive legal confrontations, however, and it may be unduly cumbersome to tackle the unique and complex nature of many environmental problems. Moreover, an exaggerated concern over scientific "proof" can slow or undermine the introduction or enforcement of much-needed environmental controls. In addition, the problems involved in adjusting standards to meet local conditions may bring about more pressure to relax the monitoring and enforcement of standards. In contrast, other systems offer much greater flexibility in the policy making procedures adopted and in the type of control measures implemented. However, they require a degree of mutual trust and co-operation between the regulatory officials and regulated firms that may not always be present. Moreover, because they entail a less visible or accountable process, they too can lend themselves to inefficiency.

The differences between these two models of regulatory intervention are possibly somewhat overdrawn in relation to environmental matters; within the institutional and informal arrangements of Member countries there are likely to be elements of both systems. Nonetheless, this brief examination of the effects of different underlying national characteristics provides a useful backdrop for the consideration in the following sections of how to improve economic and administrative efficiency in environmental matters.

3. ANTICIPATORY POLICIES FOR ENVIRONMENTAL PROTECTION

Forward-looking environmental reviews can beneficially identify early on the major environmental problems that OECD Member countries will have to tackle in the near future. Moreover, such prospective reviews can provide a valuable understanding of these environmental and resource management problems and can enable the determination of priorities for the allocation of environmental protection actions at both the national and the local levels.

The effects of economic pressures upon the scarce resources available for environmental protection makes it now even more important than ever to determine priorities.

Furthermore, OECD countries are likely to continue experiencing rapid and substantial technological and economic changes during the coming decade. This could lead to the emergence of new major environmental problems, for which the costs of remedial action could be substantial -- the costs of cleaning up abandoned hazardous waste sites being one case in point. Recent experience also shows that the formulation and implementation of appropriate policy measures to tackle emerging environmental pollution problems, such as hazardous wastes, can take considerable time. As well as causing public concern, such time lags can create problems for firms as a result of their uncertainty about the regulations to which they will be subject. Consequently, there is an urgent need to make an early start in developing appropriate anticipative rather than reactive policy measures to tackle efficiently and effectively significant emerging environmental problems.

Prevailing circumstances have led many countries to develop an incremental approach to environmental regulations, which are primarily implemented at the local level in these countries. This approach can control existing problems efficiently, but this does not detract from the benefits of performing overall prospective reviews to identify the emerging environmental problems and the priorities for action at both the local and national levels. Thus anticipatory planning can and should be compatible with the adoption of an incremental approach to the resolution of these problems.

The realisation of anticipatory environmental policies in practice, however, is subject to some significant constraints. A sound administrative capability is required to perform such prospective national reviews. Moreover, institutional arrangements are needed to co-ordinate the activities of the various government departments at the national and local levels. The second and more important constraint concerns the problems of obtaining the information required to derive valid forecasts of likely economic, technological, social and political developments and then to assess their environmental implications in the face of the considerable uncertainty that inevitably surrounds such future developments. As a result of this constraint, most countries in the past have had to resort to using curative policies and such policies are still likely to be needed to a certain extent in the future.

The environmental authorities' ability to engage in effective anticipatory long-term planning is also limited because their stretched resources are already tied up in the resolution of their current problems. To a certain extent, these current problems result from or are exacerbated by a lack of anticipatory policies in the past. For the future, it is necessary to break out of this vicious circle by undertaking effective anticipatory policies as far as possible.

Possible measures to this end include ensuring that current problems are handled as efficiently as possibly so that the authorities are able to perform such long-term plans and then to act on the results; and assessment (perhaps just in a qualitative manner) of likely future technological and economic trends and their resulting environmental implications. The effective performance of such assessments requires sound information and data on the current and likely future state of the environment. In this respect, however, it must be borne in mind that the acquisition of this information is an expensive and time-consuming process. Consequently, an iterative procedure may have to be followed, in which there is an initial review of the available information about likely future economic and technological developments and their environmental implications. If this review identified some potentially significant environmental impacts, then these would be examined in greater depth and, where appropriate, anticipatory policies would be developed. Environmental impact assessment procedures provide one potentially valuable mechanism not only for identifying environmental implications of proposed future developments but also for ensuring that appropriate control measures are implemented.

Many countries and international organisations have in fact taken steps to enhance their capacity to effect anticipatory environmental policies (see the papers for Session 1) (2)(3)(4). Many countries have elaborated national conservation and development programmes in response to the World Conservation Strategy. Australia developed an environmental management plan for the Great Barrier Reef. Recent developments in the Netherlands provide a particularly interesting indication of various measures that can be taken. The Netherlands government is currently embarking upon a system of comprehensive forward-looking environmental plans with a time horizon of eight to ten years. These plans will comprise the following aspects: description of the current state of the environment and the factors influencing it; an outline of some scenarios of possible future environmental trends which would be based on various scenarios for major economic, technological and social developments in the future; an elaboration of the environmental objectives and standards for the future; identification of any significant constraints likely and bottlenecks affecting the pursuit of these objectives and the resulting strategic choices that have to be made; elaboration of certain policy measures for the attainment of these objectives and a time schedule for their implementation; and assessment of the effects of these policy measures (5).

4. THE DECISION-MAKING PROCESS

Public concern over both damages to the environment and the economic impacts of regulations highlights the need for a sound decision-making process on environmental problems so as to identify those areas where the environmental damages are significant and corrective action is required (that is, where the quantifiable and unquantifiable environmental benefits exceed the costs of the environmental protection measures) and also to ensure that the most effective and efficient control measures are selected. This need is particularly marked at present since the public and private resources available for environmental protection are limited on account of the economic pressures in OECD countries.

4.1. The Role of Economic Analyses

Economic analyses of the costs and benefits of environmental policies can aid this decision-making process by permitting aggregation and comparison of the many heterogeneous impacts frequently associated with environmental policies, through the use of a common unit of measurement -- money. Such economic evaluations can fairly easily be derived for certain impacts items, such as the costs of pollution abatement techniques.

However, the benefits of environmental regulations are less easily measured than the costs. Economic analyses of environmental policies are subject to considerable limitations and controversy and inevitably the estimates generated by such analyses are rather imprecise. This is primarily because there is often an incomplete basis of scientific information about many environmental impacts, particularly those concerning the diverse links between the ecological chain and man. It is also partly due to the problems involved in making explicit translations of the physical assessments of environmental damages into monetary terms -- specifically, for example, the value of a human life -- which some would find unacceptable. The quantification in financial terms of non-health benefits, such as wilderness preservation or noise limitations, is even more difficult, particularly as the potential benefits may accrue very widely and not all of the participants may be canvassed for their views. However, these unquantifiable impacts may nonetheless still be important and should still be appropriately taken into account in the decision. One possible measure to assist in this is to calculate explicitly the value for these impacts that would be implied by a control decision or by the various options. Another possibility is the use of cost-effective analysis.

4.2. The Role of Risk Assessment and Risk Management

The principle preoccupation of most major environmental legislation and regulation at present is with the adverse effects of organic and inorganic compounds and particulates on human health and the ecological damage that can be caused by such substances as toxic chemicals. There is a growing awareness that potential "time bombs" were created at thousands of toxic waste disposal dumps when the concern for and knowledge of their hazardous potential were limited, and that each day tens of thousands of chemicals are used in production processes. Much more emphasis is now being put on the longer-run risks to human health arising from exposure to even small quantities of these chemical substances. Of particular concern here is whether exposure to individual chemicals can have carcinogenic effects, adversely affect reproduction or have damaging mutational effects over the span of several generations. At present there is considerable uncertainty about these impacts.

New chemicals currently entering the market place can yield important benefits to society and, in some cases, they may be used to enhance environmental protection (for example, by improving treatment techniques). Moreover, on account of the high costs of ensuring complete control of their associated hazards, zero hazard is in most cases unattainable. Therefore reasonable and timely judgements must be made (either implicitly or explicitly) about the significance of these risks and the extent to which they should be controlled. This raises the question of whether environmental economists should not only examine the concept of optimal levels of conventional pollutants with which they were customarily concerned during the 1970s, but also that of the acceptable or optimum level to which the risks associated with the second generation environmental problems (for example, toxic substances) should be controlled.

In some countries, these decisions are usually the result of a process of bargaining in which the regulatory agencies use formal standards as a starting point and then settle for a compromise that is reasonably satisfactory to both parties. There is, of course, the danger that legislators will satisfy the environmentalists by the symbolic act of passing tough-sounding pollution control legislation, and then appease industry by failing to enforce that legislation vigorously. In the continuing bargaining between firms and the pollution control agency, the results may fall significantly short of the environmental goals being pursued.

Thus the need for a sound and transparent decision-making process is particularly marked for these controversial newly emerging environmental problems about which there is considerable uncertainty. Increasing attention is currently being given to the role risk assessment and risk management could play in this.

Risk assessments involve the quantitative evaluation of a pollutant's impacts in terms of a common (physical) unit -- the risks of damages to human health -- taking into consideration uncertainty about these impacts. This can then yield risk rankings of various activities and pollutants covering different environmental media, thereby taking into account significant inter-media transfers of pollution. This can then lead to the identification of those areas where the health risks are most serious, thereby assisting in the determination of priorities for regulatory intervention and hence yielding a more efficient allocation of public and private resources for environmental protection.

Risk assessment is the scientific first step and input into the process of risk management, which involves decisions on what pollution sources to control and how strictly they should be controlled. This entails judgements about the potential risks and a balancing of the estimates of the benefits from their reduction against the control costs (6). This, in turn, moves one from the scientific to the economic dimension of the decison-making process concerning these environmental pollutants. In this respect, risk assessment is similar to the physical impact studies that form the basis for the economic evaluations of policies concerning conventional pollutants.

The performance of risk assessments and their use in risk management, however, present considerable difficulties and are subject to certain limitations and some controversy. In most cases it is not practical to apply multiple tests upon humans in controlled situations. Therefore the dose-response assessments usually involve small animals and entail dose levels that are much higher than those experienced in the environment. This raises questions, however, regarding the extent to which the results of these tests can be extrapolated to give reliable estimates of the likely health impacts for humans. The issue is further complicated by the fact that people are often exposed to various chemicals, which together may produce effects far more hazardous than those of a single chemical taken in isolation. While, to a considerable degree, this approach appears to have industry support, environmentalists and others have expressed concern regarding the difficulties of explicitly quantifying benefits and anticipating unknown risks. They fear that this may lead to insufficient consideration being given to certain unquantifiable impacts.

One final important difficulty with risk assessments is that, as with economic analyses of the costs and benefits of environmental policies, their performance can be expensive and time consuming. Consequently, there is the danger that the process of quantitative risk assessment and economic evaluation may, wilfully or otherwise, become a painfully slow, foot-dragging device. This could become particularly important given the constant and rapid emergence of new environmental problems that have to be tackled. Nevertheless, risk assessment and economic analysis can still play a useful and important role and their costs constitute a small fraction of major development projects or policy programmes. Therefore the central issue is how to strike a balance in determining the appropriate and timely evaluation technique that provides the required information for the decision-making process on complex environmental issues, while not requiring too much time or money.

4.3. How to Improve the Decision-Making Process

Some of the elements of this process are at present preoccupying the US Environmental Protection Agency, which is currently giving greater attention to these techniques of "quantitative risk assessment", cost/benefit decision models and the use of regulatory impact analyses. It is not clear, however, to what extent such techniques could be applied. Clearly they are relevant for new environmental legislation or regulations with widespread impact, or new major development projects which may have multi-faceted economic and environmental consequences. They are probably less appropriate for the day-to-day regulation of firms' pollution, where the continuing negotiations between regulating agencies and employers, which are more typical of the European systems, have already resulted in the implementation of technical or performance standards that enable achievement of the overall desired environmental goals. These standards are normally determined in a fairly pragmatic manner that takes account of both environmental and non-environmental objectives with little if any explicit reference being made to the concept of economic optimality. This is not altogether surprising in the light of the potential problems relating to the performance of economic evaluations and risk assessments, which have been highlighted in the previous two sections.

There are a number of measures that could be taken, however, to improve the effectiveness with which economic analyses and risk assessments could be applied as useful tools to aid the decision-making process on environmental problems, especially for the major developments with complex and potentially significant environmental impacts for which these techniques are particularly appropriate.

The first is improving the scientific knowledge on environmental impacts that forms the basis for both risk assessments and economic evaluations. In this respect, one of the more promising developments over the past 20 years has been the expanding interchange of information among countries on the toxic properties of various chemicals. International organisations, and in particular OECD, have played a key role in this and should continue to do so in the future.

Second, improvements may be necessary in the manner in which risk assessments and economic evaluations are performed and used and in particular in the manner in which the results are presented so that they can be a useful aid to the decision-makers. In this, explicit recognition should be made of the limitations of these techniques. In particular, certain impacts that could not be evaluated should be highlighted and relevant physical and qualitative information should be presented on these impacts so that they can be appropriately taken into account in the ultimate decision.

In those cases where the environmental benefits cannot be quantified in monetary terms, it may be necessary to use cost-effectiveness analysis, under which estimates are presented of the economic costs associated with the achievement of certain (target) environmental quality levels which are usually specified in physical terms. Such cost-effectiveness analysis can be useful in identifying the least-cost option for tackling an environmental problem that is characterised by just one major category of environmental impact (for example, risks of damage to human health). Difficulties can still arise, however, when diverse environmental impacts are involved and comparisons and trade-offs have to be made between the different levels of these diverse environmental impacts arising under the various options.

The decision-making process needs to be structured in a systematic way to take into consideration any uncertainties surrounding the environmental damages caused by a pollutant and the economic costs of control strategies. This could comprise the use of a dynamic, iterative decision-making process involving the following stages: performing an initial assessment to identify the possible environmental and economic consequences under the alternative options; identifying the key factors determining the occurrence and significance of these impacts and thereby having an important influence on the ultimate decision; and collating the available information on these factors so as to yield an indication of the probabilities of these impacts occurring. This procedure could also lead to identification of those key factors upon which further information is required. Any additional information that could be obtained would then be fed into the process of assigning the best possible estimates of the probabilities for the economic and environmental impacts and selecting the most socially efficient control strategy.

Greater openness in the decision-making process may be needed to reduce public mistrust of the tools of risk assessment and economic analysis and create greater public understanding and awareness of these tools in general and their findings regarding particular environmental problems. This may involve public disclosure and discussion of these findings at the earliest stage possible in the decision-making process on major environmental problems.

5. WHICH LEVEL OF GOVERNMENT IS MOST APPROPRIATE FOR IMPLEMENTING WHICH TYPES OF ENVIRONMENTAL POLICIES?

A number of levels of government can be involved in the formulation and implementation of environmental policies. These include the international, national, provincial and local levels. This raises the question: which level of government is most appropriate? No clear answer, however, can be given to this question. Much will depend, of course, on individual circumstances. Thus it will depend on: the size of a country; its geographical position (for example whether it is a recipient of other countries' pollution emissions); the traditional divisions of government; and various other factors such as the traditional interrelationship between governments, the private sector and the political institutions and legal systems currently in operation. A particularly important factor is the characteristics of the environmental pollutant in question.

For example, an environmental pollutant, such as acid rain, encompasses a number of jurisdictions on account of its mobility. Consequently this can be a serious source of international friction and concern both in North America and in Europe primarily because of the fact that the interests in the upstream jurisdiction benefiting from the polluting industry fail to coincide with those of the injured jurisdiction. In such cases, the resolution of such issues must take on international dimensions.

As a general rule, the national government is perhaps best suited to take account of the overall public interest since its constituents embrace the entire adult population. Equally it has or should have the legal, financial and political weight to resist the pleadings or pressures of large corporations or special interest groups. Similarly, international organisations can provide an impetus for the implementation of environmental protection measures by national governments. On the other hand, the application of a set of technically-specific standards insensitive to local conditions may be inefficient since the environmental damages in some conditions may be more serious than in others. Local authorities are usually better placed to take into account such unique local environmental circumstances. However, variations in the standards imposed by different local regulatory or enforcement authorities can create competitive distortions within an industry and therefore can give rise to political and legal disputes -- even though there may be quite valid reasons for the variations (for example, differences in local environmental conditions). What is required, therefore, is a balance which combines the uniformity and stronger enforcement powers inherent in regulations administered by a more senior government, with the flexibility required to meet local circumstances. In the Netherlands case this is described in terms of horizontal harmonization of objectives and activities among senior departments combined with vertical direction to regulating agencies or officials in the field.

6. THE INTEGRATION OF ENVIRONMENTAL POLICIES

6.1. The Need for Greater Integration

The integration of environmental policies covers three aspects. The first and most important aspect is the integration of environmental considerations into other areas of government policies, such as agriculture, forestry, transport, energy, innovation, land use planning, employment, regional and national economic policies and industrial development programmes. Where effective integration is lacking, then significant environmental implications can result from these other government policies. In such cases, the achievement of a greater integration of environmental aspects in the process of formulating these other policies represents a valuable means of enhancing the efficiency and effectiveness with which environmental protection can be achieved.

The second aspect is the integration of the policies concerning firms' discharges to the different environmental media (for example, air, water, waste). Inter-media transfers of pollution can arise from the very mobility of pollution through diverse media and also from techniques adopted to treat a specific form of pollution (for example, an effluent treatment technique leading to the generation of sludges that create waste disposal problems). Such inter-media transfers create special problems for regulating agencies and also for the regulated firms who may face uncertainty about whether they should apply certain pollution control techniques that could generate other forms of wastes. Indeed the multiple nature, media and sources of environmental degradation call administratively for a more holistic approach to environmental regulation.

The third aspect concerns the streamlining of environmental regulations. Where there are different and compartmentalised levels of government -- each with its own concern for environmental enhancement -- overlap, duplication and, in some cases, inconsistency of regulations can (perhaps inevitably) arise, especially where certain processes and activities are regulated concurrently by different jurisdictions. Moreover, in many OECD countries, many separate environmental laws have been developed (often in a rather ad hoc manner) to tackle specific problems and frequently the administration of these regulations has been incorporated within the structure of existing government departments. In the Netherlands, for instance, environmental regulation embraces 20 environmental Acts and five ministries.

While all governments are responsive to the need to avoid overlap and most have developed formal and informal arrangements to delegate or share responsibilities, almost daily a new environmental problem may emerge which may concern more than one department or level of government. Furthermore, in the case of large-scale development projects where the knowledge of the complex environmental implications is far from complete and the appropriateness of established regulations unsure, the traditional working arrangements and accommodations that mark the administration of older regulations may be found lacking. Consequently, there is a need for a greater streamlining of environmental regulations.

6.2. How Can Greater Integration be Achieved?

These considerations raise the important question of 'how can this integration be best achieved in practice?'. The inevitable fragmentation of government departments along functional lines, each with its special focus of interest, makes this difficult. These practical difficulties are exacerbated by the resource and time constraints facing the regulatory authorities in Member countries. Nevertheless, certain countries have taken steps in this direction. Most countries now have, at the national level, a single department or ministry concerned explicitly with environmental issues.

The Netherlands government has recently implemented a number of measures to achieve greater integration of environmental policies. These plans include the elaboration of comprehensive environmental plans (see Section 3) to supplement or replace the existing plans concerning specific media. These plans are designed to increase other government agencies' awareness of future environmental objectives. The environmental authorities in the Netherlands are also considering elaborating and making a greater use of national (model) standards or guidelines, introducing a greater standardisation of the regulatory procedures and moving towards a more integrated and simplified system of environmental licences. The Netherlands government primarily intends to use existing consultation procedures to achieve a greater integration of environmental policies and other government policies. The various government departments have officials responsible for co-ordination and for ensuring that environmental considerations are appopriately integrated during their policy-making processes. In addition, in 1982, land use planning and environmental protection were brought under the responsibility of one ministry, which also supervises the co-ordination between the environmental policies and other government policies. These measures should considerably increase the efficiency and effectiveness of environmental and other government policies in the Netherlands.

7. INCORPORATING ENVIRONMENTAL CONSIDERATIONS IN MAJOR INVESTMENTS BY THE PUBLIC AND PRIVATE SECTORS

The relative cost of retrofitting older plants is often considerably greater than incorporating modern emission control measures in new facilities. This has two implications for environmental policies. First, where the significance of certain environmental damages dictates that strict standards be imposed, then this can pose problems for regulators, particularly where the older plants are located in declining industrial areas. For example, few OECD countries have effectively required the retrofitting of existing coal-fired electricity generating plants. Second, this highlights the need for incorporating environmental considerations as early as possible in the planning and construction of new plant and equipment by both the public and private sectors (for example, highways, electricity generating plants), so as to avoid the expensive process of subsequently retrofitting already constructed facilities.

Environmental impact assessment procedures can provide a particularly valuable tool for this where they are employed 'ex ante' at an early stage in the planning process. To this end, the Netherlands governement is currently considering introducing a system of a basic licence, by which the regulatory authority would provide early on an indication of the environmental acceptability of a proposed project and the environmental requirements concerning this project. These environmental requirements would then be elaborated in greater detail later.

In addition, the measures described in the previous section and those discussed in the papers for Session 4 on the influence of environmental policies upon innovation will aid the attainment of this goal (7)(8). These measures include: the early announcement of imminent environmental regulations; a careful scheduling of the deadlines for the implementation of the regulations; ensuring that, wherever possible, the environmental regulations are implemented at the same time as a regulated firm's investments in the construction of new plants and equipment or the modernisation of existing facilities; effective communication between the environmental authorities and the firms during the formulation and implementation of the regulations; and the integration of environmental considerations into economic reconstruction and development programmes. A notable recent example

of this last measure is the EEC's six-year Integrated Mediterranean Programme
·which aims at integrating different policies (economic, regional development,
agriculture and social) as well as the EEC funds related to rural development
in this region (9). It was considered particularly appropriate to integrate
environmental considerations into this programme so as to ensure that the
development is compatible with the environment. This is being achieved by
performing environmentally oriented pilot projects as part of the preparations
for the implementation of this programme.

8. MORE EFFICIENT IMPLEMENTATION OF ENVIRONMENTAL POLICIES

The environmental policies implemented upon identifiable source-point
polluters may take a number of forms, ranging from those which explicitly or
implicitly prescribe the type of inputs or the emission control mechanisms to
be employed (process standards) to those setting the maximum amounts of
pollutants that may be emitted but without specifying how the target standard
should be attained (performance standards). The use of performance standards
has the advantage of leaving individual firms free to select the most
efficient, that is, least-cost method of achieving the desired environmental
goals. This advantage can be particularly important in the case of
technologically dynamic firms who are thereby enabled and encouraged to
implement more innovative and efficient pollution control measures.

However, in the case of firms that lack awareness about modern
pollution control technologies or are unwilling to implement them, then it may
be necessary for the regulatory authorities to provide such firms with
guidance about the most efficient pollution control measures for their
plants. In addition, a desire to prevent any competitive distortions within
an industry may lead to the use of uniform process standards throughout an
industry. Moreover, where the chances of error or accident are great and the
potential damage is substantial, as for example in the case of toxic
substances or nuclear accidents, then detailed process standards are needed to
provide an effective assurance that such environmental damages do not occur.
1 Another way of enhancing firms' freedom of choice regarding the
application of the most efficient method of achieving desired environmental
goals is the use of the "bubble concept", by which the authorities stipulate
the maximum emission limits for the whole firm or plant but then leave it up
to the firm to determine how to reduce emissions from its various sources in
order to meet this overall limit. Such "bubbles" have been extensively
adopted in the United States, where they have led to substantial savings in
industries' pollution control costs.

Economic instruments not only give firms flexibility regarding their
choice of pollution control measures but also provide an on-going incentive
for firms to reduce their pollution emissions. The issue paper for Session 7
shows that economic instruments such as emission charges have often been
successfully applied in OECD countries as a supplement to their principal
system of regulatory standards (10)(11).

In addition, there are economic instrument schemes that take on various
forms but basically entail the defining of an "emissions transfer market"

-- usually a geophysically bounded air or water shed -- within which the right to release stipulated amounts and types of wastes into the receiving ambient environment may be bought or sold. These rights are variously described as 'marketable emission rights', 'tradable discharge permits' or 'pollution offsets' depending on the particular case (10)(11).

Such tradable pollution rights have attracted particular attention in the United States, even though they have had limited application. Economists are attracted to such systems because they create marketable property rights and thereby set in train financial incentives that theoretically can provide outcomes that are satisfactory to all parties without the need for special government intervention. However, the fact that to date they have had limited application attests to a number of administrative and related difficulties. Basic to their application is the environmental 'shed', yet in practice it is often not easy to identify a bounded area within which to establish an overall assimilative capacity. The assimilative capacity of the receiving environment will also vary as between substances; and in most industrialised areas diverse emissions are produced and dumped into the air and water with some substances being far more toxic than others.

There is also the fundamental question of whether the assimilative capacity of the environment to accept waste should be turned into property rights. In the United States, for instance, the Clean Air Act allows for the transfer of emission rights or offsets between existing and prospective facilities to be built into the regulatory structure of each state's implementation plan for stipulated areas. However, the exact legal status of these "property rights" is not well defined, and the general public is not fully aware of the long-term implications. The fact that they have been largely given away on a first-come, first-served basis to existing polluting firms violates the basic Polluter-Pays Principle and could perpetuate the acceptance of current overall pollution levels. In addition, this reduces the economic efficiency benefits that could be yielded by such economic instruments in that this reduces the extent to which existing firms are induced to implement more efficient and effective new pollution control technologies. There are other administrative complications as well, and at least some who have been involved in their administration argue that they increase rather than reduce the administrative burden of government supervision, although such increases in administrative costs might be justified if a reduction is achieved in the firms' plus the authorities' costs of overall pollution control.

As to what types of regulatory instruments are more efficient than others, each system has its favourable and unfavourable aspects and again much depends on the environmental issue in question. Many regulations adopted in the last 20 years have been directed to stationary sources where polluting firms can be identified and their effects on the ambient conditions can be determined. In these circumstances, the use of economic instruments, "bubbles" and performance standards could be beneficial. However, a very substantial amount of pollution now comes from many non-point or non-stationary sources, such as run-offs from feed lots and agricultural lands relying heavily on pesticides, urban run-off, municipal sewage, automobiles and other transportation vehicles. Measures to deal with such multisource pollution will differ from those aimed at containing the actions of individual firms. Most countries, for instance, choose to operate central plants as public utilities for the treatment of municipal sewage, urban run-off and discharges from small firms. Thus this diversity of pollution, transporting media, and emitting sources almost inevitably calls for a variety of regulatory and non-regulatory instruments.

In the case of resource management and resource conservation on lands or in waters that are public, the problem is usually one of preserving renewable resources on some self-sustaining basis by rationing the harvesting through one means or another. In these cases, the most efficient course is usually for the appropriate level of government to take on itself or to lease to a single private agency the responsibility for managing the resource. In this way competing claims upon the common property resource can be resolved through regulations or administrative rules setting out the conditional terms of access, and the rents can be appropriated for public purposes. Generally, the most efficient rationing regulations will take the form of priced entry, and in the case of game, fish, timber, and so on, the application of harvesting quotas rather than limitations on the types of harvesting equipment that are used.

9. IMPROVING THE ENFORCEMENT OF ENVIRONMENTAL POLICIES

Effective and efficient enforcement is essential to secure the attainment of environmental objectives. This covers not only the monitoring and enforcement of emissions from specific firms but also for non-point sources of pollution (such as agriculture) as well as the monitoring and enforcement activities associated with effective resource management.

In the past, enforcement aspects have received insufficient priority and attention, especially during the formulation of environmental policies. Inadequate enforcement could become an increasingly acute problem with the growing emergence of second generation environmental pollutants, such as toxic wastes, where small quantities and concentrations of these pollutants could cause substantial environmental damages. Therefore, there is a need for the integration of enforcement aspects in a systematic manner during the formulation of environmental policies. The Netherlands government is at present considering taking steps in this direction with their Integration Plan for Environmental Protection. In addition, for the future, it will be necessary to ensure that the technological advances enabling more efficient monitoring of emission levels and environmental quality are effectively exploited.

Consideration of how to improve the efficiency and effectiveness of the monitoring and enforcement of environmental policies raises a number of questions concerning: should the monitoring be performed by the firms themselves ('autosurveillance') or by the regulatory authorities? With what frequency should the authorities visit the firms? What should be the type and level of the penalties imposed upon firms failing to comply with the regulations? And to what extent should the authorities resort to using the courts?

Evidence from case studies in France have shown that systems of 'autosurveillance' have led firms to re-examine their production processes and consequently to introduce improvements in their production and pollution control techniques. In addition, the use of such 'autosurveillance' by the firms reduces the cost of the inspections by the authorities. There are a number of measures that the authorities could take against non-complying firms. These range from warnings and fines to closing down the firm's plant. Economic measures such as non-compliance fees could be particularly useful in certain circumstances. In some cases, the authorities may have to resort to using the courts to enforce the regulations, although this may involve substantial delays and heavy legal expenditures.

The appropriate enforcement system for an individual country will obviously depend upon its underlying characteristics (see section 2) and also upon the manner in which the environmental policies are traditionally formulated and implemented. For example, in some countries, monitoring and enforcement are carried out as part of the negotiating process through, for instance, the allocation of periodic "consents" as in the British case, or licences as in the Netherlands. This gives the regulators an opportunity to examine the firm's performance and where appropriate to ease or order additional reductions in effluent discharges. In some countries, such as the Scandinavian countries, the enforcement of environmental policies is facilitated by the traditions of co-operation, social cohesion and consensus.

10. CONCLUSIONS

This paper has highlighted the importance of increasing the efficiency and effectiveness of environmental policies. The specific ways in which this could be achieved will depend upon the characteristics of an individual country and the nature of the particular environmental problem in question. Nevertheless, an indication can still here be given of a number of ways in which the planning, formulation and implementation of environmental policies could be enhanced. These include:

-- Performing forward-looking environmental planning so as to anticipate emerging environmental problems and then make an early start in developing appropriate policies to tackle them;

-- The need to make more effective use of techniques, such as economic analysis of the costs and benefits of environmental policies and risk assessment, as an aid to the decision-making process on environmental problems. Measures to this end include enhancing the scientific knowledge on environmental impacts, and improving the manner in which these techniques are performed and their results presented and used in the decision-making process;

-- Enhancing the integration between the policies concerning the different environmental media. Possible measures to this end include the elaboration of comprehensive environmental plans and policies to supplement the existing plans and policies directed at single environmental media;

-- Achieving a greater integration of environmental considerations during the formulation of other government policies with potentially significant environmental implications (for example, agriculture) through more effective co-ordination between the officials concerned with environmental matters and those involved in formulating these other government policies;

-- Ensuring that environmental considerations are incorporated at an early stage in the planning of major investment projects by the public and private sectors through, for example, the effective use of environmental impact assessments as an integral part of this planning process;

-- Enhancing the efficiency and flexibility with which environmental objectives are achieved by making a greater use of economic instruments, "bubbles" and performance standards;

-- Improving the enforcement of environmental policies. Measures to this end include: the exploitation of the technological advances enabling better monitoring; and giving greater consideration to enforcement aspects during the formulation of environmental policies through the pursuit of a comprehensive and systematic strategy relating to the enforcement of environmental policies.

These findings themselves raise various issues, particularly concerning how these measures can best be applied in practice. As yet, these issues have not been totally resolved. Nevertheless, they are currently being addressed in some countries which have successfully introduced certain measures. The challenge for OECD Member countries now is to build on these initial advances and tackle these issues of how the efficiency and effectiveness of environmental policies can best be enhanced in practice.

NOTES AND REFERENCES

1.   "The Benefits of Environmental Policies", Issue paper for Session 5 of the OECD International Conference on Environment and Economics, June 1984, Paris.

2.   "Environmental Trends, Costs and Policy Issues through 1990", Issue Paper for Session 1 of the OECD International Conference on Environment and Economics, June 1984, Paris.

3.   "Environmental Trends, Costs and Policy Issues through 1990", Background Paper for Session 1 of the OECD International Conference on Environment and Economics, June 1984, Paris.

4.   "Technological Perspectives and their Implications for Environmental Trends and Policies", Background paper for Session 1 of the OECD International Conference on Environment and Economics, June 1984, Paris.

5.   For further details see "Regulatory Reform of Environmental Policy in the Netherlands", Background paper prepared by J. Suurland for Session 6 of the OECD International Conference on Environment and Economics, June 1984, Paris.

6.   For further information and details about risk assessment and risk management see "Risk Assessment and Risk Management: Recent Experience of the United States Environmental Protection Agency", Background paper prepared by R.D. Morgenstern for Session 6 of the OECD International Conference on Environment and Economics, June 1984, Paris.

7.   "Environmental Policies and Industrial Innovation", Issue paper for Session 4 of the OECD International Conference on Environment and Economics, June 1984, Paris.

8.   "Environmental Policy and Technical Change", Background paper for Session 4 of the OECD International Conference on Environment and Economics, June 1984, Paris.

9.   Proposal of the Commission to the Council for Integrated Mediterranean Programme, EEC, OJ C251, 19th September, 1983.

10.   "Economic Instruments", Issue paper for Session 7 of the OECD International Conference on Environment and Economics, June 1984, Paris.

11.   "Economic Instruments Review and Outlook", Background paper for Session 7 of the OECD International Conference on Environment and Economics, June 1984, Paris.

SUMMARY OF THE DISCUSSION OF SESSION SIX

Mr. Robert A. Jenness

Senior Project Director, Economic Council of Canada, Ottawa

The opening and keynote remarks addressed the wide and integral nature of environmental concerns, since the environment is the basic host to life itself. Accordingly environmental issues enter many areas where governments intervene and regulate and where government departments and agencies compete for priorities and resources.. To be effective, administrators should consider these issues from the beginning when shaping their policies.

An important factor is the mobility of pollutants through the ecological chain and across media with varying degrees of damage depending on the host environment, the locality and the totality of separate pollutants. This cross-media characteristic means almost inevitably that more than one government department or agency will be involved.

In this process there are gains to be found in measures which are anticipatory, since these could be less costly in the long run than remedial measures to clean up after the damage has occurred. Reference was made to environmental auditing by corporations and private clean-up initiatives to deal with derelict waste disposal dumps.

As the realisation of environmental issues has grown there is need for better information on the chemical and biological consequences of different exposures to hazardous substances or sounds. Similarly there is a need for openness in the regulatory decision process, with public groups, trade unions and so on playing their part.

Main Issues Raised During the Debate

By and large, the discussion addressed the issues presented in the Issue Paper, in particular focussing on the following:

i) How can anticipate-and-prevent strategies be developed?

ii) How can an integrative approach to environmental protection be developed, including not only various environmental media and pollutants but also ensuring that environmental considerations are taken into account in other policy areas, such as health, transport, energy and so on?

iii) What kind of incentives (economic and others) can be used to improve the efficiency and effectiveness of environmental policies?

iv) How can better cooperation with industry and better public participation in the rule making and enforcement processes be achieved?

v) What are the respective roles of cost benefit and cost effectiveness analysis and of environmental impact statements?

vi) Should considerations and policies concerning the environment at the work-place be integrated with environmental policies and, if so, how ?

Responses

Administrative flexibility and preventative policies

The initial discussion opened on the relatively optimistic note that whereas first generation environmental policies had tended to deal with problems retroactively and had often involved the application of rigid and costly standards, second generation controls can be more preventative and built-in and consequently less costly. It was noted, though, that some of the newer environmental problems are highly complex and their resolution may involve complex and costly treatment.

In developing and administering environmental policies the need to ensure adequate flexibility was foremost, along with enlightened enforcement. Given the level of ambient standards considered acceptable, individual firms should be able to comply in the least-cost fashion. In this respect, it was recognised that the use of performance standards rather than process standards leads to more effective and more efficient responses by industry. At issue was also the question of centralised versus site or locally specific standards and regulations.

Quantitative evaluations and individual negotiations

On a more formal basis it was recognised that environmental benefit-cost analysis, despite its limitations and together with other indicators, was a useful tool in the decision making process, enabling administrators to order their priorities, to eliminate trivial matters and to address issues where the risks and damages are greatest with effective measures that require the least private and public costs. In this connection, environmental impact studies and public hearings have proved effective for big new development projects. Generally speaking, there is a strong need for data collection to provide more soundly based decisions.

At a less structured level there was recognition of the value of a continuing interaction between environmental administrators and individual firms and industries in a spirit of trust and information sharing. Environmental issues are also important at the labour-management level and, depending on the industrial relations system, trade unions have legitimate environmental concerns where their health and safety or that of consumers is involved. They can play a positive educative role in these matters.

Multi-dimensional issues and harmonisation

It was recognised too that environmental issues themselves override enterprise, national and even short and longer term boundaries, and that environmental policies must be closely integrated with social policies. Since pollution damage is often generated by multiple sources, multiple measures may be necessary to treat the problem, and, given the alternative goals that governments and societies have, there may be conflicts and trade-offs. These must somehow be harmonized.

An example of this harmonization can be found in advanced environmental planning, sometimes entailing a regulatory chain of controls dealing with toxics and other deleterious substances through the ecological cycle and across media. Inevitably this process takes time, involving various agencies and compromises, but most often it has proved worthwhile. Another example is the so called "streamlining" of regulations to ensure that polluters are subject to simplified and coherent regulations and permits addressing the various pollutants they must control (for example, air pollution, water pollution and waste).

Enforcement and compliance

Finally there was general agreement that, to be efficient, environmental policies must be complied with, and this involves not only sensible standards -- preferably performance-effective - but also monitoring and enforcement. The latter require human and physical resources which inevitably are limited and their effectiveness will depend on the severity of environmental problems and the determination of governments to deal with them. The use of legal intervention, financial penalties and incentives -- including economic incentives -- and the awarding of compensation are instruments which can supplement and add substance to traditional environmental regulations.

OECD Responsibilities

Improving the effectiveness and efficiency of environmental policies involves a great variety of complementary actions. The OECD should play a key role in this respect:

-- By reviewing and disseminating experiences of various countries;

-- By identifying the present difficulties experienced in Member countries and analysing means to overcome these difficulties;

-- The OECD should in particular study in depth the numerous policy issues raised during the Conference and act as a forum to propose and discuss the ways and means to resolve them. This covers in particular: prevention and cure, integration, public participation and incentives.

ECONOMIC INSTRUMENTS: ALTERNATIVES OR SUPPLEMENTS TO REGULATIONS?

CHAIRMAN'S OPENING SPEECH

Mr. Janez STANOVNIK

Former Executive Secretary,
Economic Commission for Europe, and
Professor at the University of Ljubljana, Yugoslavia

Thank you very much Mr. President. Ladies and gentlemen, this is then the last of the seven "working" or "discussion" Sessions. Permit me three minutes to give you a view of how I see the subject matter in front of us.

We will of course follow on from what we have developed in these discussions so far. We have so far identified problems and we have been speaking of how to plan for the problems. We come now to the real thing -- how to act! And this is the subject of this afternoon's Session.

Action during the last decade or so has been very largely concentrated on a "react and cure" formula, and therefore it should not be too surprising that the regulatory normative action has been more characteristic of governmental action than the predictive phase of action that we are considering now. But in trying to resolve the environmental problems largely through regulatory action, we have just added to an enormous host of regulatory measures that governments undertook in various other areas. It should therefore not come as a great surprise that there was a reaction to this regulation which developed the world over in this period. Therefore it is somewhat normal that today governments are more and more thinking of more indirect motivations and they call these economic actions.

In my view there is not now in principle a basic difference between the two. It is more the difference in technique, in approach and certainly not in objectives. There are many things to be said in favour of indirect economic measures.

First, in my view, they are more flexible, more adaptable, but there is one thing I would like to emphasize most strongly: in my view the indirect measures are much more stimulative in as far as innovation is concerned, and this is the basic issue now before us. May I remind you of what Keynes wrote in his Economic Consequences of the Peace. He said "... The wealth of nations is not so much determined by the amount of gold and material which the nation possesses but by hard work, brains, imagination and initiative". This, ladies and gentlemen, is the era that is in front of us: the joint approach to the environment and the economy in this tremendous challenge in which man with his creative capacities will take over the machine.

At this moment, the thinking or the instruments by which we are going to implement the goals on which there was broad agreement in the past decade -- this is the challenge before our Session. Now we have a very great advantage in having for this Session Mr. Lefrou, who in his career has experienced both academia and practice and has accumulated tremendous practical experience, and who will now help us by taking charge of our task. Let me remind you that the rules for this Session will be the same as those established at the beginning. Therefore when you hear this little bell will you please note "for whom the bell tolls". The floor is yours.

INTRODUCTION BY

Mr. Claude LEFROU

Director, Seine-Normandy River Basin Agency, Paris

In introducing the discussion, I could have confined my comments to the Secretariat's excellent Background Paper. However, in order to focus the debate on concrete problems rather than principles, I have decided instead to speak to you about the experience in France. There will be time enough when we have compared our respective experiences to return to questions of principle.

In France we have used economic instruments for over 15 years in the field of water pollution control and for almost 10 years, though far less comprehensively, in that of noise pollution. By contrast, no use is made of such instruments in the field of air or waste management.

For us, the answer to the question is clear. A policy of environmental protection can be pursued with regulatory instruments alone. They have proved signally successful in the case of air pollution. Even if economic instruments are brought into play, these do not obviate the need for regulatory action. However, they do ensure that such action is implemented more easily and more intelligently. This has been the French approach to water management.

The economists have of course demonstrated that a charge system would achieve a given environmental result at the least cost to the community. This however assumes that polluters are perfect economic agents and seek to minimise their cost outlay. No water management authority in any country has ever believed this. Hence, no-one has switched from a regulatory system to a charge one; particularly since, in many countries -- notably France and also Germany -- the actual rates charged are lower than the economic rates.

On the other hand charges have a colossal advantage over regulation in that they trigger economic reflexes on the part of both public and private users. When a polluter is monitored for compliance with the regulations and is found wanting, he looks for an excuse. When he is billed, he tries to see how he can cut down pollution in order to pay less. The two systems bring into play different parts of enterprise or community machinery and those that impinge on finances are often closer to the centres of decision.

All the charge systems introduced to date have, to my knowledge, been designed with the aim of re-utilising the revenues collected in the area where the charges were levied. In France, the river basin agencies system is regarded by users as a mutual benefit fund: the polluters participate in defining water policy and ensure equity within the charge system and in the reallocation of funds. In a country where tax evasion is a national sport, the mutual benefit concept has undeniable advantages.

Redistribution of funds collected in this way plays a key role as an economic incentive. Take one example, an industrialist, say, whose annual expenditure on pollution abatement is 100 units (50 on operation and 50 on investment). Let us assume that the charge system is so designed that the charge amounts to half that cost, the other half being accounted for by investment aids. This is roughly the situation obtaining in France today.

-- If our industrialist takes no action, this will cost him nothing if no charge system exists and 50 per cent if one does;

-- If he installs a purification system this will cost him 100 in the first case and 80 in the second (50 for operating costs, 25 for investment and 5 for the charges payable on the residual pollution).

Of course, as can be seen from this example, it costs even more to combat pollution than to do nothing and simply pay up, but the differential between the two behaviours is 100 in the absence of any system of economic incentives but only 30 under the French system. Regulation is still indispensable, but it is easier to apply.

The rates applied to the different pollution parameters, the geographic variation of the rates charged together with the geographic variation in rates of assistance, facilitate the implementation of a policy of quality objectives differentiated according to the characteristics and practices of different environments. Implementation of such a system can come up against certain hurdles, however.

i) The aim is to make every polluter pay according to the pollution he generates. In seeking to institute such a system, one swiftly discovers that there are the rich who can afford to pay and the poor whose financial position could be seriously affected by this additional burden. Furthermore, if a democratic system has been introduced whereby those who pay the charges have a say in the rate applied, the level of the charge will be determined by the ability to pay of the poorest, ruling out the pursuit of an ambitious policy. In France, this difficulty has been overcome by making the rates progressive and through government assistance to the poorest firms -- subsequently converted into contracts by industrial sectors to assist the latter to cut down pollution. The process took 10 years to carry through. Now, everyone pays without any government assistance and the costs of anti-pollution measures are built into manufacturing costs, in the same way as they are incorporated in the water rates paid by domestic users.

ii) The cost of establishing the basis for the charge system is considerable; in my agency, for instance, it represents 4 per cent of receipts. But thanks to the information compiled in this way, the agency has reliable data for managing water quality. Annual figures on pollution discharged and on the quality of the host environments serve to calibrate management models, providing a valid base for equipment planning purposes.

iii) Such a system is feasible only for types of pollution where the number of polluters is high. In France only certain pollution parameters give rise to liability: oxidizable materials, suspended solids, notrogen, phosphorus, toxic substances and soluble salts. Only pollution where there are identifiable and measurable periodic discharges is amenable to such an approach, since diffuse pollution cannot be accurately measured. A regulatory system must therefore inevitably be maintained.

ECONOMIC INSTRUMENTS: ALTERNATIVES OR SUPPLEMENTS TO REGULATIONS?

1. INTRODUCTION

The dramatic growth in the production and use of goods since World War II has increased the discharge of waste into the atmosphere, waterways, underground aquifers and ground surfaces. Environmental quality has deteriorated as a consequence of limited assimilative capacity. Growth has created a need for more environmental protection. At the same time, increased prosperity has resulted in greater demands for agreeable environmental quality.

These trends would be of less concern if environmental quality traded naturally at something resembling market prices. Prices would rise when demand shifts put pressure on limited resources, and this would drive out the less valuable environmental users. But environmental quality traditionally has been managed by public authorities, probably because of its common property and public good elements (one person's enjoyment of visibility or clean water does not necessarily detract from another's enjoyment). Thus the increased demand for improved environmental quality, the increasing desire to discharge waste into the environment and also the increased realisation of the social cost of waste discharge have combined to put unusual pressure on agencies to search for improved tools for managing the environment.

In response, various economic instruments have been adopted by OECD countries. Particularly attractive to regulating agencies have been economic instruments such as charges which, unlike traditional regulatory practices, generate revenues. Although this is not a prerequisite, such economic instruments are most often used to pay for administering environmental programmes and to finance pollution abatement expenditures. Charge-based revenues have offset the tendency in recent years to reduce public expenditures on what are regarded as discretionary public services.

Among the economic instruments are effluent and noise charges, marketable permits, fuel charges, container fees and subsidies. The common feature of all these management tools is the use of monetary incentives or disincentives to improve or protect the environment. It is this characteristic which differentiates economic instruments from the regulatory procedures which prohibit certain activities and require or constrain other pollution-related behaviour through licensing procedures or standards. Such standards directly limit physical levels of emissions, and impinge on the choice of physical inputs, outputs and manufacturing processes.

A brief historical review portraying the development of economic instruments begins with the use of effluent charges in the Ruhr River Basin in the Federal Republic of Germany. There the great industrial concentration is the source of an enormous demand to discharge waste. Moreover, the value of good water quality is also extremely high because of opportunity costs. Alternative fresh water sources for domestic use are distant and expensive. These are circumstances which invite the use of economic instruments.

Similar forces to the ones just described were among the factors which led to the introduction of an effluent charge system in the Netherlands and France at the end of the 1960s (and in 1981 in the Federal Republic of Germany). In the Netherlands and France, fewer than six physical measures of pollution were combined together to form the basis of the charge. Chemical oxygen demand, suspended solids, nitrogen and biochemical oxygen demand are illustrative components. Charges, based on actual or estimated discharges of waste into fresh sources, were paid to stipulated authorities: river basin agencies in France and water boards or the national government (in the case of national rivers) in the Netherlands.

The charges or rates, which vary across and within zones of basin agencies, are used to reduce discharge volumes and concentrations and to raise revenue. The revenues are used to support the costs of administration and to finance industrial and municipal abatement programmes through direct and indirect subsidy programmes (for example, loans on favourable terms). Charges which vary across the water boards are also used for subsidies and to finance abatement programmes undertaken by the water boards. Over time, the charge has increased and other pollutants have been added.

Economic instruments were extended to air, noise and waste management after their usefulness for improving water quality was recognised. Charges related to aircraft noise have been instituted in the Netherlands, Japan, France, the United Kingdom and Switzerland. In some cases, the noise charge resembles the effluent water charge; a limited number of physical measures of noise form the basis of the charge and the fee collected depends on the charge rate and the noise level of aircraft. The Netherlands also has factory- and automobile-related noise charges.

There are charges which vary with the sulphur and lead content of fuels in Sweden and the Netherlands, and container charges in several countries. For example, a very high tax has been levied on all non-returnable beverage containers in Norway since 1974. In Finland a special tax has been levied on beer and soft drinks in non-returnable containers since 1976; a deposit on beverage containers has been operating in South Australia since 1977. Sweden (since 1976) and Norway (since 1978) require deposits when new cars are purchased which are returned when the cars are scrapped.

A newer and more experimental economic instrument is the marketable permit system in the United States. Firms and municipalities receive (air) emission reduction credits after obtaining certification that their emissions have decreased. These credits can be sold. One kind of marketable permit is an "offset" where a new source of emission can be established in regions where no increased emissions are permitted provided that existing sources account for more than an equivalent decrease (1). At least eight OECD countries have applied economic instruments to the improvement of environmental quality.

The advent of economic policies has created a number of issues discussed in greater detail in the remaining sections of this paper. They are:

-- Are economic instruments substitutes for or complements to traditional regulations? (Section 2);

-- What are the incentive effects of economic instruments? Have they materialised? Are they large? Do economic policies accelerate the pace of innovation? (Section 3);

-- Are economic instruments easier to administer and less costly to enforce? (Section 4);

-- Are economic instruments such as charge-financed subsidies in compliance with the Polluter-Pays Principle? Do self-financed subsidies redistribute abatement costs towards polluters? (Section 5);

-- What are the future prospects for the use of economic instruments? (Section 6);

-- What are the impediments to the adoption of economic instruments? (Section 7);

-- What key elements make economic instruments feasible and acceptable? (Section 8).

2. THE COMPLEMENTARY ROLE OF ECONOMIC INSTRUMENTS

Economists have discussed economic instruments in the context of environmental management as if they were the only management instruments. In reality, economic instruments are always used in co-operation with regulatory standards. For example, effluent discharge permits are issued to all effluent dischargers by the Prefects in France and by the water boards in the Netherlands. Charges are then overlaid on this regulatory structure. Regulations have such a long historical tradition that they are unlikely to be cast aside in the near future. Moreover, many specific regulations are quite practical.

Another reason standards are surely here to stay is that setting quantity limits appeals to the predilections of many policy-makers for ensuring a given level of ambient environmental quality. The actual reduction of pollution levels is guaranteed, however, only if there is a high accuracy in the diffusion models and other necessary biological, chemical and physical relationships used to tie together target environmental quality levels and the aggregate regulations on all individual dischargers. In fact, the accuracy of the technological relationships often is low.

Another reason for using a mixture of policies is that policy-makers have multiple objectives and face multiple constraints. In such a realistic, complex setting, it is quite reasonable to expect that some mixed policy system will be necessary to achieve the efficiency and distributive goals underlying environmental management.

The world of actual policy must deal with uncertainty as well. Weitzman (2) is one of many to have shown that, given uncertainty and only the goal of efficiency, it is often optimal to use standards. In other cases it is optimal to use charges. If the real world falls in between, efficiency perforce calls for the use of some combination of charges and standards.

The final argument for orienting discussion towards a mixed system of regulations and economic instruments stems from the need to accommodate constraints. A fine example arises where environmental management agencies can design a splendid effluent charge system for municipalities but are comparatively helpless in getting the municipalities to pass the charges properly along to their customers. There is no realistic way that the agency can use a charge system alone to obtain the desired environmental quality. Under these circumstances, a very natural resolution is to use both discharge standards and charges.

Acceptance of the idea that both economic and traditional regulatory instruments will be used raises a host of unanswered questions about what are the desirable combinations of policies: for example, whether a successful mix in one country is likely to be of general use or whether it is culture specific, and so forth.

3. SHORT- AND LONG-TERM INCENTIVE EFFECTS OF ECONOMIC INSTRUMENTS

Economic instruments reward dischargers for making static and dynamic decisions that improve environmental quality. In the short term, economic instruments create an incentive for dischargers to reduce discharges by: (1) reducing product output or substituting less pollution-intensive products for more intensive ones; (2) changing the inputs, such as by using low-sulphur fuels or purchasing quieter airplanes; (3) choosing different known technologies, for example by substituting more environmentally benign pulp and paper techniques for the old sulphite processes (3); or (4) installing end-of-pipe treatment equipment. All of these actions instead reduce the cost of meeting a given standard or reduce the charge liability, or both.

Even when discharge standards have been met, firms and municipalities will engage in further abatement-related activities as long as the associated cost is smaller than the charges that would have been paid.

Economic theory indicates that the optimum rate of pollution charges is at the level where the marginal abatement cost is equal to the marginal damage cost of the pollution it is intended to abate. A "second best" but still efficient solution is to set a level of charge high enough to ensure that polluters will abate pollution to the desired level (beyond which level it is cheaper to pay the charge than to reduce pollution further). In this case, the desired environmental objective would be achieved at the lowest global cost (3). Such a level of charges is often too high to be acceptable or enforceable for political and other reasons. Thus, a "third best solution", often implemented, comprises a combination of regulation, lower levels of charges and redistribution of funds. The lack of incentive effect of low rates of charges is compensated by the subsidies paid from the charge revenues (see Section 5).

In the longer term, economic instruments are expected to quicken the pace of pollution reduction innovations. The use of charges and other economic instruments such as marketable permits, in addition to the traditional regulatory instruments, simply creates a more pronounced incentive to reduce costs. Dischargers will seek new ways to meet these standards and charges (or marketable discharge permits). This will reward those who discover better end-of-pipe treatment techniques, better substitute production technologies or better materials which reduce emissions below the standards. This in turn produces savings in the effluent charge bill or allows for the sale of some fraction of the discharge permit.

In order to learn whether charges or marketable permits encourage more innovation, it is necessary to evaluate the history of at least two comparable situations: one where there are marketable permits, and another where there are charges. This has yet to be done. Some economists argue that the pace of innovation is the same whether marketable permits or charges are used, if similar circumstances are assumed in each case. Others disagree.

It seems reasonable to argue that as the charge liability increases, it necessarily will become more of a bind on discharge behaviour and more of a profit depressant than regulations. So the reward for discovering ways to ease the bind will grow. This argument suggests an empirical study to see whether there has been more innovative activity in the Netherlands than in France, since effluent charges are substantially higher in the Netherlands, as the background paper makes clear.

It further seems reasonable to argue that the more stringent a discharge standard, the greater the incentive to innovate under a regime of marketable permits. Inevitably, regulations treat some different dischargers as though they were the same. A market in permits allows the differences to express themselves in purchase and sales of permits, with gains to all, otherwise trade would not occur. The more valuable the permits, the greater is the incentive to find innovative ways to avoid paying the higher prices for permits.

The incentive to innovation of economic instruments is important enough and the practical knowledge of its actual achievements so vague and undocumented that further discussion of this issue clearly is warranted.

The most significant empirical evidence supporting economic instruments is provided by a recent study of the Netherlands' effluent charge programme by Bressers (4). He applied statistical analysis to different charge levels and water quality improvement across the water boards in the Netherlands. The charges display substantial variation. But the regulations are much more uniform. Bressers found that "the reduction of organic pollution of industrial waste appears to correlate strongly" with the level of the effluent charge in the regions. The permits issued under the National Pollution Act "appear to be of hardly any importance when explaining regional differences".

Bressers (5) also summarises a survey of water board officials who responded to questions about the effectiveness of charges. Thirty reported either "very great" or "great" effectiveness in reducing organic pollution while there were twenty responses that policies such as informal negotiations had either "very great" or "great" effect.

The second set of empirical evidence regarding economic incentives stems from recent experience in the United States where economic instruments were introduced after conventional standards had been implemented. More than 2 000 offset transactions have taken place since 1976. Interestingly, however, less than 50 have involved a trade between companies (6), suggesting that transaction costs are high and that institutional innovations such as establishing banks for emissions credits may create substantial net benefits.

Since the economic incentives in the United States were developed after the physically oriented regulations were in place, any trade, since it is voluntary, has to have provided cost savings and profit for those making the transactions. These benefits are due to the economic instruments alone. Moreover, air quality has increased in every offset transaction.

The third result of economic incentives stems from the Norwegian and Finnish taxes on beverage containers. In Norway, beer-can production decreased from 12 million in 1973 to 1.4 million in 1975 (3). In Finland, littering has significantly decreased and the share of beer and soft drinks sold in non-returnable containers is less than 8 per cent and 2 per cent respectively of total consumption. It might also be noted that the deposit scheme for car bodies in Norway led to a 90 per cent recovery of scrapped cars.

The Federal Republic of Germany provides the fourth major source of empirical evidence regarding economic incentives (7). The national effluent charge law of 1976 was implemented only in 1981. So the evidence is scanty. Studies of discharging industries concluded that the effluent charge was the main reason for making the investment for at least one-third of the firms interviewed (8); 20 per cent of the municipalities interviewed accelerated their sewerage construction plans because of the effluent charge and slightly more than one-third of the towns and municipalities interviewed cited the effluent charge law as the principle reason for undertaking more extensive waste treatment measures. The effluent charge law induced more water quality improvement and brought it about more quickly than could have happened in the absence of the charge. These conclusions are remarkable in light of the very modest charge level: an estimate of under $6 per year per inhabitant in 1986 compared to the charges per population equivalent in the Netherlands of about Gld 49 ($17) in 1983. [See (9) for the calculation of the charge in the Federal Republic of Germany.]

The fifth source of evidence is qualitative. All of the charge, tax and fee-type programmes produce revenues which are used to administer environmental management programmes and to support pollution abatement expenses. The earmarking of particular sources of revenue for particular types of expenditures makes charges more acceptable to dischargers. In France and the Netherlands, the revenue-raising characteristic of economic instruments has resulted in more pollution abatement facilities and a more rapid improvement in environmental quality than would have occurred using only regulatory instruments. Despite the modest level of effluent charges, the revenues are substantial. For example, revenues from water effluent charges in the Netherlands amounted to Gld 1 billion ($294 million) in 1983 and to FF 14 billion ($175 million) in France in 1983.

A number of studies have estimated the hypothetical cost savings of achieving a given level of air or water quality when economic incentives are substituted for regulatory standards such as uniform reduction of discharge volume and concentrations. The merit of these studies is that they provide a feeling for the prospective gains from substituting economic instruments for physical ones.

The results of some of these studies indicate that the cost of using economic incentives varies from 10 to 60 per cent of the cost of the specified physical alternative(s). The results depend on how refined the economic instrument is assumed to be, on how primitive the regulatory alternative is assumed to be, and on how high the specified environmental quality is set. Hypothetical charges or marketable permits perform exceptionally well, saving as much as 90 per cent, if they are compared to uniform reduction of discharge across all entities and if the charges vary in time and space.

It is incontrovertibly true that economic instruments, alone or in combination with regulatory instruments, create positive incentives which lead either to cost savings or to reduced pollution loads, or both. It is important to emphasize that the magnitude of the benefits depends on the opportunities to exploit efficient options or engage in trade. These benefits decrease sharply as the stipulated environmental quality level becomes more stringent. Although orders of magnitude differences in treatment costs for phosphorus removal across dischargers are cited, cost savings are only about 30 per cent because the environmental quality level was set relatively high, at 85 per cent removal (10). This result and explanation correspond to those found in an earlier study by a group of German consultants. They estimated that a uniform charge would be about one-third cheaper than uniform standards if a reasonable ambient water quality level (removal fraction) was established.

Savings in the low range are more likely in the future if practical economic instruments such as simple effluent charges are adopted and tighter environmental quality standards are established. Even savings of 25 per cent are worth seeking when the investment costs of environmental control programmes run to billions of dollars.

4. DOES THE USE OF ECONOMIC INSTRUMENTS IMPROVE THE ADMINISTRATION OF ENVIRONMENTAL MANAGEMENT?

On balance, it appears that the introduction of economic instruments permits a more flexible response by administrators, may reduce the cost of enforcement and improves the quality of administration. Kneese and Bower (11) have argued that an effluent charge is a more flexible policy tool because it can be changed more readily than an effluent standard. Baumol and Oates (12), casting an eye towards the sluggishness of the US tax system, believe that effluent charges may not be able to change as quickly as is required. Probably all can agree that there are circumstances when charge policies respond more quickly and other instances and institutional settings when standards and other non-economic regulatory tools are more responsive.

Use of both economic instruments and standards makes it possible to benefit from adjusting either or both of the components through time. A mixture of policies produces results which track more closely the desired path of objectives. The added flexibility multiple policy tools provide is more than a theoretical point. It is part of the argument made by administrators in the Federal Republic of Germany in praise of their new system of charges and standards which replaced the old pure standards system (9).

Turning from increased flexibility to enforcement, introducing an effluent charge system raises the expected cost of non-compliant behaviour under the reasonable assumption that, if caught, one must pay the usual fines plus the charge bill for the unreported volume and concentration exceeding the permitted levels. Therefore, charges should reduce non-compliant behaviour with the result that more compliance can be achieved at the former level of enforcement costs.

Effluent charges produce revenues which are used to meet the expenses of administration and ensure environmental quality management against the vagaries of cyclic allocations from general funds. The danger is that the captive funds from charge revenues can be used for more enforcement and other administrative activities than is worthwhile. How wasteful this agency aggrandisement effect is depends on the relative power of the other claimants to the charge revenues, such as the firms and municipalities qualifying for subsidies, and on steps the policy-making bodies have taken to prevent excess administrative expenditures. Introducing an effective marketable permit policy also would improve compliance.

A polluter found to be out of compliance after having profited from the sale or exchange of a discharge permit would be more heavily fined than one caught who had not gained. Thus non-compliance should diminish with marketable permits. However, unless the sale of permits is taxed, marketable permits do not generate revenues to support improved (or excessive) environmental quality management.

It is important to learn whether and to what extent, if any, enforcement is more efficient under a system of mixed economic and legal management tools than under a regulatory system. It is a delicate issue to study. Dischargers certainly are not eager to describe their transgressions of the rules. It is risky for administrators to publicise how they are "failing" to manage so they too have a strong incentive to paint an optimistic picture of compliance. Nevertheless, a study evaluating the effectiveness of enforcement across different management systems would be a worthwhile undertaking.

5. REDISTRIBUTIVE AND EFFICIENCY-PROMOTING FEATURES OF SUBSIDIES

Financial assistance systems for pollution prevention and control are practised. There are loans available at favourable rates of interest and special accelerated depreciation tax policies for investments related to environmental protection and grants or subsidies given to reduce the costs of pollution abatement. It will be recalled that the OECD Polluter-Pays Principle (PPP) calls for the polluter to bear the expenses of pollution abatement. Nevertheless, financial assistance programmes may be an acceptable exception to the PPP objective if they are transitory, do not distort trade and investment significantly or are designed to promote a country's socio-economic objectives (13)(14).

Some aggregate information about the impact of subsidy programmes was provided in a survey conducted by OECD in 1978 (15). The report concludes that the economic and trade effects of subsidies, if any, have diminished in importance. Subsidies comprise a very small fraction of total industrial environmental investment.

Subsidies for pollution control financed by taxes and charges incident on polluters are considered to be compatible with the PPP as a means of redistributing pollution abatement costs between polluters (14). The French water management system is a typical illustration of this approach.

In theory, however, if charge systems are efficient (that is, if the level of charges is high enough) there is no need to reallocate the revenue for pollution control purposes. These funds can be considered as a "rent" paid by polluters for using the assimilative capacity of the environment; they could be paid to the general revenue of the nation (14). Any subsidy should then be judged or justified on its own merits irrespective of the origin of the funds.

In practice, the charge revenues are more often redistributed to polluters because the level of the charges that a government feels it can set is not high enough to ensure the achievement of its environmental objectives. Hence, heavy polluters with high unit costs of abatement are paying more charges which are repaid to those who can abate more pollution at lower cost. The subsidy to these polluters is justified by the fact that they are providing more clean-up at lower cost. To work efficiently, such redistributive schemes should ensure that marginal costs of abatement are equalised between polluters (3)(14); this does not seem to be the case in practice, however.

6. WILL THE USE OF ECONOMIC INSTRUMENTS CONTINUE TO INCREASE?

The record of OECD countries indicates that once economic instruments are introduced, they are increasingly used to manage environmental resources. For example, not only are pollution charges being extended to cover more dimensions of a given resource, but they are also being extended to encompass more and more resources. Charges are now being introduced in countries where they were not in use before. Charges in these countries are applied in a more widespread manner. There is more serious discussion about the use of economic instruments in countries without a charge system than there was a decade ago. In view of these trends, can one expect further adoption of economic instruments?

The case studies cited in this section illustrate the generalisations made above. Specifically, a charge on toxic substances was added to the French charge system after it had been in operation for five years. Then charges for nitrogen and phosphorus in effluents were added in 1982. The effluent charge system in the Netherlands has been extended to include toxic substances. The Netherlands' charges for the sulphur content in fuel (1970) and charges designed to mitigate road, factory and aircraft noise followed the water quality charges in the 1980s.

The dates noise charges were introduced illustrates how the use of economic instruments to manage a particular resource has been extended internationally: 1973, France; 1975, United Kingdom; 1975, Japan; 1976, Federal Republic of Germany; 1980, Switzerland; 1980-1982, the Netherlands.

In Sweden the National Environmental Protection Board (NEPB) has introduced in the last ten years: a container charge to aid in the reduction of litter; charges for fuels which exceed acceptable limits of sulphur and lead to aid in the reduction of air pollution; and charges (deposits) on automobiles to reduce the littering of the countryside with abandoned automobiles. The charge for oil discharged by ships to be introduced in 1984 and the other charge policies may also serve as examples of a country which has increasingly adopted economic instruments for purposes of environmental management and has applied them in a variety of circumstances. There is active discussion about further charges on pollution activities.

Despite these past trends, it is difficult to forecast whether the use of pollution charges will be further extended. In some countries it is claimed that when pollution charges multiply, their management becomes too complex. In some cases in order to minimise enforcement complexities, charges are implemented that have only indirect links with actual pollution discharges (for example, a tax per litre of fuel without reference to the sulphur content). Such charges are purely revenue-raising instruments with no incentive effect and are opposed by industry. In some countries, the introduction of economic instruments faces a number of political difficulties, for instance, when going through the parliamentary process.

The air and water quality management programme introduced in the United States in the late 1960s and early 1970s specified required treatment technologies and issued discharge permits for residual pollution to firms and municipalities. Since 1976 a marketable permit system has developed and has become much more sophisticated. Marketable air quality permits have been extended to cover more regions of the country. Marketable discharge permits have been introduced in Wisconsin as a further means of improving water quality.

The use of marketable permits in the United States seems likely to increase in the future. The benefits of environmental improvement may be large, but they are diffuse, with the result that per capita benefits are small compared with the abatement costs a firm or a municipality must bear.

Table 1 provides a summary of existing systems of charges. For water, most countries charge for discharges into municipal sewer systems; these types of user charges are not included in the table.

7. IMPEDIMENTS TO THE ADOPTION AND IMPLEMENTATION OF ECONOMIC INSTRUMENTS

The benefits of adopting economic instruments have been emphasized. Problems, both real and perceived, have limited the adoption of economic incentives in the past.

Table 1

POLLUTION-RELATED CHARGES AND TAXES OECD COUNTRIES, 1984 (a)

Type of Pollution			
Water (b)	Solid Wastes	Air	Noise
	Australia		
		Japan	Japan
	Finland		
France			France
Federal Republic of Germany	Federal Republic of Germany		Federal Republic of Germany
Netherlands	Netherlands	Netherlands	Netherlands
	Norway	Norway	
	Sweden		Switzerland
			United Kingdom

a)   The nature and importance of the charges vary greatly from country to country.

b)   Excluding user charges.

First, the adoption of a charge system is disruptive in a distributional sense. Firms and municipalities have to pay for the use of environmental capacity when previously such use was free. The higher the use of the charge, the greater is the incentive effect, but the greater also will be the resistance and the effort to defeat the proposed charge system.

Second, administrators, familiar with regulatory systems, quite naturally suspect that a new system will be disruptive and more difficult (and expensive) to implement. The case for economic instruments has yet to be sufficiently well documented to instil confidence in administrators.

Third, environmentalists often oppose economic incentive systems such as charges because they believe polluters are thereby given the right to pollute. It does not matter that the usual alternative, standards, "give" freely the permission to discharge which polluters would pay for under a charge system. Nor is it practically important that all productive policies legally require dischargers to restrict pollution activity whether residual pollution is paid for or not. The fact is that the often-heard environmentalist argument against charges is accepted in the political arena because economists have failed to present the full argument carefully.

Fourth, it is often argued that more information is required to implement a system of economic instruments. In reality, the advent of economic instruments brings about improved performances. Thus, it is more accurate to argue that added information requirements are associated with improved administrative effectiveness. In any event, with the dramatic decrease in the cost of data storage and processing brought about by rapid progress in microelectronics, the question of information costs diminishes greatly in importance.

8. FEASIBILITY AND ACCEPTABILITY OF ECONOMIC INSTRUMENTS

A review of economic instruments in OECD countries yields some common elements. First, economic incentives increase in their effectiveness to the degree that the charges, or the equivalent, are tied directly to discharges; a number of taxes or fees designed for environmental protection that are unrelated to actual discharges (for example, a tax per litre of fuel without reference to the sulphur content) are unlikely to produce any incentive effect.

Second, it is neither feasible nor efficient to apply an economic instrument for every individual pollutant. Some simplification is essential. In practice, charges and other economic instruments have been applied for a limited number of physical pollutants. Also, the suitability of the economic instrument depends on the pollutant and the medium; it is usually recognised that it is better to ban than to charge for highly toxic pollutants.

Third, the consequences of economic instruments are borne by those who directly and indirectly pollute and by those who benefit from an improvement in environmental quality. A durable system of economic instruments will be far more effective if all these parties participate in the political process that creates the policies.

Fourth, because policy implementation occurs in a decentralised decision-making setting, relevant political entities at the different levels must also participate in the formulation of policy. Instruments must be shaped to be administratively feasible.

Fifth, the political feasibility of charges is improved if the revenues are made available for pollution abatement expenditures or to cover costs of enforcement.

9. CONCLUSIONS

Growing realisation of the costs of environmental degradation and the increased demand for environmental quality has created the need for better environmental management. This in turn has led to the increasing use of economic instruments in conjunction with traditional regulatory policies emphasizing physical restrictions and requirements. Once adopted in a country, effluent charges, fuel charges, marketable permits, subsidies, and other economic policies have been applied to more pollutants and to more environmental resources. More countries have adopted systems of economic instruments as well.

Using a mixture of traditional regulations and economic instruments provides more flexibility and is more efficient than using either economic instruments or regulations alone. This is particularly true when there are multiple goals and constraints and when there is uncertainty.

The addition of properly designed economic instruments such as charges or marketable permits to an existing standard type system should reduce abatement costs, increase compliance, reduce enforcement costs, and improve environmental quality in the short term. In the long term, economic instruments should encourage a faster pace of innovation designed to reduce costs further or to encourage the conservation of environmental quality. Whether marketable permits or charges encourage more innovation depends on the circumstances of the comparison, in particular on the level of the charges, the severity of the discharge standards and how uniform they are. Three empirical examples of the successful use of economic instruments given in the text are as follows. (1) Statistical analysis of quality improvement and charge level across management units in the Netherlands indicates that charges, rather than standards, were dramatically effective in improving water quality. These results were further substantiated by a survey of water board officials regarding the comparative effectiveness of instruments. (2) Non-returnable container production had fallen by about one order of magnitude two years after a charge was introduced in Norway. (3) The new effluent charge programme in the Federal Republic of Germany has stimulated firms and municipalities to launch a major abatement programme in order to reduce the charge obligation. These results are remarkable, since the charge level is modest compared with, for example, that pertaining in the Netherlands.

Simulation studies suggest that savings of up to 90 per cent can be realised if charges or marketable permits are used. Even if higher and more sophisticated environmental quality standards reduce the options for economising, and thereby reduce the savings to 25 or 30 per cent, the introduction of economic instruments would be a strategy well worth pursuing.

No pure charge policies exist. It has been necessary in order to make charging effective and acceptable to combine it with redistribution of the charge revenue by subsidies to some dischargers. This has helped achieve abatement objective. However, there is a need to make the self-financing programmes more efficient by making subsidies more directly conditional on performance.

Economic instruments are not used in every instance because the perceived distributional consequences and required administrative charges are judged to be too large.

Economic instruments are more likely to be adopted if they cover a limited number of pollutants and if parties bearing the costs and benefits of the instruments and those administering them are included in the legislative process creating the policies.

NOTES AND REFERENCES

. "Emission banks" have been established to store, buy and sell credits. "Netting" permits a plant to expand its points of emission provided no increase in plant-wide emissions occurs. "Bubbles" allows plants or groups of plants to rearrange emission levels among the emitting sources provided the aggregate emissions legally permitted are not violated.

. Weitzman, M., "Prices versus Quantities", Review of Economic Studies, XLI (4), 477-491.

. OECD, Pollution Charges in Practice, Paris, 1980.

. Bressers, H., "The Effectiveness of Effluent Charges", Technische Hogeschool Twente, Enschede, the Netherlands (Summary in English.)

Bressers, H., "Dutch Environmental Policy", unpublished paper, 1983.

Palmisano, J., "An Evaluation of Emissions Trading". Paper for Air Pollution Control Association, Atlanta, 1983.

Rat von Sachverständigen für Umweltfragen (Council of Experts for Environmental Questions), "Die Abwasserabgabe, wassergutwirtschaftliche und gesamtökonomishe Wirkungen Sondergutachten" (The Effluent Charge Effects on Water Quality Management and the General Economy), 1974.

Springer, R.U., and M. Pupeter, "Evaluierung von gesetzlichen Massnahmen mit Auswirkungen im Unternehmensbereich", Munich, 1980.

Brown, G.M., Jr., and R.W. Johnson, "The Effluent Charge System in the Federal Republic of Germany". (Unpublished study prepared for US Environmental Protection Agency, Seattle, 1983.)

OECD, Economic Instruments: Review and Outlook. Background paper for the International Conference on Environment and Economics, Session 7, Paris, 1984.

Kneese, A.V., and B. Bower, Managing Water Quality: Economics, Technology; Institutions, Baltimore, 1968.

Baumol, W., and W. Oates, The Theory of Environmental Policy, Prentice Hall, Englewood Cliffs, New Jersey, 1975.

OECD, OECD and the Environment, Paris, 1979.

14.   OECD, The Polluter-Pays Principle, Paris, 1975 and OECD, An Assessment of the Implementation of the Polluter-Pays Principle, Paris, 1981.

15.   OECD, Notification of Financial Assistance Systems for Pollution Prevention and Control: Results of 1978/1979 Notifications, Paris, 1982.

SUMMARY OF THE DISCUSSION OF SESSION SEVEN

Professor Karl-Görar MÄLER

Stockholm School of Economics

Issues

i) In the late 1960s and early 1970s environmental policies were exclusively conducted by the use of regulations. The spread of inflationary pressures through the OECD economies and the decline in productivity and economic growth led to the re-examination of the regulatory approach in many fields, including the environment. The obvious question asked was: What role could economic instruments play in the free market economies of the OECD countries in the implementation of environmental policies?

ii) The Polluter-Pays Principle, accepted by the OECD countries as a guiding principle for environmental policies, aimed at ensuring that the cost of environmental control fell in the first place on the polluters, thereby ensuring that market forces took these costs into account and that resources would be allocated accordingly in production and consumption. The Polluter-Pays Principle is in fact an economic instrument. Other economic instruments include charges on emissions, charges on the disposal of waste, transferable emission rights, compensation payments and insurance. How do these instruments work and what are their advantages?

iii) In spite of the significant claims made for the various advantages of economic instruments, relatively few countries have introduced economic instruments on a large scale. What has been the experience so far with economic instruments? Have they led to the efficiency expected from them? Can experience with economic instruments in one country be transferred to other countries? What have been the main obstacles to the more widespread use of economic instruments?

iv) As pollution costs rise and some of the inefficiencies of the regulatory system become more obvious the search for more efficient means of implementing policies continues. What are the prospects for a significant extension of economic instruments? What are the limits and, if any, in what areas, on the use of economic instruments?

Responses

i) Environmental regulations are different from most other regulations in the sense that they are aimed at correcting the malfunctioning of the market system, which fails to take account of the externalities created by production and consumption. Because of this, the general view was that regulations are essential to environmental policy implementation, but that they can be and indeed should be supplemented by economic regulations.

ii) The main arguments advanced for the use of economic instruments were:

-- They are more efficient; that is, they achieved the same environmental objectives at lower social and private costs and they can be more efficiently administered;

-- They gave more flexibility; greater flexibility was also given to polluters to respond to policies and also greater flexibility to adapt to changing conditions;

-- They could also have a strong incentive effect for innovation in pollution control;

-- As redistribution charges, they could substantially assist pollution control in general;

-- In general, economic instruments are more open and transparent than regulations, are less at the discretion of the bureaucratic system and can be easily kept account of.

iii) In the discussion it emerged that while economic instruments were used everywhere in conjunction with regulatory standards, there were great disparities in their use. First of all there are a number of barriers: instruments, charge programmes, transferable emission rights, compensation payments, insurance schemes. The use of these vary widely; in fact most countries use only charge programmes, but even within charge programmes there are great variations. They are most commonly used in the field of water, but also for noise pollution. There are fuel charges as an aid to air pollution abatement and there are waste charges including charges on packaging.

iv) Marketable permits are being examined and developed only in a limited number of countries, but the claim was made that they could result in savings of up to 50 per cent in pollution control. Cost savings although not of this magnitude have been claimed for most charging systems.

v) In general business representatives were cautious about the use of economic instruments and preferred regulations combined with voluntary agreement. At least one country with experience of this type of "agreement" approach testified to its usefulness. There were others who pointed out that voluntary codes are easily eroded and difficult to implement under the systems presently obtaining in OECD countries. The voluntary code on multinational companies was quoted as an example of a voluntary agreement which is consistently broken.

vi) The inefficiencies of the regulatory system were enumerated and it was suggested the economic instruments would help to overcome these inefficiencies:

-- Regulations set equal standards for everyone and therefore are either too weak or too costly; '

-- In spite of the complexity of regulations, emissions continue to increase and rarely decline;

-- Regulations cannot keep pace with economic developments: old industries keep going too long, keeping new ones out.

vii) There was considerable debate about the transferability of experience with economic instruments from one OECD country to another; the advantages of economic instruments could vary considerably from country to country. One view was that with some modification in line with the institutional and economic structure of the country concerned, these instruments have wide applicability.

viii) A major point in the debate was the potential use of funds collected through charges. One view was that charges are effective only if they are sufficiently high, in which case they have substantial redistributive effects and results in a surplus over and above the operating cost of the scheme. In some cases these surpluses are redistributed to polluters who have successfully reduced pollution, and it was argued that this is a redistributive incentive effect. In general there was opposition to treating charges as revenue raising and lumping income from them with other tax receipts. If this were done then any incentive payments to polluters who successfully reduced pollution would have to be regarded as subsidies.

ix) Insurance schemes can be usefully employed as economic instruments in a number of cases, such as with hazardous waste. Nevertheless, a number of problems remain; for example, in what form the funds should be held against potential damage in the distant future, and also the possible disappearance of insurance companies over time. One country expressed considerable reservations about the use of private insurance in this field.

x) On the whole economic instruments have been used successfully in a number of countries but their use is still limited. The USA, Germany and France see further expansion in the use of these instruments while a number of others expressed reservations about their advantages over a flexible system of regulation. However, these reservations were not on economic grounds.

OECD Responsibilities

i) OECD should examine the transferability of economic instruments that have been successfully employed in some OECD countries: in particular, how far different existing regulatory systems lend themselves to adjustment and to complementing economic instruments.

ii) In the light of the doubts expressed about full compliance with the Polluter-Pays Principle, the OECD should continue to monitor and assess the implementation of the Polluter-Pays Principle and to examine how the Polluter-Pays Principle could be improved in the light of past experience and of new circumstances.

iii) Given the possibility of rapidly rising control costs in some areas and the potential savings offered by economic instruments, the OECD should continue to explore new economic instruments and new areas for their use, and to encourage countries in their implementation.

SESSION EIGHT

FUTURE DIRECTIONS FOR ENVIRONMENTAL POLICIES

CHAIRMAN'S OPENING SPEECH

Mr. William RUCKELSHAUS

Administrator,
United States Environmental Protection Agency

Twelve years ago this month the delegates of 113 nations met at Stockholm to discuss, in Barbara Ward's phrase, "The Care and Maintenance of a Small Planet". What a remarkable job they did defining for the first time an international environmental ethic, and what a remarkable job has been done in the years since in putting those ideas into effect. Throughout the industrialised world we have seen heartening evidence that environmental degradation can be stopped and that the environment can recover.

Even more dramatic has been the change in attitude on the part of industrial and government leaders throughout the world. Those of us who were involved in the infancy of environmental protection remember the difficulty of convincing hard-headed businessmen and politicians that environmental protection was not a transient fad that courted national bankrupty. All developed nations now understand that they can, indeed must, select actions that protect the environment and public health while at the same time maintaining a competitive economy.

Our discussion of future issues for environmental policies at this Conference has become increasingly important and timely in the context of the recent London Economic Summit's declaration on the international dimension of environmental problems and the role of environmental factors in economic development. The summit declaration invites Ministers responsible for environmental policies to identify areas for continuing co-operation in this field. In previous Sessions of this Conference, we have already covered these issues quite thoroughly. A major goal of this Session will be to identify further our priority concerns and potential areas of co-operation for the remainder of the 1980s and possibly into the 1990s. In the very near term, we can also provide "food for thought" for the next meeting of the OECD Environment Committee at ministerial level which will be held in June 1985.

Certainly environmental policy remains contentious, but the controversy concerns means not ends, issues not of whether, but of how, how much and when. These are more subtle and difficult questions than those we had to confront when we urged action against scores of immediate and pressing threats. Now the crusade, it seems, has entered a new and equally important phase: environmental protection is more traditional and vital "react and cure" strategies and programmes are being further complemented by "anticipate and prevent" strategies where feasible.

208

This new situation, as I see it, arises from the status of environmental amentiy and public health protection as social goods that people in developed nations want to "buy" in ever-increasing quantities. Given stable or slowly growing national resources, "buying" more of one thing means "buying" less of another. Environmental protection thus inevitably involves some kind of trade-off, a balancing among different kinds of environmental protection, or between environmental protection and other social goods. Of course, different nations strike the balance differently, depending on their economic development, the perceived severity of their pollution problems and their national value system; the point is that there is always a balance.

Acknowledging this balance becomes more and more important as we begin to deal with the remaining increments of pollution and with the many potentially toxic products produced by modern industry. In recent months the Environmental Protection Agency has begun to focus special attention on the way that we analyse environmental problems and the way we make these necessary trade-offs. Our goal is to make our whole system for doing this as rational and consistent as possible, and to make the hard choices involved in the most explicit and public fashion. We feel that public understanding of how and why we make such choices is essential to the proper functioning of our Agency, and to the efficient achievement of national environmental goals in the United States.

We have begun to use the term "risk management" to stand for the way that we take into account the probable effects of pollutants on human health and the environment and the economic and social effects of a regulatory programme. There are some general principles that govern the way we do this. First, we are careful to distinguish between risk management, a process that may legitimately involve politically important values, and risk assessment, which is a scientifically-based estimate of the extent of the risk posed by exposure to a particular pollutant.

Because of the tremendous uncertainty involved in such estimates, it is essential that they be governed by well-understood guidelines on how to make judgements under such uncertain conditions, and that the eventual quantified estimates of risk are rendered without interference from the political sphere. Development of such guidelines for important classes of risk data is currently a major effort at EPA.

Second, we must expose to public scrutiny the assumptions that underlie our assessment and management of risk. The point of quantitative analysis is not coming up with the single "right" answer, but rather the orderly exposition of the values we hold and the reasoning that travels from some set of values and measurements to a decision.

Third, we must demonstrate that reduction of risk is our main concern and that we are not driven by narrow cost considerations. Because we are obliged to be efficient with Agency resources and society's resources, cost will always be a factor, but where we decline to control some risk we should do so because there are better targets or because there are more efficient ways of getting the same or similar benefits. Risk management is largely a matter of focussing resources on the most important environmental problems.

Finally, we must admit the limits of quantification. There are some cherished values that resist being quantified or squeezed into monetary terms, but are no less real for that. Agents of democratic societies are responsible to the people, but we should remember that "the people" refers not only to the working majority that actually makes current decision, and not even to the whole of the living population, but to those who came before us, who provided our traditions and our physical patrimony as nations, and to those who will come after us and who will inherit what we leave behind. Decisions in the environmental arena often touch on this broader sense of public responsibility, and we cannot afford to lose it among the numbers.

And increasingly, as our world shrinks further, the decisions of each nation will affect the people, in that same broader sense of all the nations. For this reason, we must make sure that international co-operation on the environment continues and flourishes. I believe that the kind of approach we have developed at EPA can be extended to international management of environmental risk.

With all of its limitations, quantified analysis gives us a common basis for comparing the many risks we must handle and deriving joint priorities for controlling them. A common basis for assessing risks would be invaluable in dealing with such problems as the risks connected with substances in international commerce and with the natural transport of pollutants across international borders.

At the minimum, we must begin to speak the same analytic language so that we can begin to make sense out of the complex and confusing problems that affect our global commons. We have some evidence that chemicals used in cooling systems and aerosol sprays have the potential for disrupting the ozone layer that protects the earth from radiation. We have evidence that carbon dioxide produced by fossil fuel combustion has the potential for creating major climatic changes. Although this evidence and the actions it may require remain controversial, we must continue to expose issues of this magnitude to international scrutiny.

International interest and co-operation should also be drawn to the protection of the major ecosystems -- the tropical forests and the oceans -- which are vital to the health of the planet. We must continue to seek the co-operation of the developing world in this effort, as was done so successfully at Stockholm.

In order to cope with these problems we are going to have to take a longer view than most governments are comfortable with taking. With these kinds of problems it takes a long time to figure out what to do and an even longer time to do it. The alternative to making such long-term commitments is a succession of unexpected and shattering crises. Think of how much better off we would all be if the nations of the world had launched major programmes of acid rain research 10 years ago.

Lord Keynes pointed out that in the long run we are all dead, and while this is true of individuals, the human adventure goes on. Putting as much energy and talent as we can afford into the longer view is, I think, the only way of insuring that it does go on, in the long run.

Stockholm demonstrated that from time to time the nations can turn from their daily business and do just that. This Conference is, I hope, another demonstration of this, and of our continuing commitment to create, in the words of Rene Dubos, "Humanised environments that are stable, profitable, pleasurable and favourable to the health of the earth and the growth of civilisation".

INTRODUCTION BY

Mr. Maurice F. STRONG

Chairman, Canada Development Investment Corporation, Vancouver

The Issue Paper prepared by the Environment Directorate for this Session and the opening remarks we have had from our distinguished Chairman, Mr. William Ruckelshaus, have provided an excellent basis for our discussion on "Future Directions for Environmental Policies". And the discussions at the previous Sessions of the Conference have provided some important additional insights and perspectives from which we can draw in our deliberations this morning.

The issues are set out very well in the Issue Paper. I will not attempt the difficult job of trying to improve on them. We should focus our attention especially on the four general directions pointed up in Section 4 and the suggested means of giving effect to these directions. Personally, I would strongly endorse the high priority which Mr. Ruckelshaus accords to anticipatory rather than reactive policies. These in turn require better scientific data and risk assessment capability, as well as more effective use of benefit-cost and cost-effectiveness analyses and environmental impact assessment. In my view the biggest single challenge is to ensure that all available knowledge is brought to bear on evaluation of environmental considerations at the earliest possible stage in the decision-making process. In most governments the internal procedures in respect of decision and policy making have still not sufficiently accommodated to this need and the same is true in the private sector, except to the extent that environmental impact statements are required by law.

However, in these introductory remarks I have neither the time nor the need to be comprehensive. I would like rather to direct my remarks to some very fundamental changes now taking place in the world econmy which I believe profoundly affect the context in which the future directions for environmental policies of the OECD nations must now evolve and add immensely to their importance. I am referring to the changes in the world's industrial landscape as a result of the growing industrialisation in the developing world.

While the industrialised countries of the OECD and the socialist countries of eastern Europe still account for most of the world's industrial production, the "north" no longer has the monopoly it once had on the production of an increasingly wide range of industrial products. The process of industrialisation of the developing countries is well under way. And this process will continue, as it must, for industrialisation is an indispensable ingredient of their development if the needs and aspirations of their people are to be met. It will be retarded but cannot be reversed by the impediments industrialised countries continue to place on access to their markets, by the high costs of capital and by continuing political and economic uncertainties.

A recent World Bank study revealed that developing countries as a whole have maintained substantially higher growth rates than developed market economies in practically all industrial sectors in the period 1966 through 1980. During this period they experienced an average growth rate of 6.5 per cent in manufacturing output as compared with 3.4 per cent for the developed market economies, and 8.1 per cent in heavy manufacturing as compared with 3.9 per cent. And although there was a marked slowing down in the growth of world industrial production after 1973, developing countries experienced the smallest reduction despite the severe impacts of the energy crisis.

The developing countries' share of aggregate world manufacturing output rose only modestly from about 7 per cent in 1966 to 10 per cent in 1980. This makes it extremely unlikely that they will reach the ambitious goal of a 25 per cent share by the year 2000 which was set at the Lima Conference.

But relative growth rates do not tell the whole story. Because world output grew so substantially during this period, the statistics tend to understate the performance of developing countries. While their growth has been concentrated in the labour-intensive sectors such as textiles, wearing apparel and footwear, wood products and basic metals, developing countries have also increased their share of the growth in the more skill-intensive industries such as chemicals, metal products and machinery.

And, as we all know, the performance of some of what we now call the "newly-industrialising countries" has demonstrated the degree to which developing countries are capable of rapid and extensive industrialisation. Brazil is a major producer of automobiles and machinery and a successful competitor in world markets for such sophisticated products as aircraft; Taiwan, Korea and Singapore are important producers of electronic products; and the oil-producing countries, particularly in the Gulf region, are using the comparative advantage of their immense reserves of oil and gas to become major producers of petro-chemicals. These are but a few examples of the way in which the industrial geography of our world is changing.

I am drawing your attention to this issue because I believe its environmental implications have had far too little attention. The Stockholm Conference recognised that environmental problems and priorities of developing countries are somewhat different from those of our industrialised societies and relate primarily to the undermining and destruction of the renewable resources of soil, forests and plant and animal life which provide the principal basis for their development. More recently these issues were very cogently pointed up in the World Conservation Strategy. And I don't want to detract in any way from the high priority which these issues must be accorded in suggesting that developing countries are now facing on an increasing scale the threat of severe environmental impacts that result from the processes of industrialisation.

These impacts cannot be isolated from their need to develop their non-renewable resources on a basis that will be sustainable. Indeed, industrialisation can add to the problems of conserving the renewable resource base. And it has an even more direct impact on the other area in which the environmental problems of the developing countries are most acutely manifest

-- their rapidly-growing urban areas.

In short, the pollution problem is moving south.

The growth in the industrial-related environmental problems of the developing countries has at least paralleled the growth in their industrial capacity. While air pollution levels in most of the major cities of the industrial world have been reduced in the past decade, they have become increasingly severe in many cities of the developing countries, as for example Mexico City, Santiago and Ankara. Growing pollution of water threatens the water supply of many of these same cities. Pollution of surface water and streams as a result of Brazil's programme of "gasohol" production has caused widespread damage to the water supplies of rural areas there. Lake Managua in Nicaragua has become what was described in a recent report as a "stagnant, malodorous dump". And plans for large-scale increases in coal production and use in China and India raise the prospect of a growing problem of "acid rain" in Asia.

I spend a good deal of time in the developing countries and you can just see it happening. Not only are they now experiencing virtually all of the same environmental problems that were at the time of the Stockholm Conference perceived primarily as problems of industrialised societies -- air pollution, pollution of rivers and streams and water supplies and contamination of the food chain -- but they are experiencing them in many cases even more acutely and under conditions which affect the health and well-being of much larger numbers of people. Indeed, I am now deeply convinced that the pollution problems of developing countries are on the way to becoming much worse than the pollution problems of the industrialised countries.

They will certainly be more difficult to deal with. Developing countries will seldom be able to afford a "react and cure" approach. "Anticipate and prevent" strategies will almost always be the only real options available to them.

Far from being peripheral to the interests of developing countries, environmental issues must now be seen as absolutely central to their development prospects. We must now recognise that this is as true of pollution as it is of the need for sustainable development of renewable resources and the problems arising from explosive urban growth. In each of these areas the developing countries face environmental pressures which will dwarf those we in the older industrialised societies have confronted. The principal environmental battles in the period ahead will undoubtedly be fought in the developing countries and the future security of the global environment will depend on the outcome of these battles.

This is, I submit, of the greatest relevance to the OECD countries and to the future directions of your environmental policies.

The continued growth of the economies of the developing countries offers the principal prospect for the renewal of growth in the world economy as a whole. Although our countries will experience short-term difficulties in accommodating to growing competition of developing countries in a wide range of industrial products, as well as their traditional resource and agricultural products, this will be more than offset in the long run by the growing markets they will provide for the goods and services of the OECD countries.

Much if not most of the industrialisation carried out in developing countries will involve the participation of OECD countries as investors, joint venture partners, contractors, marketers or sources of technology and expertise and the multinational corporations of the OECD ountries are in the vanguard of this process.

In addition, I would submit that by accepting and co-operating in the process by which developing countries are allowed to exploit their comparative advantages in industrial development, we will be helping in the evolution of the kind of competitive and efficient world econmy from which all can benefit.

From the environmental point of view, the co-operation of developing countries will be essential if we are to deal effectively with such global environmental risks as pollution of the oceans and atmosphere, the CO_2 problem and common interests such as conservation of wildlife, tropical forests and genetic stock.

All of this, I submit, underscores the need for the OECD countries to give high priority in the period ahead to strengthening international co-operation in all the ways pointed up in the issue paper. The experience of OECD countries and the policies, practices and standards they have developed as a result of this experience, must be made available on a much broader scale to developing countries, recognising that they will have to be adapted to the often varying needs, conditions and priorities of these countries. In some cases, developing countries will have a legitimate comparative advantage because of the lower scale and intensity of their industrial development, which will enable them to adopt less demanding standards than those of OECD countries. But they will need to draw very heavily on the knowledge and experience of OECD countries in evaluating the potential environmental impact of industrial projects to ensure that they have a full understanding of the potential costs of accepting lower standards than have proven necessary elsewhere.

The development assistance programmes of OECD countries provide a major mechanism by which their experience is made available to developing countries and there is an urgent need for much closer co-operation between the environmental ministries or agencies of these governments and their development assistance programmes. At the multilateral level, the World Bank has taken an important lead in this respect and a number of national development assistance organisations have made a start, but so far on a scale that is far short of what is needed. It seems to me that a good deal could be done by OECD through the combined efforts of the Environment Committee and the Development Assistance Committee to accelerate this process.

I would also attach very high priority to the early adoption of the "Environmental Guidelines for Multinational Enterprises" which is now under active consideration in OECD. I believe these Guidelines provide an important basis for ensuring that the multinational corporations of OECD countries provide both positive channels for transmission of environmentally-sound practices and procedures to developing countries and good examples of environmental responsibility.

Finally, I would place strong emphasis on the need to press on with the development within the OECD region of the legal and administrative measures and modalities which will give practical effect to the principles articulated in Articles 21 and 22 of the Stockholm Declaration concerning transboundary environmental impacts. It is important, too, that OECD countries take the lead in enabling these principles to be applied globally.

In conclusion, let me simply lay before you my strong plea that the growing environmental problems of the developing world, particularly those which result from the processes of industrialisation in which OECD countries have had such vast experience, be given high priority in shaping the future directions for environmental policies of our countries. Our experience gives us a special responsibility and our interest in the development of a more secure, prosperous and sustainable world society makes it imperative for us.

ISSUE PAPER: SESSION 8

FUTURE DIRECTIONS FOR ENVIRONMENTAL POLICY

1. INTRODUCTION

What new emphases and directions should OECD Member countries be giving to environmental policy at the national and international level? There are a number of reasons why this question has come to the front of the stage: the past decade's unfinished agenda of environmental pollution issues; this decade's new and broader agenda, which includes not only environmental pollution issues but also critical concerns in resource management and the quality of urban life; the projected environmental consequences of certain economic, social and technological trends; and today's improved economic prospects which present governments with both new demands and new opportunities. Each of these is discussed briefly in the first part of this paper.

The paper continues with a comparison of react-and-cure and anticipate-and-prevent strategies, the two broad strategic approaches now reflected in the environmental policies of OECD governments. To what extent can, and on economic grounds should, the mix of environmental policies be changed in favour of anticipation-and-prevention? And how should they be changed both to improve their economic efficiency and their cost-effectiveness. The paper concludes with a number of suggestions concerning future directions for environmental policies.

2. WHY NEW DIRECTIONS?

2.1. An Unfinished Agenda

There are a number of compelling reasons why now is the right time to consider future directions for environmental policies. First, the progress of the past decade-and-a-half in addressing the backlog of air and water pollution, in controlling certain chemicals, in extending parks and nature protection areas, in improving the quality of life in urban areas and in managing certain resources, while measurable and indisputable, was distributed unevenly throughout the OECD region and has left much to be done (1)(2).

New environmental agencies had to become established and operational, and new environmental programmes had to be implemented during a period of economic recession in the wake of two energy shocks. While higher energy prices tended to reduce overall emissions in many countries as a result of improved energy efficiency, the economic slowdown, with its budget cuts in the public sector and reduced profits in the private sector, reduced the pace of progress in institutional and policy development and in programme implementation. Some countries found it necessary to delay a start on their backlog of environmental problems, and even those countries that made the greatest progress continue to suffer black-spots of pollution.

The realization that water pollution from non-point sources has actually worsened (2); that evidence is accumulating about the adverse environmental and economic effects of certain air pollutants transported long distances and falling as acid rain (3); that disasters such as Seveso can occur; that past failure to properly manage hazardous wastes is imposing a heavy financial and economic burden on certain jurisdictions (2); that comparatively few of the more than 80 000 chemicals in commercial use have been adequately tested for their effect on human health and the environment (4); that noise pollution is a serious and increasing problem in OECD countries, and that the natural environment continues to deteriorate does not alter the basic finding of the OECD's State of Environment Programme that there has been a significant improvement in environmental quality in several Member Countries over the past decade (1). It does, however, highlight the fact that the battle against conventional pollutants is far from won, and that the economic costs they impose on our societies continue.

2.2. A New Agenda

Second, there is increasing concern with a new generation of pollution issues, some more complex than those presented by conventional pollutants and some implying potentially heavy financial and economic consequences, whether action is taken or action is delayed. The gradual realization, thanks to ever more sophisticated methods of measurement and analysis, that a large number of organic chemical and metal pollutants are found in air, water and soil is altering the perception of actions to be taken to control pollution (2). Similarly, the growing evidence that air, water and land pollution are interconnected is forcing a re-appraisal of compartmentalised approaches to their management. Underground water -- a major source of water for drinking, agriculture and industry in many communities -- is threatened in many regions from contamination by abandoned hazardous waste sites and by nitrates (2), the latter often originating in part from the overuse of fertilizers, sometimes encouraged by certain agricultural policies (2). In some places, groundwater supplies are also threatened by depletion, again often from overuse, sometimes encouraged by water pricing policies (5). Air pollution control has focussed with good reason on outdoor air, and on occupational risks in factories, workshops and mines. But evidence is now accumulating that under certain conditions the quality of the air in residences and commercial areas may also pose serious problems (6). There is also an increasing awareness of the potential risk to the public at large from possible accidents in areas where dangerous industries are concentrated.

These issues are local and regional in scale. Others are global. Rising levels of CO_2 in the atmosphere related to the burning of fossil fuels, for example, could cause a warming trend leading to climatic changes in the next century with massive physical, economic and social consequences. If counter-strategies are to be developed in time to be effective they need to be considered soon (7)(8).

2.3. A Broader Agenda

Moreover, the field of environmental concern has expanded beyond pollution to embrace a new range of critical resource issues. These include: the degradation of soils through erosion, salinisation and pollution; the loss of cropland and amenity areas through encroachment from other uses; the continued depletion of and increasing damage to forests in spite of long-standing commitments to sustained-yield management; the loss of wildlife habitat; depletion of marine natural resources and the loss of the planet's biological diversity, essential to maintaining the genetic strength of the world's principal crops and livestock (7)(9).

These problems raise complex issues of interdependence between sustainable economic development and practices to maintain the resource and environmental basis of that development. Many of these problems stem from the lack of effective policies in certain areas, in some countries especially policies governing land-use planning and development control. Other problems originate in or are aggravated by development policies (for example, in agriculture, forestry and fisheries) that neither take sufficient account of their impact on the very resource on which they depend, nor possess a sound economic rationale themselves (7)(9)(10).

While most of these problems are domestic in cause as well as effect, some arise from the incidental effects of economic, trade and other policies in the OECD region as a whole. Others, including some of those that have the greatest effect in Third World countries, result from the impact of the material demands of OECD economies on countries that lack the laws and policies needed to protect their own environment. Some are significant to the OECD region because they are closely related to the North/South debate or because concerted policy action by OECD countries could assist in finding solutions (7)(10). The potential benefits of prior environmental assessment of certain types of projects as a condition for development assistance are currently being assessed by the OECD, as are means to encourage more environmentally responsible behaviour by multinational enterprises (7).

2.4. New Economic, Social and Technological Perspectives

Third, the environmental consequences of economic growth in the coming years will be far from negligible, especially if current trends toward higher growth can be sustained and extended worldwide. The introduction of new technologies, changes in the structure of economic activity, changes in patterns of consumption, investment and trade, and growth in per capita income will all have significant implications for trends in environmental pollution and resource development through the turn of the century. Such changes will also determine the need for, and cost of, improved or new policies as well as the conditions under which they may be deployed (2).

To illustrate this, imagine a future scenario in which emission standards are frozen at 1978 average levels and in which the technology available to abate emissions is also assumed to remain at essentially 1978 vintage. Given low (1.0 per cent) to medium (3.0 per cent) economic and energy growth trends, this condition would imply a significant increase in emissions, with 1990 levels rising 10 to 30 per cent above those of 1978. It would also imply an increase in associated health, property and environmental damage costs. Control costs, however, would show only a small increase.

Now imagine another scenario in which total emissions, rather than emission standards, were held at 1978 levels but environmental technology remained at its 1978 vintage. With emission standards tightened appropriately in step with low to high economic and energy growth trends, there would be no increase in the level of conventional pollution nor in associated damage costs, but there would be an increase in control costs. And in some areas this increase would be significant.

Of course, technology has not remained stable. Fortunately, there have been significant advances in environmentally-favourable product designs (in automobiles, for example), in processes for production and recycling (in chemicals, for example), and in emission-control technologies (in energy, for example) (11). Some industries have introduced these developments to the benefit not only of the environment, but also of their balance sheet (12). Many industries, however, appear to have been much less innovative and others have encountered major obstacles in the introduction of new designs, processes and clean technologies. A period of economic prosperity may create a better climate for innovation, but changes in environmental policies and programmes will also be needed (13)(14).

One can therefore imagine a third scenario in which emission standards would be further tightened and total emissions would be reduced below 1978 levels. Improved product designs, processes and abatement technologies, combined with more efficient and effective policies, would constrain increases in control costs. Some OECD countries are probably in a position to project such a scenario.

It must be stressed, however, that while many future technologies will have favourable consequences for environmental management, the consequences of others could be adverse. Take as an example the effects of releasing genetically engineered micro-organisms into the open environment for agricultural purposes. At present not enough is known about these possible effects. This in itself is an important finding and points to the need to develop effective 'early warning' assessments of emerging technologies (13).

2.5. New Demands and Opportunities

Fourth, future developments in OECD countries have implications not only for the state of the environment and the shape of environmental issues, but also for the political climate in which policy will be developed and implemented. This climate could create both new demands and new opportunities. In many countries, unfortunately, this comes at a time when budgets are severely constrained.

As for demands, a major continuing challenge will be to find and hold the right balance between quantitative and qualitative development. It is of considerable interest to note in this regard that throughout the recent recession and slow recovery the demand for higher environmental quality was sustained in most Member countries, and that public support for environmental measures remained high (15). There is ample reason to believe that a positive relationship exists between per capita income and the demand for environmental quality. With continued improvements in income, education, information and awareness, that demand should continue to change and to increase.

As for opportunities, a return to economic growth should provide several new opportunities to satisfy demands for environmental goods in an economically efficient and cost-effective manner. Structural change may result in a shift from polluting to less polluting activities. With appropriate government policies the modernisation of plant facilities should provide opportunities to modify the design of products and build in less-polluting processes. Profitable firms should be better able and more willing to adopt an innovative response to environmental regulations and to invest in clean technologies and efficient resource management. Governments, too, may be better able to formulate policies that encourage practices which have a positive effect on the long-term sustainability of the resource base of agriculture, forestry and fisheries (16).

3. ENVIRONMENTAL POLICIES: STRATEGIC CHOICES

The environmental consequences of likely growth patterns for the medium-term -- and the growing scale and complexity of environmental issues -- call for changes in some existing strategies and policies for environmental improvement. While the desired nature of these changes will vary greatly, two general points can be made about them. First, they should improve the economic efficiency and cost effectiveness of environmental policies. Second, in order to achieve this, they should promote the integration of environmental considerations into overall economic policy and especially into those policies concerning energy and resource development.

3.1. The Strategic Choices Defined

More specifically, two broad strategic approaches can be distinguished to expose the issues starkly for argument. They are "react-and-cure" strategies and "anticipate and prevent" strategies. One useful criterion for distinguishing between react-and-cure and anticipate-and-prevent strategies is the distinction between new and existing activity. If an activity exists and is having an impact on the environment, society can respond only with react-and-cure measures. If the activity is new and has not yet had an impact on the environment, society can anticipate-and-prevent. Thus, one can draw a distinction between an existing and a new substance (such as existing and new chemicals); between an existing and a new product; (such as last year's and next year's model of a motor vehicle); between an existing and a new project; or between an existing and a new policy (such as an economic, tax, energy or transportation policy).

Pursuing this criterion further, a policy requiring the testing of all new chemicals before they are put on the market would be an example of anticipate-and-prevent; a policy requiring the systematic testing of existing chemicals would be an example of react-and-cure, if accompanied by measures for victim compensation or clean up. Similarly, requiring all new industrial plants to meet clear performance standards would anticipate-and-prevent future damage; retrofitting old plants would be reactive and, depending on associated measures, curative. In general, policies requiring the prior assessment of a new activity are designed to anticipate and, if they lead to measures being built into the activity, to prevent. Examples of this include assessment before a product is constructed (such as a new housing estate, industrial park, dam or irrigation project), manufactured (such as a new automobile design), marketed (such as a new chemical), put on the statute books (such as a new law), or announced (such as a new budgetary measure or fiscal policy). The establishment of future water quality standards may also be anticipatory and preventive providing all new activities are required to comply with them.

Another useful criterion for distinguishing between the two policies is the distinction between short-term and long-term. The consequences of certain activities can be anticipated, but they may emerge only slowly and over the longer-term. Counter-measures also often require long lead times before they can be negotiated, agreed, planned and implemented. Measures undertaken today to assess and develop strategies concerning the emerging problem of CO_2 and climatic change would thus be anticipatory and preventive. If nothing is done, in two to three decades they would be reactive and curative.

Actual environmental policies, of course, have in the past and will in the future reflect different mixes of both strategies, with the chosen mix depending on each country's legislative and institutional framework for environmental management, its stage of development, its priority issues, the pressure of events and the cost to society of those strategies.

3.2. React and Cure

Under this strategy, governments tend to react to issues and problems as they emerge with a range of policies to reduce further damage, to clean up the damage already done and, if possible over time, to reverse the damaging process and roll it back to one in which the ecosystem in question is restored, in whole or in part. Increasingly, too, under this strategy, governments have to adopt policies to ensure equitable compensation of victims.

The past decades provide many examples where react-and-cure strategies were made to work: Lake Erie and the River Thames in the field of water pollution; London and Tokyo in urban air pollution; and Mercury and DDT in chemicals. Resource management examples abound: conservation measures to halt erosion on the Great Plains of North America; retrofitting irrigation schemes with drainage to arrest salinisation; planting exotic species to replace lost native forests.

Most OECD countries are currently deploying react-and-cure strategies in a range of situations: most notably, perhaps, with regard to certain air and water pollutants and existing chemicals and hazardous waste sites, but also with regard to schemes to halt erosion, salinisation and deforestation, and to control groundwater pollution and urban air pollution in Southern Europe.

These strategies are marked by certain characteristics. They are usually activated only after considerable damage to health, property and the environment has been sustained and is obvious, and where popular demand for action assures political support for the control measures needed. They usually reflect centralised decision-making by a government agency aimed at specific point sources. They are necessarily interventionist and usually involve reliance on regulatory instruments that can be put in place rather quickly, setting discharge or emission limits, for example, and occasionally mandating the technologies to be used to reach them.

In terms of economic and financial consequences each case is unique and general conclusions are difficult. It can be said, however, that react-and-cure strategies often involve, first of all, the costs of retrofitting existing plants or schemes with abatement technologies so as to avoid or reduce future damage to health, property or ecosystems. Depending on the nature of the past damage, react-and-cure strategies can also involve the costs of measures to clean up affected sites or, to the extent possible, to rehabilitate property and restore land and water ecosystems affected. These costs, of course, do not affect the costs of the damage to health, property and ecosystems that were incurred before action was taken and, indeed, in political terms, are usually the source of demands that action be taken.

Retrofitting existing industrial plants, property or resource developments can be very expensive, much more so than building-in environmental measures from the start. According to the Polluter-Pays Principle, all these costs should be charged to the polluter who may, to the extent that competitive conditions permit, reflect them in the prices of his products. But in reality, the costs are frequently shifted to the public, that is to citizens and communities which in many cases end up paying: first, for the health, property and ecosystem damage incurred before action is taken; second, as tax payers for the publicly financed part of retrofitting schemes, of clean-up and reclamation programmes, and of victim compensation measures; and finally, as consumers, for increased product prices to cover the privately financed part of retrofitting schemes.

There are, of course, many variants of this distribution pattern, up to and including almost total transfer to the public sector, with tax-supported schemes for victim compensation, clean up and rehabilitation, as well as subsidies for industry. Whatever the distribution, it is society as a whole that pays in the end, either through taxes, prices or damage costs to health, property and ecosystems. From the point of view of economics and the efficient allocation of resources, the question of how society pays for the environmental costs of human activities is second only to the question of how much society pays. This leads to consideration of the second broad strategic approach.

3.3. Anticipate and Prevent

Under this strategy those responsible for making decisions on economic policy and development are required, or induced by various means, to anticipate the probable impact on health, resources and the environment of a given activity, and, where possible, to plan to create environmental and economic benefits from the opportunities offered by a policy or development or, where necessary, to take measures to prevent or reduce the external damage that might result.

The past decade provides many examples where anticipate-and-prevent strategies were made to work: new source standards, for example, that reduced pollution by major stationary sources as well as air and noise emissions from motor vehicles; effluent charges that have induced plants in several industries to engage in a wholesale rethinking of their products and

223

production processes thus leading to greater recycling and less waste (12)(13); impact assessments of major new development schemes that have either induced cost-effective changes to prevent avoidable damage, or that have stopped certain development schemes altogether where the economic and social costs of project-induced damage to the ecology and resource could have exceeded the economic benefits sought by the development (17). Land-use policy can be used to anticipate the environmental consequences of a proposed activity and, if associated with effective development controls, can ensure environmentally acceptable development.

Most OECD countries have developed or are developing legislation and policy instruments of an anticipate-and-prevent character, notably in the area of chemicals control, by requiring the assessment of all new chemicals for impact on health and the environment before rather than after they are put on the market; and in the area of hazardous wastes, by encouraging maximum recycling and cradle-to-grave control. In the field of air pollution, new source standards in many countries are being tightened to avoid aggravating future "react-and-cure" situations associated with damage to forest and water bodies.

Anticipate-and-prevent strategies are also marked by certain characteristics. Generally, they try to ensure that the environmental dimension is taken fully into account at the earliest possible stage of any major decision affecting the environment. They also consider the entire product cycle from design and development through to marketing, use and disposal and they tend to focus on the forward design-and-planning end rather than on the use-and-waste disposal end. This is true whether the cycle concerns a new chemical, as in OECD's programme to foster pre-market assessment; or energy, as in pricing policies to encourage increased efficiency of energy use, or to induce the use of low sulphur fuels; or agriculture, as in taxes to discourage the overuse of fertilizers in sensitive areas.

Formulated within a longer-term perspective, anticipate-and-prevent strategies can be pursued through a wider range of instruments, including assessment, planning, financial and economic instruments as well as regulatory instruments. Where regulatory instruments are used they tend to stipulate enforceable performance standards, without mandating the process or technology to be used, leaving the industry concerned free to choose the most effective and efficient means. In the case of existing industries, they would also establish reasonable deadlines for compliance with performance standards to enable the industry to take them fully into account in redesigning products, in rethinking processes and in planning plant restructuring and modernisation.

Anticipate-and-prevent strategies also try to induce a search for and development of innovative and cost-effective means to meet performance standards. This they would do by supplementing performance standards and reasonable deadlines with appropriate economic instruments, including emission charges, marketable pollution rights and taxes.

3.4. The Strategies Compared

When comparing react-and-cure with anticipate-and-prevent strategies, it is customary to advance social and political arguments in favour of the latter.   The case is evidently a good one.   But the economic arguments favouring anticipate-and-prevent strategies are also often convincing.   The reason for this is that by building preventive measures into the design of a product, process, plant or resource development plan society usually pays less for those measures than it would later when they were added on through redesign or retrofitting.   Moreover, while still using the assimilative capacity of the environment in question, society can avoid future damage to health, property and the environment and hence future costs of clean up, rehabilitation and restoration, as well as the future need for and costs of victim compensation measures.   In the case of environmental pollution, these damage costs avoided can be quite large, as witness recent cases involving certain chemicals and hazardous waste dumps and the growing evidence concerning the adverse effects of acid rain on the productivity of soils and forests.   They can be heavy in the case of resource projects, too;   witness, for example, the economic and social impact that uncontrolled forestry operations can have on erosion and floods, or that irrigation projects undertaken without adequate drainage can have on affected soils and communities.   As for victim compensation costs, witness those associated with certain chemical and air pollutants in Japan (18), with asbestos in the United States, with hazardous waste dumps in the Netherlands and the United States, and with aircraft noise around many airports in the OECD area.

In spite of the fact that they can be demonstrably more efficient and effective, anticipate-and-prevent strategies involving direct regulation are often difficult and sometimes impossible to put in place.   This is because unlike react-and-cure strategies, they are activated before considerable damage to health, property and the environment has been sustained and, hence, before popular demand for action assures political support for the measures needed.

Increased use of well-designed economic instruments may offer one way out of this dilemma.   If an economically justifiable charge is placed on the use of the environmental resources in question, the market induces those who generate wastes or resource impacts to seek least-cost methods of minimising them through changes in designs and processes as well as through changes in methods of treatment.   While this does not reduce the need for public monitoring and enforcement, it does lead to more built-in prevention and reduces the need for an ever-increasing number of decisions by central agencies.

In spite of the comparative attractiveness of anticipate-and-prevent strategies from the point of view of economic efficiency and cost-effectiveness, society will have a continuing need for react-and-cure strategies.   The origin of environmental issues in economic and social development, the range of future impacts built into past patterns of development and the uncertainty that surrounds most issues regarding either their precise causes or consequences or their response to control measures, assures that this will be the case.   At best, react-and-cure strategies can be gradually supplemented and reinforced by anticipate-and-prevent strategies.

4. FUTURE DIRECTIONS FOR ENVIRONMENTAL POLICY

In light of the above, what new emphases and directions should be given to policy at the national and international level in order to deal with environmental issues in a more economically efficient and cost-effective manner? The answers to these questions are clearly complex and will vary between countries. But at least four general directions seem to stand out:

1) Integrating environmental considerations into overall economic and sectoral policies by:

-- Recognising the interdependence between environment and the economy;

-- Improving institutional arrangements;

-- Improving aids to decision-making, including benefit-cost analysis, cost-effectiveness analysis, risk assessment and other means;

-- Increasing public information and involvement.

2) Developing a stronger basis for anticipate-and-prevent strategies by:

-- Improving environmental information and statistical systems;

-- Increasing scientific research on priority environmental issues;

-- Extending impact assessment to policies as well as programmes and projects that have potentially significant implications for environmental and resource management;

-- Including environmental considerations in planning, especially land use planning, zoning and development control schemes.

3) Promoting greater efficiency in environmental policies, by:

-- Management and conservation of the environment on a sustainable basis;

-- The consistent application of the Polluter-Pays Principle;

-- Supplementing regulation with the extended use of economic instruments;

-- Streamlining and improving regulatory systems;

-- Adopting a multi-media approach to management.

4) Strengthening international co-operation on certain critical environmental and resource issues, by:

-- Extending state-of-the-art assessments on the science of the issues;

-- Developing better information on the economic, social and trade dimensions of the issues and sharing it;

-- Assessing the impact of economic, trade and other policies on the issues;

-- Investigating policy options and encouraging harmonized approaches to the issues.

Each of these general directions and some of the suggested means are discussed below.

4.1. Integrating Environmental Considerations into Economic and Sectoral Policies

Sustaining future growth in the economy and in the quality of life of people will depend increasingly on recognising and managing the natural resource and environmental basis of that growth. Development trends in all OECD Member Countries present significant opportunities for long-term economic gains through sound management of the environment, as well as risks of major losses. If the gains are to be realised and the losses minimised, however, environmental considerations need urgently, and as a matter of priority, to be brought into the centre of national decision-making on overall economic policy and, more specifically, on investment policies for industry, energy, transportation, forestry, agriculture and urban development.

Reconciling economic and environmental objectives at the earliest stages of policy formulation and planning can result in more economical development. Energy development, for example, is often accompanied by potentially high pollution loads. The early co-ordination of energy policy with environmental policy can identify significant opportunities for mutually beneficial development, whether such development involves hydro-electric dams, coal mines, electric power plants, or measures to improve end-use efficiency. Policy co-ordination can also ensure that the environmental costs of alternative choices are reflected in decisions. And co-ordination can help to avoid heavy downstream costs to society in the form of damage to health, property and environment. Society, of course, would pay for the costs of preventing this damage but that payment could and -- from the point of view of economic efficiency should -- be reflected in the cost of energy and associated goods and services (19).

The same can be said for resource development projects where building environmental considerations into policy and planning could prevent or reduce potentially heavy future costs associated with erosion, salinisation, groundwater pollution and the destruction of watersheds, habitat and landscape. Again society would pay the costs of prevention but it would enjoy the economic benefits associated with the damage avoided, such as more productive soils and forests. Avoidance of future loss has present worth and may make the best economic sense.

In most countries environmental deterioration is most severe in congested urban areas. The economic and social costs of inner cities in decline have become starkly evident in the last decade (20). Urban policies, however, can also be given a strong environmental component; with it, they can do more than aim at cleaner cities. They can aim at amenity-rich cities. Amenity conservation and improvement is an important environmental objective; it usually encompasses quietness, beauty, privacy, social relations, cultural heritage and other non-measured elements of the quality of life; it also includes the rehabilitation and renovation of urban neighbourhoods. Rehabilitation and renovation are usually a better investment than demolition and reconstruction, and their resource content is different: they utilise more labour, less energy, fewer raw materials and less capital. And renovation often makes better economic sense, as reflected in that most conventional of indicators, property prices.

4.1.1. Improving Institutional Arrangements

The means to achieve integration of environmental and growth policies are available. They include special institutional arrangements, programme and budget review procedures, and other arrangements to ensure continuing interaction with central policy agencies, with treasury and finance departments, and with other ministries, especially at an early stage of policy development. These instruments are usually difficult to deploy, however, and even more difficult to make work. They require broadening the basis of policy, programme and budget analysis, some better means of assessment and, perhaps most difficult, sensitive means to deal with the entrenched mind-sets of venerable bureaucracies. An essential first step, however, is to accord environmental policy the priority and the professional and other resources needed to become an effective partner in integrated decision-making processes.

4.1.2. Improving Aids to Decision-Making

Certain aids to decision-making can be helpful when assessing proposed environmental measures against the criteria of efficiency and effectiveness. These include benefit-cost analysis, risk assessment, cost-effectiveness analysis and impact assessment of various kinds.

The choice of the most appropriate method depends on the nature of the policy or project being assessed, and the laws and policies under which a decision is to be made. All such methods assume, however, that there is an advantage in expressing relevant parameters in a quantitative fashion, so data availability is a critical consideration.

Benefit-cost analysis enables a comparison of the benefits and costs of a policy, programme or project by reduction of variables to a common monetary unit. It has long been used and remains a powerful technique. The requirement that the benefits and costs be measured and expressed in a common monetary unit represents the method's principal attraction. But the monetary evaluation of benefits remains one of the most difficult tasks facing economic analysts. Although significant progress has been made over the last ten years in developing the methodologies for estimating benefits -- mostly in the form of avoided damage costs which in certain cases has reached a high degree of sophistication -- comparatively few studies have yet been carried out. There is also an unequal geographic distribution of studies. Most evaluations have been made in the United States and relatively few in other countries, making comparisons difficult and potentially misleading.

The measurement of damage cost in monetary terms often depends on prior measurement in physical terms. Here a major obstacle is the lack of background data. The same applies to risk assessment. To cite one example, there is a serious lack of epidemiological data vital to sound assessment of the health effects of a pollutant.

Benefit-cost analysis is not suitable for all types of projects. It has a built-in bias against unquantifiable benefits which, in some projects, can be critically important. Given the nature of discounting, it is not helpful on projects involving issues of irreversibility, intergenerational transfers and interdependence between the aggregate effects of many projects.

When monetary evaluation of benefits is impracticable, or subject to major uncertainties; cost-effectiveness analysis can provide a useful alternative. Cost-effectiveness analysis is used in selecting the least costly manner of attaining environmental targets, which are often based on expert advice, public demand, or national and international norms. It provides decision makers with information on the additional cost of a given improvement in environmental condition (for example, air quality, health, or reduction of damage) in a given unit of measure. Such analysis also allows comparison of the results of different but equally costly policies.

With further development, risk assessment could also provide a better basis for decisions in certain areas, for example, those having to do with the management of risks from chemicals, toxic wastes and other hazards. Risk assessment attempts to estimate the probable changes in the incidence of some effect (for instance, on health, property or the environment) associated with the presence of a certain agent at a certain level in the environment (21). With such an estimate, based on the best available scientific evidence and objectively defensible for that reason, decision-makers can determine what, if anything, to do about the risk in the light of other relevant considerations: economic, social, and political (22).

On the other hand, there is a wide gulf between the manner in which the lay public and technical experts assess the hazards of complex technologies (23). There is also a wide difference between the way these two groups assimilate these assessments into decisions regarding acceptance or rejection of technological options. Every action, including inaction, has some risk associated with it (24). It has been suggested that the best decision is reached by estimating correctly the number of people who may benefit from a correct action, or suffer from a wrong action. For example, overestimating the potential harm to man and the environment which might result from undertaking a specific course of action, could cause a project to be delayed or even scrapped. Conversely, underestimating the harm could lead to the expenditure of significant resources for a programme which might ultimately result in unacceptable health and/or environmental consequences. But, having already proceeded, cessation of activities would cause severe financial difficulties (such as experiences with certain nuclear power plants).

Quite apart from the practical and political considerations involved in using risk assessments, decision-makers have to deal with the uncertainties inherent in the risk estimates themselves. Descriptions of risk, whether presented quantitatively or qualitatively, generally express a range of possibilities, in some cases involving several orders of magnitude. Consideration of control options to reduce risks, and their associated costs, also will reflect these uncertainties. Techniques such as decision analysis and sensitivity analysis have therefore been advocated as means to assist decision makers in coping with uncertainty. At the very least they can help a decision maker to make his assumptions more explicit and to evaluate how sensitive different decision outcomes are to different assumptions. While these techniques have been advocated for several years, little practical experience has been gained from their use to date.

Impact assessment of various kinds can avoid some of these problems and, provided it is used selectively and kept reasonably simple, can be a useful aid to decision-making. In the real world, public and private, decisions need to be taken without too much delay and on the basis of the best available knowledge. Under imperfect conditions, the best available information, if marshalled well, can be a powerful aid to decision-making. Even before full understanding of -- or full agreement on -- the potential effects of a given undertaking has been reached, a great deal can be learned, for example, about the kind of opportunities and damage that can be anticipated; the number of people and the area likely to be affected; and the range of possibilities, that is, the variation between the more pessimistic and the more optimistic scenarios, as well as the direction of trends (for example, towards probable future improvement or deterioration in existing conditions). At the same time, it is often possible to develop an approximate estimate of the economic benefits which would be foregone were the project in question to be altered or abandoned. Comparing these two groups of estimates and recognising their limitations can be an extremely useful exercise especially, as is often the case, when the two differ by several orders of magnitude. In this way, or in similar ways, important decisions are taken every day, in crucial domains such as health, education and defence, not to mention environment.

4.1.3. Increasing Public Information and Involvement

Integrating environmental, economic and other policies can often be facilitated by ensuring that the public is in possesion of the relevant facts -- including facts about risks, benefits and costs -- and by ensuring that it is in a position to express its preferences concerning the proposed responses of governments and enterprises. Governments can support informed public involvement by providing better information through the media; by ensuring consultation through elected representatives; by holding public hearings, by providing third-party access to the courts; and by backing local referenda. Some OECD countries have had considerable experience with public involvement and a critical assessment of this experience could be of value to all.

4.2. Developing a Stronger Basis for Anticipate-and-Prevent Strategies

Although anticipate-and-prevent strategies often appear comparatively attractive from the point of view of economic efficiency and cost-effectiveness, they are difficult to apply. This is because they call for action in advance of demonstrated damage and the scientific certainty and political support that such damage can provide, and also because the knowledge base needed for anticipatory analysis is often weak. Strengthening the knowledge base through improved information and statistical systems is clearly necessary, as is increased scientific research on priority issues. Extending impact assessment to policies as well as programmes and projects was proposed by the OECD Environment Ministers in 1979. Including environmental considerations in planning -- and especially in countries where it has not yet been done in land-use planning, zoning and development control schemes -- is essential.

Ensuring the availability of objective and policy-relevant information and data is more feasible than ever, given the technologies now available to measure, monitor, store, send, transmit, process and share data. Some progress has been made in this field, but it has been unevenly distributed. Much remains to be done. Moreover, the recession, with its associated budget cuts, has not spared publicly-supported information systems and there is a danger that the information base for environmental policy, always weak, could become weaker before it gets stronger.

Information on the state of environment of a community, province or nation, and on the direction of trends, provides an essential basis for assessing the efficiency and effectiveness of existing policies and programmes, and a useful underpinning for debate on new policy needs and options. State of the environment assessment and reporting can be put on a much stronger basis not only locally and nationally in all OECD countries, but also internationally. Comparative assessments are particularly useful. But they depend on the availability of nationally and internationally comparable data. OECD's emerging set of internationally comparable data can make a significant contribution in this regard.

As has been pointed out, there is also an urgent need for more and better data to underpin risk assessment, benefit-cost analysis cost-effectiveness analysis and impact assessment. Especially critical in this regard are better data on the health, property and environmental impacts of exposure to a wide range of industrial and agricultural chemicals, of certain air depositions and hazardous wastes, of land use, and on the costs of policy measures. While the assessments in which these data would be used would remain unique to each situation, the data themselves could be transferable among countries. There is, therefore, a strong basis for cost-effective international co-operation in this field.

4.3. Promoting Greater Efficiency in Environmental Policies

While the deployment of anticipate-and-prevent strategies may often improve the effectiveness and efficiency of environmental policies, other means are also available. Among them are consistent application of the Polluter-Pays Principle; supplementing regulation with the extended use of economic instruments; streamlining and improving regulatory systems; and adopting a multi-media approach to management.

4.3.1. The Consistent Application of the Polluter-Pays Principle

The Polluter-Pays Principle aims at the internalisation of the potential costs of environmental pollution and aims at avoiding distortions in trade by discouraging subsidies.

An economic efficiency principle, the PPP is a useful guide to governments in determining both who should pay for environmental protection, and how and when they should pay. In the final analysis, of course, society pays. But there is a fundamental difference, from the point of view of economics and the efficient allocation of resources, whether society pays for the environmental protection required by a given industry in the form of the increased costs of the goods and services provided by that industry (which, within the limits of competition, PPP would encourage), or in the form of tax-supported subsidies for environmental technology, or, where protection is dropped or deferred, in the form of damage costs to health, property and the environment (28).

231

The PPP could be applied in various ways to become an essential part of policy on several current and emerging issues such as control of hazardous wastes, air pollution including acid rain, chemicals and groundwater pollution. If applied consistently, PPP could induce producers to pass on the full costs of meeting performance standards, resulting in the inclusion of pollution costs in product prices and enabling consumers to take into account the full environmental costs of their purchasing decisions. Over time this policy would induce a shift in relative prices in favour of low pollution industries. It would also enable a reduction in government subsidies and expenditures.

4.3.2. Greater Use of Economic Instruments

The increasing demand for environmental quality and the growing costs of environmental degradation create a need for better management of the real costs of utilising environmental resources for production and consumption. This calls for greater use of economic instruments with their reliance on market signals, in conjunction with regulatory instruments emphasizing performance standards.

Certain OECD Member countries have now acquired a considerable body of experience with economic instruments such as effluent charges, non-compliance fees, fuel charges, and marketable permits, including "bubbles" offset and similar transactions. A recent analysis establishes their effectiveness in a variety of cases (22). Where well-designed economic instruments are added to an existing regulatory system of standards, the result is both an increase in environmental quality and a reduction in abatement costs in the short-term. In the longer-term these results are magnified, because economic instruments encourage a faster pace of innovation designed to further reduce costs and achieve higher levels of quality. Results thus far of the marketable permit programme in the United States indicate savings of more than $130 million for just the bubble portion of the programme. Simulation studies suggest savings of up to 90 per cent in comparison with traditional command-and-control instruments if charges or marketable permits are used. Even if higher and more sophisticated environmental quality standards reduce the options for economising, and thereby reduce the savings to 25 to 30 per cent, the introduction of economic instruments is still well worth pursuing.

Appropriate economic instruments supplementing performance standards not only enable those whose activities generate wastes to seek out least-cost options for reducing discharges into air, water and on land, including changes in product design and process as well as recycling and self-treatment, but should also positively induce them to do so. If charges are imposed, they may also provide revenues to finance at least a part of construction and operation of waste treatment plants, and thus reduce the burden on government budgets.

User fees and taxes of various kinds could also be extended to resource management in order to encourage, for example, a more efficient use of water resources by agriculture, industry and households; recycling of materials; reuse of beverage containers; restoration of strip mines; reforestation after harvesting; the use of low sulphur fuels, etc.; or to encourage the use of harmful products as phosphorus detergents. At the same time, many existing fiscal systems (e.g. subsidies, depreciation allowances could lead to the overuse either of environmental resources or of potentially harmful products.

4.3.3. Strengthening and Improving Regulatory Systems

Environmental institutions, regulations and methods of enforcement have grown with great rapidity during the past two decades. In many cases, institutions and regulations were simply added on to the existing framework both reflecting and re-enforcing an "add-on" approach to management.

The consequences have been manifold. One has been a significant increase in decision-costs, especially in decisions on the siting of certain large scale projects, stemming from growing time-lags in review and control procedures. While this has often resulted in siting and design modifications to prevent avoidable damage to health, property and the environment and the economic losses associated therewith, it seems probable that streamlined procedures, accompanied by earlier and more open dialogue, could reduce decision-costs without jeopardising environmental gains.

Another consequence has been inconsistency and unnecessary duplication and overlap within and between jurisdictions and regulatory regimes, national, regional and local. This, too, has led to loss of economic efficiency in the implementation of environmental measures, and no gain in environmental effectiveness.

A case in point is chemicals control. In many OECD countries, laws and institutional arrangements have developed over time on a piecemeal basis in response to the need to control an expanding range of chemical types -- food additives, pesticides, pharmaceuticals and, more recently, industrial chemicals. Responsibility to administer these laws has been lodged in a variety of ministries, agencies and laboratories and, in federal states, different levels of government. The result is a patchwork control system, with duplication, fragmentation -- and holes (26).

Chemicals control in OECD countries is increasingly conducted within an anticipatory framework, and in a way that can come to grips with the thousands of new products entering the market each year. In this field, however, as in many others, a second generation environmental problem is being managed by an institutional framework dominated by first generation characteristics.

Some countries have already begun or are planning to review their institutional frameworks and regulatory regimes with a view both to streamlining decision-making processes and to improving coherence in policy and consistency in regulation. At a minimum attention needs to be given to means to improve the flow of information and the co-ordination of policy between agencies concerned with similar problems within and between different levels of governments. Beyond that, the OECD's work would argue for a number of specific improvements in the design and delivery of regulation (27).

-- Regulations should, as far as possible, stipulate performance standards without mandating the process or technology to be used, as is often the case today.

-- Establishing reasonable deadlines and a timetable for compliance with performance standards is also essential: indeterminate time limits, or the prospect of influencing their continual change and postponement, simply fosters uncertainty and inaction.

-- Increasing the level of consultation with firms and experts knowledgeable about conditions in the industry is also essential, especially in establishing reasonable deadlines and a timetable for compliance.

-- The most appropriate and cost-effective points in the total cycle of a product at which to tackle the pollutant in question may not be at the end of the cycle, or at the "end of the pipe," although in the case of react-and-cure situations, there may be no choice. Regulations designed to facilitate prevention should meet at least three criteria: they should enable a search, in consultation with industry, of the most effective points in the cycle of a product, up to and including its design, testing and marketing, at which to tackle the problem in question; they should provide suitable and enforceable performance standards; and they should induce the development of cost-effective methods of compliance.

4.3.4. Adopting a Multi-Media Approach to Management

The institutional and regulatory framework that emerged during the 1970s is proving deficient in another respect: it treats pollution problems as individual islands of concern occurring in different media: air, water or land. Yet toxic substances tend to be present in more than one part of the environment. So, for example, efforts to control water pollutants may result in increased air pollutants. Moreover, air pollutants may be a significant source of land and water pollutants, as in the case of acid rain. Scrubbing sulphur oxides out of the air emissions of a coal-fired power station creates a problem in solid waste management.

Multi-media problems like these are becoming more and more evident but, to-date, they have seldom been attacked in an integrated manner. Nor is it clear how existing environmental institutions, laws and regulations, which in most countries are compartmentalised into air, water and land, could be effective in dealing with these problems. A difficult re-design of certain programmes would appear necessary, requiring a substantial commitment of imagination and determination.

4.4. Strengthening International Co-operation

The international dimension of environmental and resource issues has long been recognised and was among the principal reasons why the Member countries of the OECD decided in 1970 to establish an Environment Committee to examine issues of common concern, to propose policy options and to encourage the harmonization of environmental policies among Member countries. While the priority issues have changed over the years, the Committee has always focussed strongly on their economic and trade dimensions (28).

More recently the growing interdependence of the international economic and political system has become a central question for governments as they examine the critical issues likely to dominate the world scene to and beyond the turn of the century (29). This interdependence is seen to cover not only population, energy, food and technology, but also environment and, increasingly, the effective management of the resource and ecological basis for development (7). It has been the subject of a number of recent reports (30) and has been considered by the OECD's Council at Ministerial level and also by various summits of Heads of Government e.g., Williamsburg.

Rising levels of CO_2 and climatic change, ozone depletion, chemical control, acid rain and transboundary movements of hazardous waste raise economic and social issues of concern not only within and between OECD countries, but also between OECD and non-OECD countries. The same is perhaps even more true of the accelerating loss of food-producing land through erosion, salinisation and desertification, the gradual depletion of tropical forests and the loss of genetic resources and marine pollution.

The Third World comprises three-quarters of the planet's population, and in many parts of it population growth and poverty conspire to place destructive pressures on the environment. One of the many observable consequences is the fuel wood shortage and the erosion and desertification that follow in its trail. Ecological destruction in large parts of the world will not leave OECD Member countries unaffected; indeed, many of these issues, including those that impinge most immediately on developing countries, stem largely from the activities and policies of the industrialised countries of OECD, and few can be addressed effectively in the absence of collective policies on their part (31).

What can OECD countries do? They might try the following for a start:

a) Include environmental impact assessment in their project evaluation procedures.

b) Consider environmental deterioration as a priority area in their aid programmes.

c) Deepen their support for indispensable international efforts to establish international regimes for the oceans, the atmosphere and the other commons of mankind.

How can international co-operation through OECD contribute? Several forms of co-operation have proved effective to date and could be extended and deepened.

-- Given its composition and mandate the OECD would seem well placed to encourage and facilitate the development of an improved capacity on the part of Member governments to undertake co-ordinated and integrated analysis of these issues.

-- It could do more to assist in developing periodic "state-of-the-art" papers on the emerging science of these issues, as well as identifying degrees of consensus and areas where further work is needed.

-- With the needed support of government, industry and other groups, it could develop better information on the economic, social and trade dimensions of these issues and share that information widely.

-- Many of these environmental issues are aggravated by the economic, investment, trade and other policies of the OECD region (30) and it would be useful to identify and assess those policies that have the greatest potential impact.

-- The OECD could also broaden its work in identifying and assessing policy options and in encouraging harmonized approaches to the issues.

NOTES AND REFERENCES

1. The State of the Environment in OECD Member Countries, OECD, Paris, 1979.

2. Environmental Trends, Costs and Policies to and through 1990. Background paper for Session 1 of the International Conference on Environment and Economics, June 1984.

3. Proceedings of the 1982 Stockholm Conference on Acidification of the Environment, June 21-30 1982, Swedish Ministry of Agriculture, Stockholm, Sweden.

4. National Research Council Report on Chemicals Testing, Washington, DC, 1984.

5. Pricing urban Water, The South western Review of Management and Economics, 1981, Vol. 1, No. 1.

6. Environmental Effects of Energy Systems: the OECD COMPASS Project, Chapter 4, p. 78, OECD, Paris, 1983.

7. Economic and Ecological Interdependence, OECD, Paris, 1982.

8. This very point was recently mentioned as being of primary importance in an outline of policy initiatives prepared by the US. D.D., Ref. P. S. Daley, Pollution Engineering, Feb. 1984, pp. 30-33.

9. Environmental Policies in New Zealand, OECD, Paris, 1981.
    Environmental Policies in Greece, OECD, Paris, 1983.

10. Environmental Challenges for the '80s, OECD, Paris, 1981.
    Environmental Policies for the 1980s, OECD, Paris, 1980.

11. Cost of Coal Pollution abatement; Results of an International Symposium, OECD, Paris, 1983.

12. Royston, M., Pollution Prevention Pays, Pergamon Press, 1979.

13. Background paper for Session 4 of the International Conference on Environment and Economics: Technological Perspectives and their Implications for Environmental Trends and Policies and Environmental Policies and Technical Change.

14. Low or Non-Pollution Technology through Pollution Prevention. Paper prepared by 3M Company for UNEP.

15. Public Opinion Poll on Environmental Pollution; Japan Environment Agency, Tokyo, 1982.
The Europeans and their Environment; Commission of the European Communities, Brussels, 1983.
Ladd, E. C., Public Opinion and Public Policy on the Environment; in Public Opinion, Washington, D.C., 1982.

16. Royal Commission on Environmental Pollution, Tenth Report, Tackling Pollution -- Experience and Prospects, Cmnd. 9149, HMSO, London, February 1984.

17. Berger, Thomas R., Northern Frontier, Noerthern Homeland: The Report of the Mackenzie Valley Pipeline Inquiry; Minister of Supply and Services, Ottawa, Canada, 1977. Two volumes.

18. Environmental Policies in Japan, OECD, Paris, 1977.

19. Background paper for Session 6 of the International Conference on Environment and Economics: Effective and Efficient Environmental Regulations: the Economic Rationale.

20. Managing Urban Change; Vol. 1: Policies and Finance, Vol. 2: The Role of the Government, OECD, Paris, 1983.

21. Risk Assessment in the Federal Government; the National Research Council, National Academy Press, Washington, D.C., 1983.

22. Fischoff, B., S. Lichtenstein, P. Slone, S. L. Derby and R. L. Keeney, Acceptable Risk; Cambridge University Press, Cambridge, 1982, Chapter IX.

23. Spangler, M. B., Risk Analysis, 2 (2), 101 (1982).

24. Berg, G. G. and H. H. Maillie, editors, Measurement of Risks; Env. Sci. Resources number 21, Plenum, 1981.

25. Background paper for Session 7 of the International Conference on Environment and Economics: Economic Instruments, Review and Outlook.

26. Managing Chemicals in the 1980's, OECD, Paris, 1983.

27. Issue paper for Session 4 of the International Conference on Environment and Economics: The impact of environmental polices on industrial innovation, Issue paper for Session 4 of the Internatonal Conference on Environment and Economics.

28. OECD and the Environment, OECD, Paris, 1979.

29. Facing the Future, OECD, Paris, 1979.

30. The Environment: Challenges for the 80's, OECD 1981; The Global 2000 Report to the President, Washington, US Government's Printing Office, 1980; Global 2000, Implications for Canada, Toronto, Pergamon Press 1981; Basic Directions in coping with Environmental Problems; Ad Hoc Group on Global Environment Problems; Government of Japan, 1980; North – South: A Programme for Survival: Pan Books, 1980.

31. Statement by Secretary General, E. van Lennep, The Environment: Challenges for the 1980's, page 10.

SUMMARY OF THE DISCUSSION OF SESSION EIGHT

Professor Claude HENRY

Director, Econometrics Laboratory, Ecole Polytechnique, Paris

There was broad agreement on the four general directions for environmental policies as set out in the Issue Paper for Session 8. These future directions were:

    i) Integrating environmental considerations into overall economic and sectoral policies;

    ii) Developing a stronger basis for anticipate and prevent strategies;

    iii) Promoting greater efficiency in environmental policies;

    iv) Strengthening international co-operation on certain critical environmental and resource issues.

The discussion went into considerable detail on these points, enlarging on them and adding a number of new ones.

Issues

    i) Future environmental trends in developing countries have international implications and raise important issues of policy for developing countries as well as for OECD countries. These future trends concern increasing pollution arising from industrialisation in developing countries and from the consumption of their natural resources. Both of these trends have worldwide implications for the environment, for the conservation of disappearing species and for action that the OECD countries might take to ensure the sustainability of these resources worldwide and to maintain the environment of the developing countries.

    ii) For the OECD countries the contentious issues in the field of pollution are how; by how much and when pollution should be reduced and to what extent "anticipate and prevent" strategies are feasible.

    iii) In confronting these major questions, the main challenge is how to ensure that all available knowledge is brought to bear on the evaluation of environmental considerations at the earliest possible stage of decision-making, and therefore how environmental

239

problems are analysed and how the necessary trade-offs between environmental protection and other social goods are made.

iv) In the OECD countries themselves there is the complex issue of the interdependence between sustainable economic development and the practices necessary to maintain the resource and environmental basis of that development. These practices must include measures to prevent the degradation of soils through erosion, salinization and pollution; the loss of cropland and amenity areas through other uses; the continued depletion of and increasing damage to forests; the loss of wildlife habitat; loss of biological diversity; and the depletion of marine natural resources.

Responses

i) There was a reaffirmation of the important role governments must play in the field of environment, at both the national and the international level, and of the necessity that international needs might in some cases over-ride short-run narrow national interests. International agencies could take the initiative in assisting Member governments to achieve improvements in environmental quality; all speakers emphasized that by the end of the 1980s environmental quality should be improved beyond that obtaining at the end of the 1970s.

ii) The view was put forward by some speakers, but not endorsed by everyone, that a new international authority might be needed to deal with global environmental problems such as the greenhouse effect, depletion of the ozone layer and pollution of the seas. An additional point put forward was that international bodies to deal with these and similar problems might need a degree of financial independence obtained, perhaps, from international tax on resources.

iii) Greater international co-operation is needed to deal with the emerging pollution problems in developing countries . It was recognised that developing countries should be allowed to exploit their comparative advantages in industrial development and that they have been assisted in dealing with the externalities of industrial development, which have manifested themselves in various forms of pollution and in urban blight. The resolution of the North/South conflict in the world depends partially on solving economic conflicts also requires control of the environmental impact even of relatively slow economic growth.

iv) To this end various suggestions were proposed:

-- Economic development programmes should contain environmental impact assessments for the various projects;

-- The experience of OECD countries, their policies, practices and standards, must be made available to developing countries on a much wider basis. This should also include innovative technologies of pollution control;

-- OECD countries should also ensure that the multinational companies investing in developing countries provide both positive channels for the transmission of environmentally sound practices and procedures and good examples of environmental responsibility.

v) OECD countries should also assist developing countries in the sustainable development of their renewable resources: soil, forests and plant and animal life, which are of common interest. The economic needs and conservation objectives of OECD and developing countries should be harmonized.

vi) The approach to environmental problems in the future should be as rational and consistent as possible and the choices must be explicit and public. It was suggested that decisions about pollution control programmes should take into account the probable effects of pollutants on human health and on the environment and the economic and social effects of a regulatory programme. Clearly the decision involving trade-offs must finally be based on political judgements taking present and future societal values into account. However, risk assessment relating to health and environmental impacts involving great uncertainties must be scientifically based, without political interference, and must be governed by well-understood guidelines. The majority of participants emphasized the importance of the use of appropriate benefit-cost analysis and similar evaluation techniques.

vii) There was a general agreement that the data base, both scientific and economic, of environmental consensus should be strengthened for better decision making and to give the data credibility with governments, business and the public in general. There is a need to share this information widely, and decisions made on the basis of it should be explicit and transparent.

viii) There was strong advocacy of the multi-media approach to pollution for both reactive and anticipatory policies in order to make environmental policies more efficient in the near future. Such an approach would include: (i) focussing on all pollutants from a single source; (ii) focussing on one geographic area; (iii) focussing on single pollutants and controlling them at the most efficient point as they flow through several media; (iv) co-ordination with all media regulators.

ix) Following up the London Summit Meeting of Heads of Governments, which recognised the international dimensions of environmental problems and asked governments to act, the United Kingdom government indicated a number of steps: (i) identifying areas for co-operation by the end of 1984; (ii) inviting the OECD Secretariat to contribute; (iii) transmitting results to the OECD Ministerial meeting.

OECD Responsibilities

i) The OECD should ensure that the experience of OECD countries with regard to policies, practices and standards developed is made available on a broad scale to developing countries and should ensure closer co-operation between the environmental ministries or agencies and their development assistance programmes. Such co-operation between the OECD's Environment Committee and Development Assistance Committee is essential.

ii) The OECD should aim for an early adoption of the "Environmental Guidelines for Multinational Enterprises".

iii) The OECD should accelerate progress in developing the appropriate principles and the legal and administrative framework to deal with trans-boundary environmental impacts and should take the lead in enabling these principles to be applied outside the OECD countries.

iv) The OECD should develop a common basis for assessing risks associated with pollution. Such a common basis for assessment would assist Member governments in dealing with pollution within their boundaries as well as on an international basis.

v) OECD should initiate a co-operative effort amongst OECD countries for the protection of the major eco-systems -- the tropical forests and oceans -- which are vital to the health of the world community.

vi) OECD should continue to strengthen its work on the economic aspects of environmental protection, in particular in the assessment of anticipatory policies.

<u>BIAC STATEMENT TO THE INTERNATIONAL CONFERENCE</u>
<u>ON ENVIRONMENT AND ECONOMICS (1)</u>

This Statement was prepared by the Secretary-General of the Business and Industry Advisory Committee to OECD (BIAC) for transmission to the participants in the Conference.

1. Introduction

The main themes of this Statement are:

-- The relationship between environment and economics;

-- The benefits of environmental policy and job creation;

-- Improving the efficiency of environmental policy.

While BIAC reviewed the Background and Issue Papers for the Conference, it is not our intention to comment on these papers in detail.

Although this Conference has been organised relatively shortly after the 1979 OECD Conference on Environment Policy and Economic Issues, BIAC welcomes the initiative of OECD. It especially appreciates the Session on improving the efficiency of environmental policy.

2. The Relationship between Environment and Economics (Sessions 1 and 2 of the Conference)

Industry is committed to conducting its operations in an environmentally sound manner, irrespective of the level of economic growth. Indeed, the state of the environment has improved; considerable money has been invested by industry and, moreover, there is a heightened sense of awareness within industry of environmental requirements. Economic growth, however, remains an important condition, not only in terms of the general welfare, but also from the environmental point of view. Growth is essential for investments in environmental measures, and represents the driving force for technological change, for instance in the further development of cleaner technologies. A more efficient implementation of environmental policy is further needed to improve investment conditions; for example, by decreasing the time delays resulting from licensing procedures.

There should be a balance between environment policy and economic policy. Especially in a situation of low growth rates, low profit margins in industry, structural over-capacity in many sectors of industry and a high rate of unemployment, new and costly environmental measures should be carefully assessed for their need, their method of implementation and their impact on industry.

OECD notes in several statements and documents that industrial and public expenditure on environment protection is relatively low in terms of GNP. This may be misleading; one should take into account the following factors:

-- Most statistics cover only end-of-line technologies and not in-plant techniques, which are increasingly used in industry;

-- The rapid increase in operating costs: these can equal 10 to 30 per cent of capital expenditure and recur annually. For some companies these costs are increasing at a rate of about 10 per cent per year.

-- The major part of industrial expenditure comes from a very important but also relatively small part of industry (for instance, the chemical industry, the oil industry, the base metal industry). Investment in environmental measures in these sectors can be up to 20-25 per cent of total investment costs.

One should therefore be careful when making general statements based on macro-economic figures like GNP. In fact, environmental expenditures and GNP should not be discussed in strict relationship to one another. A more micro-economic approach, taking into account the relative position of the sectors concerned, is essential for a clear insight into the real effects of environmental policy.

3. Job Creation and the Impacts and Benefits of Environmental Policies (Sessions 3, 4 and 5)

The benefits of environment policy and job creation are often stressed by OECD.

BIAC recognises that OECD takes the view that in certain short-term circumstances some net employment benefits may accrue from increased work on protection of the environment. But BIAC has warned in the past that benefits may be at the expense of investments in productive manufacturing industry and therefore can result in increased production costs and in negative effects on employment.

It should also be taken into account that there are only a very limited number of studies available on this subject. Moreover, they are in some cases contradictory or very difficult to compare because of the differences in their assumptions. While the positive effects can easily be identified, the negative effects (such as lack of investment in other areas and plant closures) are much more difficult to identify.

There is also a tendency to undertake studies in order to establish the real costs as against elements such as health protection, damage avoided to monuments and so on. A systematic use of this type of analysis is, in BIAC's opinion, not realistic. These studies have clear limitations in assumptions and evaluation methods; general conclusions based on only some or on outdated studies should also be avoided.

What is needed is a cost-benefit analysis that compares the costs for environmental control programmes with the benefits (positive impacts) to the environment. Especially in cases of emission restrictions or the implementation of emission limit values, cost-benefit analysis is essential in order to use scarce economic and technical resources as effectively as possible.

4. Improving the Efficiency of Environmental Policies
   (Sessions 6 and 7)

This is rather a new element in OECD's activities; in BIAC's opinion, it is a crucial topic. Environmental regulations in most OECD countries have usually been developed on a sectoral basis within a relatively short time frame. This has led in many cases to scattered, complicated and sometimes conflicting regulations. Developing national and international strategies to achieve environmental objectives as simply as possible may be the best way to ensure compliance and the attainment of objectives.

In some countries, such as the Netherlands and the United States, initiatives for better integration of legislation, reduction of time delays and better pre-screening and post-evaluation of regulations have been undertaken. The "bubble concept" is an example of more flexible and cost-effective regulation: it is an alternative to complicated, detailed and costly emission restrictions for installations. These economic instruments are very important to industry as incentives to use its innovative potential to improve technologies and hence to improve environmental protection. These initiatives could be further stimulated by exchange of information within the OECD group and eventually by OECD recommendations on this subject.

In BIAC's opinion, the following elements should be included in discussions on this subject:

i) Flexibility in policy. It is not always necessary to enact legislation; voluntary agreements between government and industry can be a better and more effective solution, both as an alternative to legislation and as a way to implement it. Such voluntary agreements have been made with regard to chlorofluorocarbons in Germany and the Netherlands and phosphates in detergents in Sweden;

ii) Pre-screening, evaluation. Pre-screening of potential legislation is valuable, not only in the economic sense, but also in relation to the choice of instruments; the time schedule of implementation; the resulting time delays in, for example, licensing procedures; the (administrative) burden for local authorities; and eventual effects on appeal procedures and so on. The USA regulatory impact analysis and the recent Dutch experiences are interesting examples of such pre-screening of legislation. Evaluation afterwards can also be a useful instrument for legislation with important economic or regulatory impact on industry.

iii) Flexibility in the use of instruments. A careful evaluation of instruments is necessary. There are alternatives to the current detailed emission restriction requirements. An example is the "bubble concept", originating in the USA and under study now in some EC countries. This concept, despite some limitations, gives opportunities to improve both the environment and the cost-effectiveness of measures and also gives incentives for a technological approach to problems. A further study of some additional elements, like offset, marketable rights and others is worthwhile in order to fit these elements within current practices in OECD countries;

iv) <u>Integration, transparency of the decision-making process</u>. Integration of sectorally constructed legislation would in many cases be useful, in order to eliminate duplication, to improve the transparency of regulations, and to make better use of existing legislation instead of creating new laws. The time delays resulting from notification, licensing and other procedures should be better taken into account. Also essential is a better integration with other elements of government policy: energy, economy, industrial/innovation policy;

v) <u>Risk assessment</u>. It is important to separate risk assessment and risk management processes in regulatory policy development. Risk assessment must involve an evaluation of the potential hazard. This requires a critical review of the epidemiological and experimental data bases, the evaluation of dose-response data and an assessment of exposure and characterisation of the risks. This work should be based on sound scientific information and principles and must be subject to objective peer review. The risk management process should take the outcome of the risk assessment and balance it with the economic, legal and social factors to arrive at regulatory decisions.

Pollution charges are also an element of this theme. From the beginning, industry has accepted the Polluter-Pays Principle, which means that each company is responsible for and pays for the measures to prevent or cure its own pollution. However, charges to finance public expenditure on the environment or to regulate products have been rejected by industry. Such charges are in fact an additional instrument in relation to legislation and should never be regarded as a regulatory instrument as such, because of their inflexibility and bureaucratic nature.

5. Conclusions

These elements should be incorporated in the Conference Conclusions:

i) Economic growth and efficient regulations are key factors for current and future environmental policy;

ii) Better integration of environmental policy with other policies (economy, energy, innovation);

iii) Increased international cooperation and harmonization, since many environmental problems can only be resolved on an international scale;